PRAISE FOR *THE NEW ROARING TWENTIES*

"Well written, thoughtful, and persuasive."

—David Kruger, chairman and chief executive officer, The Fiore Companies

"Whether you are an entrepreneur, employee, a gig worker, this book is a clever, insightful look forward to what the next ten years may hold for everyone. Paul Pilzer and Stephen Jarchow offer up their wealth of financial expertise and in-depth knowledge in current matters of business and economy to both forecast and reveal what lies just ahead, so you can take the path that's right for you."

**—Jeanette B. Milio, motion picture executive
and award-winning UCLAX lecturer**

"Solid and sound advice for understanding, acting, and shifting the mind in the area of finances. As times change so should we as guardians of our money and assets. Volatile times may not go away soon, and I believe this book is ammunition for survival."

—Dr. Kat Smith-Hudak, author and motivational speaker

"Have you ever wanted the ability to predict the future? *The New Roaring Twenties* may not look like a crystal ball, but it's close. Rarely do you find authors that can provide such a clear viewpoint and thoughtful context for current and forthcoming trends. *The New Roaring Twenties* serves as your clever, entertaining guide to an exciting and more prosperous future."

**—Paul Colichman, chief executive officer, Here Media Inc.,
and Emmy-winning film and television producer**

"A must read to understand the economic issues facing the nation."

—Tino Balio, professor emeritus, University of Wisconsin

THE *NEW* ROARING TWENTIES

ALSO BY PAUL ZANE PILZER

Other People's Money
Unlimited Wealth
God Wants You To Be Rich
The Next Trillion
The Wellness Revolution
The Fountain of Wealth
The New Health Insurance Solution
The Next Millionaires
The New Wellness Revolution
The Entrepreneurial Challenge
The End of Employer Provided Health Insurance
Becoming an Entrepreneur

THE *NEW* ROARING TWENTIES

Prosper in Volatile Times

PAUL ZANE PILZER
WITH STEPHEN P. JARCHOW

Matt Holt Books
An Imprint of BenBella Books, Inc.
Dallas, TX

The New Roaring Twenties copyright © 2023 by Paul Zane Pilzer

BenBella Books, Inc.
10440 N. Central Expressway
Suite 800
Dallas, TX 75231
benbellabooks.com
Send feedback to feedback@benbellabooks.com

BenBella and *Matt Holt* are federally registered trademarks.

Printed in the United States of America
10 9 8 7 6 5 4 3 2 1

Library of Congress Control Number: 2022949866
ISBN 9781637740972 (hardcover)
eISBN 9781637740989

Editing by Katie Dickman
Copyediting by Scott Calamar
Proofreading by Jenny Rosen and Isabelle Rubio
Indexing by Amy Murphy
Text design and composition by Aaron Edmiston
Cover design by Brigid Pearson
Cover image © Shutterstock / vectorkat
Printed by Lake Book Manufacturing

I dedicate this book to you, my reader.

CONTENTS

PREFACE   *Economic Possibilities for Our Grandchildren*....xi

INTRODUCTION   *The Twelve Pillars* 1

PART I: THE WORST AND THE BEST OF TIMES

CHAPTER ONE   The End of the World As We Knew It...... 15

CHAPTER TWO   The Great Recovery: Did You Miss It?...... 23

PART II: THE SIX ECONOMIC PILLARS

CHAPTER THREE   Technology-Driven Wealth 45

CHAPTER FOUR   An Energy Revolution 63

CHAPTER FIVE   Structural Unemployment 87

CHAPTER SIX   The Robots Are Coming 99

CHAPTER SEVEN   The Gig Economy 121

CHAPTER EIGHT   Universal Basic Income 137

PART III: THE SIX SOCIAL PILLARS

CHAPTER NINE   The Millennials Step Up................ 151

CHAPTER TEN   The Sharing Revolution 163

CHAPTER ELEVEN Consumer Surplus 177
CHAPTER TWELVE Gross National Happiness 189
CHAPTER THIRTEEN The China Challenge 199
CHAPTER FOURTEEN The Russian Wild Card 217

PART IV: STRATEGIES FOR THE NEW ROARING TWENTIES

CHAPTER FIFTEEN Should You Quit Before You Are Laid Off? 227
CHAPTER SIXTEEN Business-Opportunity Businesses (BOBs) .. 235
CHAPTER SEVENTEEN You Ain't Seen Nothin' Yet 243
CONCLUSION Some Thoughts for You 251

Acknowledgments 253
Index 255

PREFACE

ECONOMIC POSSIBILITIES FOR OUR GRANDCHILDREN

We want to pass on a better world to our children and grandchildren. This is the ultimate reason to prosper in volatile times.

The great economist John Maynard Keynes (1883–1946) completed *Economic Possibilities for Our Grandchildren* in 1931. He forecast what our world would look like in ninety-nine years.[1]

Today, 165 million people, about 50 percent of the 330 million people living in the US, are in the workforce. In 1931, 60 percent of the US population was in the workforce. Keynes predicted that in 2030, only 33 percent of our total population would be in the workforce, and those who did work would work about three hours a day. Keynes said that due to massive technological innovation, this working one-third would be so productive that they would supply all the needs of our entire population. Many people would become rich because innovation would allow them to accomplish the work of up to three people in as little as one-third of the time—an up to a 9x lift in average personal productivity. Keynes effectively predicted the Great Resignation of the 2020s, as well as the impact of technology on productivity.

Keep in mind that Keynes's predictions were made during the Great Depression, a period of economic collapse after the buoyant period known as

---

1   Elizabeth Kolbert, "No Time," *New Yorker*, May 19, 2014; John Maynard Keynes, *Essays in Persuasion* (W.W. Norton & Co, 1963).

the Roaring Twenties. The original Roaring Twenties (1920–1929) came in
the aftermath of disastrous wars and a massive flu pandemic that killed fifty
million people worldwide.[2]

Keynes's 1931 forecast poses the following questions: What will the
nonworking two-thirds of the population do with their free time? How will
they feed, clothe, and house themselves? How will society redistribute the
extreme bounty received by some of the one-third of our population that do
work?

To these three questions I pose a fourth: What can you or I do now
to ensure that we become among the people experiencing a 9x lift in
productivity?

This book will attempt to answer these four questions, but it will focus
mostly on the last one—how you and your business can become up to nine
times more productive during the next ten years.

One reason it took Keynes three years to write his optimistic
long-term economic forecast was the stock market crash of
1929, which Keynes wrote had produced a "slump which will . . .
over the long run prove to be just a minor interruption in a much
larger, more munificent trend." In the final version of *Economic
Possibilities*, published in 1931, Keynes urged readers to look
beyond the Great Depression's "temporary phase of maladjust-
ment" and "into the rosy beyond."[3]

Keynes's economic forecast, in which he predicted, on average, a four
to eight times increase in Gross Domestic Product (GDP) per person, has

---

2   Keynes's work, *The Economic Consequences of the Peace*, condemned the hypocrisy of the
     reparations imposed on Germany after World War I and predicted the resulting future
     devastation of Europe, i.e., World War II. Nonetheless he still held a positive long-term
     view.

3   Keynes is arguably the greatest economist of the twentieth century. His best-known
     work, *The General Theory of Employment, Interest and Money*, published in 1936, was a
     fundamental text for future economic theory and practice. He was a member of the
     Bloomsbury Group, a Cambridge salon of the best and brightest in arts, sciences, and
     economics.

already proven itself correct—a decade earlier than expected. GDP is the monetary value of all finished goods and services made within a country during a specific period, typically annually.[4]

From 1930 to 2020, total US real GDP grew twentyfold. Adjusting for the growth in the US population from 123 to 330 million, real GDP per person rose from $8,130 in 1930 to approximately $63,593 in 2020—an eightfold increase in the economic output and wealth of the average American.[5]

Sadly, this "average" doesn't exist for most Americans. The average annual income in America today is about $52,000, and the median income is about $67,000. However, more than 50 percent of the US population today earn less than $30,000 per year.[6] We will examine this problem and its cure in chapter eight, "Universal Basic Income."

Keynes's other forecast for 2030—that there would be far fewer workers, each working fewer hours because they would have achieved their economic goals—has not come true for several reasons.

First, women have almost doubled the size of our workforce. The percentage of women participating in the US labor force rose from 24 percent in 1930 to 57 percent in 2019, mostly because the nature of work itself changed to favor brains over brawn.

Second, Keynes miscalculated a fundamental characteristic of human behavior, one that has ruled our economy since World War II—unlimited demand. As will be explained in chapter three, "Technology-Driven Wealth," the more you get, the more you want—there is no limit to consumption, especially for the baby boom generation that has dominated the US economy for the last fifty years. However, as explained in chapter nine, "The Millennials Step Up," our nation's insatiable desire for more stuff may be waning somewhat now that the millennials have become the largest US generation.

---

4   Until 1991, Gross Domestic Product (GDP) was referred to as Gross National Product. Its definition is provided by a number of national and international economic and social welfare organizations, such as the Organization for Economic Co-operation and Development (OECD) and the International Monetary Fund (IMF). Typically adjustments are made to GDP to facilitate comparison over time and place, as well as for inflation.

5   World Bank National Accounts Data, OECD National Accounts data, Tradingeconomics.com.

6   www.indeed.com, www.payscale.com, www.salaryexplorer.com, www.ziprecruiter.com.

The original Roaring Twenties (1920–1929) was a period of dramatic social and political change. The nation celebrated a return to normalcy after World War I (which resulted in over twenty million deaths and over twenty million wounded) and the devastating flu pandemic (resulting in over fifty million fatalities). The US national wealth doubled, and for the first time, more people lived in cities rather than on farms.

The Eighteenth Amendment to the Constitution enacted in 1919 banned the manufacture and sale of intoxicating liquors. Drinking then went underground in illegal speakeasies, the distribution often controlled by bootleggers and other criminals. Some felt that Prohibition was a way to control unruly immigrants and undesirables. The National Origins Act of 1924 set immigration quotas excluding many Eastern Europeans, Asians, and Africans.

The first commercial radio station was opened in 1920, and by the end of the decade, there were radios in over twelve million households. Three-quarters of the American population visited a movie theater every week. The automobile started the decade as a luxury and by the end of the decade became a necessity. This was the first era of mass communication and marketing.

It ended with the Wall Street crash of 1929, the most devastating stock market collapse in US history. The market did not return to its 1929 highs until 1954.

It's easy to see why Keynes, writing during the Great Depression and before the baby boom, did not appreciate the possibility of unlimited demand. Back in 1930, when every household yearned for a single-family home with an indoor bathroom and an automobile, it was unfathomable to think that, once achieving this goal, most families would be willing to work even harder for a larger home with multiple bathrooms and two or more automobiles. Looking ahead beyond the economic crisis of the 1930s, Keynes foresaw the day when most Americans would have a car and a four-bedroom, one-bathroom house. He once warned President Franklin D. Roosevelt that when most people had fulfilled the American dream, they would lose part of their incentive to work. These productive Americans, Keynes felt, would shift from spending their increasing incomes to saving it, until the economy would grind to a halt—a victim, as it were, of its own success.

Today, due to massive increases in innovation, Keynes's forecast of rising GDP, from fewer workers working fewer hours, may finally be realized, at least to a certain extent. In the next decade, our current 165-million-person workforce may shrink substantially while our $22 trillion GDP grows 50 percent—just as GDP grew almost 50 percent during the original Roaring Twenties (1920–1929).

While one-third of our workforce in 2023–2033 might lose their jobs, the remaining two-thirds of our workforce could receive a raise in excess of $10 trillion per annum in increased GDP—that's a $102,000 average raise for each person remaining in the workforce. Whether you are a businessperson working for a large company or an entrepreneur working for yourself, it's time to get your business and life ready for a period when unlimited demand, technology, and other forces may cause a massive increase in disposable income. This will be one of the most interesting times in world history, filled with surprises and volatility: *The New Roaring Twenties*!

INTRODUCTION

THE TWELVE PILLARS

A few years ago, before the pandemic, my children started asking questions about their future in a world of rapidly changing technology. They wondered what they should study in college, if they should even go to college, and how they would support themselves as adults. Their questions started me researching the long view—how our lives will change over the next few decades. I realized that they were not alone in their questions, and that there was a need for this book.

Specifically, for the US and other developed nations, I envision the following possibilities by 2033:

- The foundation of our lives will be resting on six economic and six social pillars that will revolutionize society and our workplaces, changing everything.
- The economic wealth of the US as measured by GDP will soar. The personal economies of millions will plummet, however, along with the poorest one-third of the world's population. This will be especially hard in the United States, which has arguably the weakest safety net of any developed nation.
- Individuals and businesses that understand the pillars will be rewarded by retooling their economic lives, whether they work for a traditional employer or for themselves.

The twelve pillars of our new society and economy are:

Economic

- Technology
- Energy
- Structural unemployment
- Robots
- The gig economy
- Universal basic income

Social

- Millennials
- The sharing revolution
- Consumer surplus
- Gross national happiness
- The China challenge
- The Russian wild card

Each of these twelve pillars is a chapter in this book.

The coronavirus disease initially looked like it was going to destroy the world's economy as whole segments closed down. Sheltering in place, facial masks, and social distancing became a major part of our daily routine. Individuals and businesses saw their foundations tremble.

Although millions of individuals and businesses suffered, many survived. Some even thrived and retooled for the new, post-pandemic era. Often this required higher productivity. Now we face a long battle with the coronavirus disease in all of its variations, as well as the pervasive effects of long-term COVID.

To place this in context, small businesses employ approximately one-half of the workforce. Over one-third of all small businesses closed during the pandemic, many never to reopen. Meanwhile, very small businesses (fewer than ten employees) grew, often with an online component. Americans created almost three million more online businesses in 2020 than 2019. An entrepreneurial spirit prevails, albeit somewhat battered.

While the pandemic affected each person or business differently, one effect was universal among the surviving and the thriving: the speed of change. All of the surviving individuals and businesses adopted technological change much faster during the pandemic than before. Digital capabilities became increasingly important for small firms.

Many societal and economic changes I previously thought would take three decades to become ubiquitous will now become universal in one decade—or less. This rapid adoption of innovative technology, along with great societal changes, will cause a period I call "the new roaring twenties" (2023–2033).

SUMMARY OF THE PILLARS

The New Roaring Twenties explains how our post-pandemic economy rests on six economic and six social pillars that are changing everything. Individuals and businesses who understand these twelve pillars will succeed in the decade ahead.

The Six Economic Pillars

The six economic pillars provide a framework for understanding what the major economic drivers will be in the new roaring twenties. Extraordinary technology and energy developments are coming, but with a painful path buffeted by volatility, inflation, supply chain issues, and war.

Technology

Throughout history, wealth (W) has equaled physical resources (P) multiplied by technology (T)($W = P \times T$). The wealth of a person or a nation consisted of their physical resources (e.g., farmland, minerals, fossil fuel, fresh water) multiplied by the technological era in which they lived and used these resources (e.g., the Stone Age, Bronze Age, Iron Age, electronic age). Since technology was a constant over the lifespan of most human beings, the only way a person could get wealthier was to acquire more physical resources, often by violent means.

This changed after World War II when humankind became an active participant in managing the growth of technology. Advances in information technology took on an exponential life of their own, effectively changing the central equation to $W = P \times T^n$ where n refers to the exponential impact advances in information technology have on all technology.

The old adage was that technology for an industry or a nation simply advances along with its economic growth. This is no longer correct. Now the advance of specific technologies causes economic growth of a business, industry, or nation in the first place. Then, increasing information/digital technology dramatically raises the level of all technology.

For example, mechanical fuel injection doubled fuel economy in the 1970s from ten to twenty miles per gallon (mpg), effectively doubling our supply of gasoline.

As digital information technology connected to electronic fuel injectors in the 2000s, fuel economy doubled again to 40 mpg. Electric vehicles (EVs) will soon make the equivalent of 100 mpg vehicles commonplace. Getting 100 mpg versus 20 mpg is financially equivalent to getting your former $5.00/gallon tank of gasoline filled up for $1.00/gallon.

In our lifetimes, the relative value of physical resources has plummeted so much that wealth often equals technology. Period. Managing physical resources for most of us is no longer part of our decision-making process. John D. Rockefeller became the first US billionaire through fossil fuels in the early twentieth century. Today, 80 percent of American billionaires acquired their wealth either through supplying information technology to others (e.g., Apple, Alphabet, Microsoft, Cisco) or applying technology built by others, such as e-commerce, to a traditional business (e.g., Walmart, Amazon, Tesla, Netflix).

Energy

Many experts today are predicting abundant energy due to increases in the supply of power from new sources such as fracking and wind and solar. They are only half right. Another equal amount of savings will come from applying better technology to our devices that use energy, like electric vehicles, heating and cooling systems, home construction, and LED lighting—which also yield instant localized monetary savings and reduced pollution.

For example, 22 percent ($2 trillion) of the world's $9 trillion annual energy production is used for illumination. The simple substitution of an LED light bulb for an incandescent reduces energy consumption for illumination by up to 90 percent (a 10x lift) and initial cost by 95 percent (a 20x lift, because it can potentially last twenty times as long). This one change alone could save the world from wasting up to $2 trillion per year in fossil fuels, equivalent to about half the total economy of Japan. This is enough to give an annual stipend of $267 to every one of the eight billion people on the planet.

Structural Unemployment

Most governments reacted to the 2020–2021 pandemic economy by providing multiple stimulus packages to extend unemployment benefits until the economy recovered and people were called back to their prior jobs. While this may have been necessary for political stability, this was a cruel joke played on many of the unemployed. Most of those unemployed during the pandemic may never be called back to the jobs they held regardless of what happens to the economy—because their jobs have permanently disappeared due to robots armed with artificial intelligence (AI), the gig economy, and the rest of the pillars. Others may not wish to return to low-paying menial jobs but rather to retool their skills.

> Show me a company or work organization of one hundred employees doing $10 million in sales, $100,000 per employee, and I'll show you how with restructuring it can either have the same sales with fifty employees, $200,000 per employee; or keep one hundred employees and double sales to $20 million, also $200,000 per employee, although not necessarily the same one hundred employees.

Some of us have already seen this happen to certain service providers during the pandemic. Those that survived have maintained and in some cases increased sales and profits through new technologies and different staffing that the pandemic forced them to implement.

The Robots

Many people think robots will take away many of our jobs in the 2020s and beyond. This is only partially correct. Robots will take away most of our existing jobs because that's what robots are designed to do—replace work formerly done by humans. The substitution of technological tools for labor has been around for millennia, but we've never had to deal before with the substitution of tools for virtually every job, including managerial positions. In chapter six, "The Robots Are Coming," you'll learn how potential fortunes await the entrepreneurs, many of them displaced former employees, who create the first robots for their industry, transferring the knowledge they learned in their prior professions to self-learning machines with artificial intelligence.

The Gig Economy

The conventional wisdom is that almost everyone can be an entrepreneur when it comes to producing new products or services, but that few have the personality and temperament to succeed when it comes to sales and marketing. In my experience with many entrepreneurial ventures, there is no typical entrepreneur.

Entrepreneurship is literally a possibility for everyone, particularly as opportunities open dramatically in the gig economy. This is a labor market characterized by short-term contracts and freelance work as opposed to permanent jobs. Gig workers are independent contractors, online platform workers, contract firm workers, on-call workers, and temporary workers. The definition and structure of work is changing.

The establishment and traditional employers often fight the gig economy every step of the way—from Marriott challenging the legal existence of Airbnb's hotel rooms to California's ballot-box attempt to reclassify Uber drivers as employees entitled to costly benefits. Chapter seven, "The Gig Economy" explains why these challenges to the new order are generally failing. The biggest entrepreneurial business opportunities often are those that facilitate the creation of recurring gigs for other entrepreneurs—see chapter sixteen, "Business-Opportunity Businesses."

Universal Basic Income

The economist John Maynard Keynes predicted that we would face a crossroads in approximately 2030 where only a third of the population would work and for only fifteen hours a week, but that this third would be so productive that 100 percent of the world's population could live an abundant life. Today, when only half (165 million) of the US population (330 million) is employed, we are arguably approaching this crossroad.

This raises the possibility of a universal basic income (UBI) of, say, $1,000 per month per household ($500 per person), no matter how rich or how poor. The conventional wisdom is that many people will become lazy and not work when given UBI. As you'll see in chapter eight, "Universal Basic Income," most working people will work harder than they already do when given a supplement to improve their lives. Moreover, switching from entitlements of things (public housing, food stamps, Medicaid) to entitlements of money (cash to buy things) will more than pay for itself. It will create a whole new $1.6 trillion UBI industry, serving up to one hundred million Americans who have previously been left out of our economy. It will create millions of jobs for the entrepreneurs who serve them. Additionally, UBI for everyone will dramatically improve the quality of life of all Americans, poor and rich, and will pay for itself in economic growth.

The Six Social Pillars

The six social pillars will have both an important social and corresponding economic impact in the new roaring twenties. They will help determine our quality of life and whether there will be any kind of life at all

The Millennials

The millennials are stepping up with Generation Z right behind them. They are here to stay as your employees (and in some cases, your employers) as well as your customers. They are the largest demographic in the US and currently number eighty-three million, versus seventy-two million baby boomers. Your knowledge of millennials and the advent of Generation Z is going to influence your success or failure in the new roaring twenties.

Millennials are interested in fairness. It guides their purchasing and is revolutionizing our society, particularly after the pandemic. Millennials will also create a housing boom of smaller living spaces, partly by desire and partly out of necessity. In the 1930s the average American lived in about two hundred square feet of space, versus six hundred square feet today. Now we may see a meaningful downsizing of living spaces. Just retooling our housing and retail sectors to serve the values of millennials will support a substantial part of the entire US economy.

The Sharing Revolution

In the sharing economy of the 2010s, you could get many of the things you wanted at half the price because you shared the cost and use with a stranger—from a Uber pool taxi ride to a Airbnb guest bedroom. However, in the sharing revolution of the 2020s, you will get the same 50 percent price benefit (a 2x lift), plus the product may be twice as valuable because you've met a new friend or potential business associate (another 2x lift, or 4x total). You may at some point be choosing your next restaurant seat by who is sitting at your table, either someone you already know or someone you want to get to know. See chapter ten, "The Sharing Revolution."

Consumer Surplus

The old business adage "give the customer what they pay for" is now a recipe for disaster. In today's world, where most products and services are approaching a zero- to low-marginal product cost, you've got to give your customer more (and more) of what they pay for just to keep them from going elsewhere. In the new roaring twenties you can afford to do so. Economists call this "consumer surplus," and it's the most important factor behind the success of Amazon, Uber, Airbnb, and many other companies. These successful companies typically measure the consumer surplus of every transaction with a scale called Net Promoter Score (NPS). You can too, as explained in chapter eleven, "Consumer Surplus."

Gross National Happiness (GNH)

In 1971, economist Simon Kuznets was awarded the Nobel Memorial Prize in Economics for creating in the 1930s a quantitative universal scale to measure human economic progress: gross national product (GNP) now known as gross domestic product (GDP). Because he did this during the Great Depression when many people barely had enough to eat, Kuznets assumed most people wanted products and services more than the happiness originally promised by the US Constitution (e.g., "Life, Liberty and the Pursuit of Happiness"). Chapter twelve, "Gross National Happiness" explains how since 2012 economists worldwide have been using a new measuring tool called gross national happiness (GNH), which measures what people really want. Surprisingly, GNH shows that most people prefer having more security and stability to having more money. Many of the fastest growing companies today have a new senior manager: the director of happiness.

This new GNH scale for measuring human progress balances being human with being prosperous. To quote the world's most popular book:

For what shall it profit a man, if he shall gain the whole world, and lose his own soul? (Mark 8:36 KJV)

The China Challenge

The US and China together roughly account today for 22 percent of the world's population and 50 percent of the world's GDP. Many experts view China as an economic and existential threat to the United States and its prosperity. As outlined in chapter thirteen, "The China Challenge," the Chinese-American relationship poses the greatest socioeconomic opportunity for both nations to establish a new paradigm through universal free trade. For the first time in history, the prosperity of the two most powerful nations in the world is tied together at the hip, to the world's mutual advantage. Both nations have much to learn from each other. It is my view that this relationship will ultimately change the world for the better.

The Russian Wild Card

World news in 2022 focused on the Russian invasion of Ukraine. In order to understand why this has happened, one needs to be familiar with Russian history and the tortured relationship between the two countries. In addition, one needs to look into the mind of President Putin and see why he feels completely justified in his actions. The impact of all this is mixed—a new cold war, the reinvigoration of the West, and some unintended consequences.

Russia is the wild card of the new roaring twenties posing a tactical nuclear threat not really seen since the Cuban missile crisis in 1962. The invasion affected supply chains, wheat, and fossil fuel availability, as well as economic and political security throughout the world.

STRATEGIES FOR THE NEW ROARING TWENTIES

The greatest political and socioeconomic challenge facing the world in the new roaring twenties is how to maintain political stability during periods of rapidly advancing technology and increasing structural unemployment. The solutions are part of the twelve pillars. Your understanding of this challenge can help inform your personal strategies.

Should You Quit Before You Are Fired?

This is a pervasive question facing readers, chapter by chapter. The answer is not just *yes* for millions, but a yes response that begs a second question: *When?* The answer to this second question for many readers is a most resounding *now*. Chapter fifteen will help you figure out the best time for you to strike out on your own or stay where you are.

Business-Opportunity Businesses: The New Business of Creating Business Opportunities

Airbnb and Uber started out in the sharing economy to provide opportunities for homeowners and car owners to earn extra cash when they weren't fully using their homes or their autos. However, a close examination of the largest individual producers for Airbnb or Uber today reveals that these companies are as much in the business of providing business and employment opportunities to new entrepreneurs as they are in the business of providing lodging or transportation to consumers. The average Airbnb provider owns or controls multiple properties in the same area and is thus more likely to be a specialty and user-friendly hotelier than a single property homeowner. Ditto for Uber, where individual entrepreneurs own and manage multiple Uber vehicles (which may soon be self-driving). Ditto for Amazon, which started out to be an online bookseller, but ended up being an affiliate marketer where it turns its online customers into entrepreneurs with their own online stores. See chapter sixteen, "Business-Opportunity Businesses" (BOBs) to learn whether you are best suited to become a customer of a BOB or one who offers BOBs to others, or most likely, both.

You Ain't Seen Nothin' Yet

There is reason to be optimistic despite the challenges and volatility we face. In chapter seventeen, we take a final look at the extraordinary impact of technology on our businesses and our lives. The twelve pillars will lay the foundation for prospering in the new roaring twenties, particularly by helping others.

In his play *The Tempest*, William Shakespeare observes that "What's past is prologue," meaning that an understanding and appreciation of the past informs our strategies in the future. However, we can't go back to the "good old days." Technology continues to change everything. You cannot get to your destination looking in the rearview mirror all the way.

I believe America, one nation under God, will survive and thrive. Its best days lie ahead.

The Worst and the Best of Times

PART I

The new roaring twenties has the potential to be one of the most meaningful times in your life, but it comes on the heels of a worldwide pandemic with massive economic, physical, and psychological trauma. It also comes as the world experiences tremendous technological innovation, reevaluation of life and work goals, and perhaps somewhat of a reawakening to what really matters. Not to mention the inspiring heroism of healthcare workers, first responders, and the families affected by the pandemic. It has been the best and the worst of times.

Chapter One

THE END OF THE WORLD AS WE KNEW IT

In order to understand where the economy is going in the new roaring twenties, you need to understand where the economy has most recently been.

In this chapter we'll examine:

- How good and bad the US economy really was before the pandemic began, starting with employment.
- Where you were when you realized the pandemic was upon us, a moment you will probably remember for the rest of your life.
- How the pandemic affected one family, mine— a franchisee for Planet Fitness gyms—during the business lockdown period in 2020.

The US economy at the end of 2019 was very strong. It had a low 3.45 percent official unemployment rate; relatively low interest rates due to abundant capital; rising real GDP due to increasing household disposable income;

and the highest stock market ever recorded. Moreover, paradoxically, it had remarkably low inflation—1.81 percent, despite what then seemed to be a very high annual federal deficit of $984 billion (4.6 percent of GDP).[1]

Over the longer term, the economy was also enjoying the longest economic expansion in history. This expansion ran more than ten years since the end, in July 2009, of the eighteen-month-long 2007–2009 Great Recession. Coincidentally, 2009 was also the highest federal deficit ever recorded to that point, at $1.41 trillion, designed to end the Great Recession, which eventually it did.

The Great Recession and ensuing crisis followed an extended period of expansion in US housing credit and mortgage-backed securities. High-risk subprime mortgages were offered by lenders who repackaged these loans in collateral pools as securities.

A decline in housing prices coupled with aggressive and irresponsible underwriting practices led to a near or actual collapse of major securities and investment firms (including Bear Stearns, Lehman Brothers, AIG, Merrill Lynch, Bank of America, Citigroup, and Goldman Sachs). All required billion-dollar bailouts by the Federal Reserve and US Treasury. This was the deepest recession since World War II, and the recovery took several years.[2]

At the end of 2019, all signs pointed toward more years of prosperity. That's when I began my research on the twelve pillars that I felt were going to reshape our lives.

Importantly, not everyone was enjoying this new economy in early 2020, nor were the reported unemployment numbers accurate when compared to prior years.

In addition to the 3.45 percent (5.7 million) officially unemployed in the 165-million-person US workforce, there were 5 percent (8.3 million)

---

1   Bureau of Economic Analysis, US Department of Commerce, US Bureau of Labor Statistics.

2   "The Great Recession and Its Aftermath," Federal Reserve History; Benjamin Bernanke, "Monetary Policy and the Housing Bubble," Annual Meeting of the American Economic Association (January 3, 2010); Benjamin Bernanke, "Monetary Policy Since the Onset of the Crisis," Federal Reserve Bank of Kansas City Economic Symposium (August 31, 2012). See also Bill Bamber and Andrew Spencer, *Bear Trap* (Brick Tower, 2008); Bethany McLean, and Joe Nocera, *All the Devils are Here* (Penguin Group, 2010, 2011), and Greg Farrell, *Crash of the Titans* (Crown, 2010).

more unemployed people (14 million total) who economists technically call "discouraged."

In the United States, a discouraged worker is generally defined as "a person not in the labor force who wants and is available for work . . . but who is not currently looking because of real or perceived poor employment prospects." This is someone who has looked for a job during the last twelve months, but not in the last month.[3]

Since 1967, the US Bureau of Labor Statistics does not count these discouraged as unemployed because they are deemed to be no longer actively looking for work. Moreover, these additional unemployed were just the tip of an iceberg.

Let's look beyond these numbers. These 14 million (5.7 + 8.3) total unemployed have millions of spouses, children, parents, grandparents, and others who live with them and are, or were, supported by them. The average US household size in 2020 was 2.53 people—meaning 35 million (14 × 2.53) people were living in a household with an unemployed member of the workforce (including discouraged). Thirty-five million people living with unemployment in their household is a lot more than the official government classified figure of 5.7 million unemployed—614 percent more.

Moreover, many of the 165 million people who had a job in 2019 didn't fare much better. Despite record high "average" household incomes and per capita GDP, 50 to 75 percent of Americans lived paycheck to paycheck without a safety net if they lost their income—plus 575,000 Americans were homeless and 42 million lived below the poverty line! The unemployment rate for Black Americans was twice the rate for White Americans—indirectly leading to violent riots and looting in many cities following the murder of George Floyd in Minneapolis on May 25, 2020.

COVID-19

Then came COVID-19. The pandemic put economic misery on steroids for almost everyone, making even worse the sum of all fears. Official

---

3   US Department of Commerce, US Bureau of Labor Statistics.

unemployment, excluding the discouraged, skyrocketed in 2020 from 3.45 percent in February, 4.4 percent in March, to 14.7 percent in April—more than 30 million Americans lost their jobs in just the spring of 2020.

COVID-19 emerged in Wuhan, China, in December 2019. By the middle of 2020, it was directly affecting the lives of every person, every job, and every nation on the planet. Supply chains were disrupted and prices of many materials increased.

Where Were You at 4:04 PM on March 20, 2020?

The coronavirus disease was officially declared to be a pandemic on March 11, 2020. Nine days later, on March 20, 2020 at 4:04 PM, with the economic catastrophe from the pandemic in full swing, I was giving a speech via Zoom on how the economic recovery sputtered during the Great Depression. I paused to take an urgent phone call from my wife, Lisa. She was at Primary Children's Hospital in Salt Lake City where our fifteen-year-old son had been admitted three days earlier. Lisa reported that, while our son was still extremely ill and unable to breathe on his own, he had tested negative for COVID-19. I said a prayer of gratitude, and realized that I would forever remember where I was at that moment, just as I vividly remember where I was during six other historical moments that, at the time, I thought might forever change my life:

1. **The assassination of JFK on November 22, 1963.** At 2:38 PM (EST), my fifth grade teacher, Miss Holiday, was summoned from the classroom. She returned a few minutes later, in tears, and walked slowly and quietly to her desk. She then announced that President Kennedy had been assassinated.

2. **The murder of Lee Harvey Oswald on November 24, 1963.** At 12:21 PM (EST), my mother was making our family lunch while my older brother, Steven, was watching television in the basement. Steven screamed to our family upstairs that Oswald had just been shot by Jack Ruby.

3. **The resignation of President Nixon on August 8, 1974.** At 9 PM (EST), I had just left a Fortran programming class at Hunter

College on Sixty-Eighth Street in New York City. I was walking along Park Avenue and noticed that pedestrians were gathered in groups around stopped cars and taxis, all listening to President Nixon's resignation on the vehicles' radios.

4. **The stock market falling 22.6 percent on "Black Monday," October 19, 1987.** At approximately 10 PM (EST), I was attending a social function in the West Wing and watched President Reagan's eyes swell with tears as he described how his parents lost faith in the American economy during the Great Depression.

5. **United Airlines Flight 175 crashing into the South Tower of the World Trade Center on September 11, 2001.** At 9:03 AM (EST), I saw the second plane strike while I was driving across the Manhattan Bridge with my pregnant wife and our one-year-old daughter. I remember wondering what was happening to our world and what our lives would be like from now on.

6. **The Great Recession (December 2007–June 2009).** During this eighteen-month period, there were several terrible moments when I lost faith in the resilience of the American economy. I'm glad that my immigrant father wasn't alive at the time to see me lose faith in the nation he loved so much.

7. **My son testing negative for COVID-19 (March 20, 2020).** While I was overjoyed to learn that my hospitalized fifteen-year-old son did not have COVID-19, I knew that his condition was still critical and that a new segment of our lives was about to begin.

What is the most significant moment in your pandemic experience? At what moment did the pandemic segment of your life or career begin?

For a biologist in Wuhan, China, it might be December 31, 2019, the moment your team first identified the novel virus. For a woman in Queens, New York, it might be a day in June 2020, when your mother died in a coma, while on a respirator—alone, because regulations denied family members access to patients' rooms. For an entrepreneur in Los Angeles running a restaurant with a $100,000 a month payroll, it might be the moment you received your first CARES PPP SBA "forgivable loan" of $250,000 (2.5x payroll) and realized that your business, thanks to government assistance, might survive.[4]

Throughout 2020, it seemed like the world, as each of us knew it, was coming to an end. Then, almost as abruptly as it began over a one-to-three-month period in early 2020, the world didn't come to an end. Not only did the world not end, the world economy, starting with the United States, recovered at rates and to new heights no one ever thought possible.

Planet Fitness and the Business Lockdown of 2020

Since 2010, my wife and I have owned two franchised Planet Fitness gyms in Salt Lake City. On Tuesday, March 17, 2020, we were ordered by our franchisor (and later by the state of Utah) to close due to a statewide lockdown of most businesses—which quickly became nationwide. All membership dues being collected, then about $350,000 per month, had to be credited back or not charged to our 16,000 members, who were no longer legally allowed to use any gyms. On a single day, my wife and I went from owning a family business earning about $100,000 a month profit, a positive $1.2 million a year, to owning a business losing $167,000 a month, a negative $2 million a year. Ouch!

In early May 2020, we were told by our franchisor that they would allow us to reopen after May 18, 2020, if, and only if, our local city, state, and county health departments allowed all gyms to reopen; subject of course to wearing masks, social distancing, and other cleaning and health safety regulations. A lot of challenging things happened during the sixty-two days that we were forced to close, but the worst thing was the uncertainty. Each day we had to think about whether to let the business go under, or pay $40,000 a week in bills so we'd have something left to reopen if and when the time came. In addition to keeping in touch with our 16,000 local gym members who were no longer being billed dues, each day our Planet Fitness employees,

---

4   CARES is the Coronavirus, Aid, Relief, and Economic Security Act. PPP is the Payroll Protection Program. A forgivable loan is one that you don't have to repay if you spend at least 75 percent of the loan proceeds on payroll. SBA is the Small Business Administration, which administers the program.

landlords, banks, cleaners, trainers, and other vendors tried to find out when we were reopening and when they could resume their lives—and we had nothing we could tell them.

To put our personal crisis into a national perspective, we only owned two of the 2,039 US Planet Fitness gyms that collectively had more than fifteen million members in 2020. The 2,039 US Planet Fitness gyms represented less than 2 percent of the 102,148 gyms, health, and fitness clubs in the US, which, in 2020, were all in same predicament. And this 102,148 gym figure represented less than 0.3 percent of the 32 million small businesses in the US—most of which were similarly forced to close without any idea of when they would be allowed to reopen.

Then, on Monday, May 18, 2020, our franchise was part of a small group of 155 US Planet Fitness gyms allowed to reopen in a handful of smaller states. Each month for the next nine months more corporate and franchisee Planet Fitness gyms were allowed to reopen. Meanwhile, our franchisor developed online and in-store programs, including free online exercise programs for nonmembers, to help people maintain their physical and mental health during a business lockdown never before seen in US history.

The pandemic has infected approximately ninety million persons and killed over one million in the United States. The toll worldwide has been immense, over a half-billion cases and close to fifteen million deceased. And counting.[5]

Each case reflects intimate human suffering as well as personal and economic dislocation. The empty storefronts in many cities reflect lost or delayed dreams.

The shutdown of many businesses, face mask requirements, shelter-in-place, and social distancing have changed our perceptions of reality and our relationships with one another. Each of us has our own story of the pandemic and how it ended the world as we knew it.

---

5   Helen Branswell, "WHO: Nearly 15 million people died as a result of Covid-19 in first two years of pandemic," STAT, May 5, 2022. Fatalities reported by countries are known to exceed seven million. WHO believes the real number is close to fifteen million.

Chapter Two

THE GREAT RECOVERY: DID YOU MISS IT?

Don't worry if you missed the economic recovery from the pandemic. If you're like most upper-middle class Americans reading this book, you may have missed most of the pandemic recession in the first place. Economically speaking at least, you made it through. However, the impact on many others has been devastating and enduring.

In this chapter, we'll examine six reasons the pandemic didn't and won't cause a major depression. The actions taken by our private and public sectors helped lay the foundation for the economy in the new roaring twenties.

1. Big-box retailers and manufacturers dodging the lockdown entirely by offering "essential services";
2. The unprecedented government spending on the pandemic;
3. The unpredictable stock market;
4. The intrepid survivors on Main Street, starting with your local pub;
5. Unlimited capital and relatively low interest rates; and

6. Companies adjusting to remote work, changing the way business is done.

THE RECESSION THAT ALMOST GOT STARTED

A recession is generally defined as two successive quarters of a negative economic indicator, such as declining GDP or rising unemployment. The US economy certainly met these criteria in the first two quarters of 2020; GDP fell 5.0 percent in Q1 and 31.4 percent in Q2, 36.4 percent total—the largest decline ever recorded in the history of the United States!

However, in Q3 and Q4 2020, GDP roared back 33.4 percent and 4.3 percent respectively, 37.7 percent total—making up entirely for the Q1–Q2 decline and then some—finishing out full-year 2020 GDP up 1.3 percent. There was no recession at all for the US on a full-year 2020 basis.

Double-digit changes like this in GDP typically take place over decades, not over months in a single calendar year!

Then the economy continued its meteoric rise in 2021—at 6.4 percent annualized for Q1, 6.5 percent for Q2, 2.3 percent for Q3, and 6.9 percent for Q4. I anticipate similar increases in GDP will continue, on average, throughout the 2020s, just like GDP did during the eras' 1920s namesake.

U.S. GDP 2020–2021			
		U.S. GDP	Cumulative
Q1 2020	GDP fell	-5.0%	-5.0%
Q2 2020	GDP fell	-31.4%	-36.4%
Q3 2020	GDP rose	+33.4%	-3.0%
Q4 2020	GDP rose	+4.3%	+1.3%
U.S. GDP in 2021			
Q1 2021	GDP rose	+6.4%	+7.7%
Q2 2021	GDP rose	+6.5%	+14.2%
Q3 2021	GDP rose	+2.3%	+16.5%
Q4 2021	GDP rose	+6.9%	+23.4%

WHY DIDN'T THE PANDEMIC CAUSE A MAJOR RECESSION OR DEPRESSION?

A recession is a reduction in economic activity—so how did we escape a major recession (or even a depression such as occurred after the original Roaring Twenties) in 2020 when it seemed like everything shut down? Let's examine the six reasons the pandemic did not cause a major recession or depression in 2020. Then let's identify a seventh über-reason, the twelve pillars, which suggests our overall economy may thrive in the new roaring twenties and beyond.

1) Big-Box Retailers Offering Essential Services

When the business lockdown was mandated in almost all US states in March 2020, big-box retailers and other staple and food providers (e.g., Walmart, Apple, Costco, Target, Sam's Club, grocery chains) were deemed to be essential services and thus exempt from the lockdown and potential recession— keeping needed food, goods, and services flowing to individuals and businesses. Here are just two examples of thousands of essential services providers and how they fared.

Walmart

Allowing Walmart and others to remain open in the US had the added benefit of maintaining the GDP from the largest companies in America. They were permitted to operate in an almost normal manner. In addition, Walmart significantly expanded its e-commerce capabilities.

Walmart worldwide sales were $510 billion in 2019, $519 billion in 2020, and $555 billion in 2021. Walmart annual US sales increased from $341 billion in 2019 to $370 billion in 2020—what recession? Walmart and other large companies supplied the goods every household and business needed to stay open in 2020.[1]

Walmart's biggest challenge during the pandemic was labor. Walmart is the largest private employer in the US, with 1.6 million employees. In 2021 there were 240 million customer visits worldwide. In 2020, the US

---

[1]   *Marketplace Pulse* (May 28, 2021); Statista Research Department (January 27, 2022).

experienced its largest labor shortage—in part because tens of millions of Americans received more unemployment compensation benefits than they did net wages, in some cases, up to two to three times more!

Walmart has been implementing for years different models of robots for just this sort of labor conundrum. In addition to traditional self-checkout robot cashiers, these models include: (1) RFID-reading robots that allow shoppers to just walk out of the store with their purchases without stopping to check out;[2] (2) chip robots built in to smartphones that monitor what shoppers put into their cart; and (3) web-based shopping algorithms that greatly improve the online shopping and delivery experience—so much so that millions of Walmart shoppers chose to forego entirely the in-store experience—shopping only over the net. This may eventually eliminate the need for up to half of its in-store retail employees (mostly cashiers), a promising and troubling development.

Apple

On March 13, 2020, Apple closed all its retail stores outside of China and got ready to hunker down for the business lockdown—the government enforced closure of most retail outlets not deemed to be selling "essential services."[3] Apple had a market capitalization (value) that day of $912 billion or $57 a share. A few days later, on March 26, Apple stock surprisingly rose to $62.50 a share, making it the first company in US history to reach a $1 trillion market valuation. At this all-time record high of $1 trillion, at the beginning of the pandemic, Apple seized on the opportunity of implementing new technology to be the world's leading hardware supplier for remote learning and home offices. Apple laid off many of its retail employees, invested heavily in online sales technology, and doubled its online direct sales in 2020.

Wall Street reacted to what happens to earnings when a retailer retools for online sales. In the five months following March 26, Apple's market capitalization doubled to $2 trillion on August 24, 2020. It took Apple forty-four

---

2   RIFD stands for radio-frequency identification. An RIFD reader is a network-connected radio frequency transmitter and receiver that can read and write information to an RIFD tag. The transponder is in the RIFD tag itself.

3   Although Apple closed all its retail stores in 2020, its products were deemed to be essential. Apple's retail stores could have stayed open.

years to become a $1 trillion valuation company in the prior economy, but only five months to grow a second $1 trillion in value (to $2 trillion total) during the pandemic economy. As I write this, the market cap is approximately $2.5 trillion.

Watching the experience of Apple and other pandemic economic winners in 2020 led me to a realization regarding speed. Changes I originally thought in 2020 would be implemented over the next three decades would now in many cases be implemented over the next decade.

2) US Government Spending

A billion here, a billion there, and pretty soon you're talking real money.
—Senator Everett McKinley Dirksen, 1896–1969

Let's review some basic definitions before we speak about "real money."

Debt – The amount of money owed at a moment in time by the federal government of the United States, mostly through US Treasury bills (less than one-year maturity), notes (two to ten years), and bonds (ten to twenty years).

Deficit – The amount of federal tax and all other revenues collected less than the amount of government spending, assuming it's negative. If it's a positive figure, it's called a surplus.

Stimulus – Money paid directly to all US individuals who earned below a certain amount on their prior year's tax return, typically $75,000.

Stimulus tax relief – Credits given to US taxpayers to pay their taxes as part of a stimulus package (effectively the same as "stimulus").

One million dollars – One thousand $1,000 bills. Since there haven't been one $1,000 bills since 1969, a more accurate definition would be ten thousand $100 bills. To get an idea of how big a million is, it would take someone about twelve days, twenty-four hours per day without breaks, to count to one million.

One billion dollars – One thousand million-dollar bills (which don't exist). It would take someone about thirty-two years to count to a billion.

One trillion dollars – One million million-dollar bills (which again don't exist). It would take someone 32,000 years to count to a trillion.

Now, before I tell you how much money the United States government paid out in 2020 to stimulate the economy, let's add a human perspective. There are roughly 330 million residents in the United States—including both legal and undocumented residents.

In 2020, to counter the economic effect of the pandemic, I estimate that the US government spent $6.5 trillion more than it took in, consisting of $3.1 trillion in deficit, $2.6 trillion in stimulus, and $900 billion in stimulus tax relief.[4]

This $6.5 trillion is four and a half times larger, 450 percent, than the previous record-setting federal deficit of $1.4 trillion set in 2009 to deal with the Great Recession.

To put this in perspective, if you gave $6.5 trillion, divided equally, to every US resident, each would receive about $20,000. Or, if you gave this sum only to the forty million officially poor US residents, they would each receive about $162,500 ($650,000 for a family of four)—enough to eliminate US poverty, at least for a while.

At the time I am writing this book, I am expecting the US federal debt to exceed $30 trillion at the beginning of 2023.[5]

WARNING: Spoiler Alert!

---

4   *Forbes*, May 28, 2021.
5   Statista.com; Datalab.usaspending.gov; Treasurydirect.gov; Bureau of Public Debt; US Department of the Treasury Quarterly Bulletins.

You are about to read: (a) the truth about the US $30 trillion federal debt, and (b) what I think about the $6.5 trillion the US government spent on the 2020 pandemic.

The Truth About the US $30 Trillion Federal Debt

The current $30 trillion size of the federal debt doesn't matter.

You are reading my words as a lifelong member of the Republican Party, a former Republican candidate for US Congress (in Texas no less), and a former economic advisor to two US Republican presidents.

Again, the $30 trillion in US federal debt doesn't matter.

What does matter when it comes to the federal debt? The debt service.

Think of the first mortgage you ever had on a home. Did you worry about the principal, or did you worry, perhaps between jobs, about making your monthly payment? If you owe someone money—what's more important: paying off the principal or making your monthly payment?

It's making your monthly payment, and what your lender may legally do to you and your family if you don't make your agreed-upon interest and principal payments.

So, who owns the largest share of our $30 trillion in US federal debt? You do—you, your friends, your business associates, your parents—the largest investors in US federal debt are our Social Security trust fund (16 percent), the Federal Reserve (12 percent), mutual funds (6 percent), and many more benign organizations owned almost entirely by the citizens of the United States. These organizations should be the least of your worries.

About 33 percent of the US federal debt is held by foreigners; but look at who's on the list— it's not owed to Russia or North Korea! The five largest foreign debt holders in 2021 were: China ($1.08 trillion), Japan ($1.28 trillion), the UK ($368 billion), Ireland ($300 billion), and Luxembourg ($267.8 billion).

Frankly, I appreciate the fact that these nations have so much confidence in the full faith and credit of the United States. God bless Luxembourg, along with about one hundred other nations who are putting our (US) citizens' welfare ahead of the welfare of their own citizens. Each dollar lent to the US goes to improving the lifestyle of Americans by the same amount.

Moreover, the people and governments who lent the US money have traditionally only gotten back a fraction—one-ninth or about 11 percent—of what they gave us, due to inflation. One thousand dollars in 1960 is worth $9,000 today in purchasing power. With increasing inflation, this may well continue to be the case.

If you are concerned about the US federal debt and what it could mean to you, read ahead to the section "Unlimited Capital and Relatively Low Interest Rates." There I explain why people line up from around the world to lend (give, really) money to the United States, at almost no cost and will continue to do so for at least the foreseeable next few decades. This largesse of the world to the United States could alone justify an economic boom in the next decade.

You may be legitimately concerned that a potential increase in interest rates will increase the debt service on the federal debt. Don't be. As you'll also learn in a few pages, interest rates are not going back to double digits any time soon—I've been correct about this since the 1980s, when US Treasury rates peaked at 14.97 percent. And even if interest rates did increase to an unmanageable level, just the personal net worth (savings) of American citizens, $137 trillion, is much more than enough to handle any situation if we ever wanted to pay down, or off, our $30 trillion in national debt. As a practical matter, don't be terribly worried that your savings will be used to pay off the national debt.

However, there is something you should be concerned about when it comes to rampant government spending above what people really need—waste and immorality. In chapter eight, "Universal Basic Income," you'll learn how my late brother's life was destroyed by a phony government disability program that paid him more money to stay at home than he could earn at work.

What I Think About the $6.5 Trillion Spent on the Pandemic

Second, I promised to tell you what I think about the $6.5 trillion the US government spent in 2020 (alone!) on the pandemic.

The government of the United States did a very good job saving our economy—it was $6.5 trillion well spent! The Republican Party (which held power in 2020) did great in 2020 by pouring trillions in stimulus into the

United States economy and giving money directly to individuals and businesses. The Democratic Party (which held power in 2021) did an equally great job continuing the stimulus payments in 2021. The results, as evidenced by the Standard and Poor's 500 (S&P), speak for themselves—the stock market completely recovered in the second six months (Q3–Q4) of 2020, all and more than it lost in the first six months (Q1–Q2) of 2020.

In 2007–2009, our nation faced an economic crisis then second only to the Great Depression—but this time it wasn't caused by something a vaccine could fix. Back then it took six years, not six months, for the S&P to recover by 2013 what it lost.

"We" (both national parties) did great in 2020–2022, learned a lot from 2007–2009, and applied what we learned to the betterment of our nation—laying an economic and social foundation for the new roaring twenties.

3) The Unpredictable Stock Market

The initial negative impact in 2020 of the pandemic on the stock market far exceeded the negative impact of the stock market crash of 1929, but then completely bounced back, and then some, in the same calendar year. This upswing prompted confidence that recovery was possible. Then, of course, the market declined in 2022. I expect significant stock market swings throughout much of the new roaring twenties. Of course, predicting the stock market is a fool's errand.

It is my view that GDP and employment are better indicators of the economy performance than the stock market. Often, stock market valuations are not based on earnings and profit margins, but rather on hype and so-called momentum. In fact, in some cases, earnings are not necessary at all for a high valuation. Value is based on projections, which are at best a guess at the future.

My father was born in 1903 and lived through sixteen of the nation's forty-seven recessions. I once asked him: What's the difference between a recession and a depression? He replied, citing a popular joke: "That's easy. In a recession your neighbor loses his job. In a depression, you lose your job."

For most of us, our "depression" (our firsthand experience) came sometime during the first or second quarters of 2020 when the entire country, and soon the world, entered the "business lockdown" and "social distancing" period. Unlike during the Great Depression of the 1930s, which was caused by the economic laws of supply and demand, this 2020–2022 catastrophe was caused by the laws of biology, which meant that everyone, no matter how rich or how poor, was affected.

During the second quarter of 2020, GDP decreased at an annualized rate of 31.7 percent. To put this in perspective, during the first three years of the Great Depression, annual GDP only fell 8.5 percent in 1930, 6.4 percent in 1931, and 12.9 percent in 1932.

Unlike the Great Depression, where virtually everything fell in value and stayed that way for a decade, the pandemic economy was resilient. Incredibly resilient! Right after GDP fell an annualized 31.7 percent in the second quarter of 2020, GDP bounced back in the third quarter of 2020 and increased at an annualized rate of 33.1 percent. GDP increased 1.3 percent for the full year in 2020.

The Standard and Poors 500 (S&P) is a stock market index of 500 large companies. It was at an all-time high of 3,855, worth about $30 trillion, on January 25, 2020, just before the pandemic became widespread. Over the next fifty-four days, the S&P index fell 40.2 percent to 2,237 on March 23 and then came roaring back 44.58 percent over the next seventy-seven days to 3,232 on June 8. This decrease, and subsequent increase, were each the fastest decrease and increase ever seen in history—both occurring back-to-back in less than six months during the same calendar year! The stock market was reflecting the public's ever-changing opinion of how businesses would be impacted by the pandemic, interest rates, geopolitical events, and other extraneous factors and how they would deal with it. As I write this, the S&P is at 3,650.

4) Survivors on Main Street

The pandemic economy was creating losers and winners on Main Street. Most importantly, it gave certain business owners the opportunity to retool and bounce back stronger than ever. This is a case of "survive, then thrive."

Although I didn't realize it at the time, I initially saw this survive-then-thrive phenomenon on May 18, 2020, when my family went out for our first dinner together since the business lockdown began on March

17, 2020. We went to visit a local restaurant close to our home called Skier's Pub (name changed).

Skier's Pub is a standalone 150-seat family restaurant located in Park City, Utah. My children grew up going there, and it was our first choice when we heard that a few local restaurants would be reopening on Monday, May 18, 2020, under "special conditions."

I had phoned this restaurant and checked their website in early May, only to be told that they didn't know when they would be allowed to reopen. This changed, seven days before their reopening.

The Skier's Pub phone recording and their website stated that only seventy-five of their 150 seats would initially be available to facilitate "social distancing." No one would be allowed inside the building unless they were wearing a mask and had made a reservation online with an app on their smartphone. The recording apologized for the restrictions and noted that they were mandated by our county health department, which could close the restaurant anytime if their rules were not followed. Later, I learned that our county health department required a cell number to trace patrons of any open business in case there was a COVID-19 outbreak from that business.

We made a reservation for 6 PM on Monday, May 18, using just my cell phone number and without speaking to a person. I later found out it would have been quicker on their website. When we arrived, there was a hostess outside with an iPad who confirmed our reservation by my cell number, directing each group of diners to enter one table at a time. Because the restaurant was not full, this same hostess was also able to make instant reservations if needed for some customers wanting to dine right away, as well as for future visits.

Once inside, a different host, Jesse, confirmed the last four digits of my cell phone, and I received a text telling me to "Please follow host Jesse to your table."

When we arrived at our table, Jesse took our drinks order and entered them into his iPad. He then explained that we could only access the menu, and order food, using a cell phone and a QR code posted on all four sides of a two-by-two plastic cube on our table. Jesse told us to look at the menu on our phones, determine what we each wanted, and then wait until a server returned with our drinks to answer questions about the menu. Any of our group could access the online menu and order food with their own smartphone provided they had my cell number. Shortly thereafter, a different server arrived with our drinks and then directed us to order using the menu on our smartphones.

Our food arrived much sooner than expected. When we were almost done eating our entrees, another server arrived in a similar fashion, asking what we wanted for dessert and coffee—and he entered our responses into his iPad. When we finished our complete meal, I signaled to a different server to find and tell our server that we were ready for our check. This server told me that we didn't need a check: any of our cell phones would function as a cash register, including tipping, as long as the user had the original cell phone number (mine) that was used to make the reservation.

I charged the meal to my credit card using my iPhone, noting that the price was less than I had expected. I then realized the bigger picture. All of the employees we had encountered, from the hostess outside to the last waiter who told me how to pay my bill, were electronically connected and could do any required function in the public areas of the restaurant. It was as if each employee's brain was synchronized when it came to giving great service—with each employee able to cover for each other. No server would have to tell a patron "I'm not your server" or "I'll have to check if we still have any those left." The restaurant had retooled its entire operations using standard, off-the-shelf SAAS (software-as-a-service) programs, accomplishing what every coach ultimately wants from every member of their team—the ability for each player to function as one.

I had arrived with lowered expectations—just wanting a safe place to dine and get out of my house with my family. Skier's Pub exceeded all my expectations and, in doing so, fulfilled the fundamental requirement for happiness: Happiness = Reality less Expectations. Moreover, as you'll learn about in chapter eleven, "Consumer Surplus," Skier's Pub had delivered true consumer surplus—a product or service for which I would have happily been willing to pay more.

Everything Skier's Pub had changed so far was originally done to survive, just to meet the health and safety requirements of our local authorities. Once the coronavirus came under control in 2021, the restaurant was set to thrive, not just survive. The technology they implemented for survival had given them the operational potential to double their former sales by auto-mating most of their take-out business, reduce prices so more people could afford to go out, and hire more employees who had fewer skills yet needed less time to train and who were each less critically needed when they got sick or just wanted a few days off.

5) Unlimited Capital and Relatively Low Interest Rates

One of the main economic reasons for the escape from serious recession and the eventual prosperity in the next decade will be an abundance of capital and relatively low interest rates. Despite the return of inflation and resultant interest rate increases, rates are still historically low and growth capital is available.

Economically, on a total basis, the US sailed through the pandemic, partially at the expense of depositors from other nations who tripped over themselves to loan the rewards from their labors to the United States Treasury and to the American people.

I live in Park City, Utah, a ski town that used to be a mining town. In the 1800s, thousands of immigrant miners traveled to Park City to try their luck at striking it rich. When a miner found a strike of gold or silver, he would work his claim day and night. He would bring his newfound wealth for safe-keeping to one of the banks on Main Street.

There were three banks to choose from. They were among the largest buildings in town, and each had a prominent walk-in safe and armed guards. Unlike banks of today that pay interest, depositors paid storage charges to the bank for safeguarding their wealth, mostly raw gold. In those days, you picked the bank with the strongest guards and the most secure safe versus choosing the bank that paid the highest interest—it wasn't called "the Wild West" for nothing!

Today, particularly after the Great Recession of 2007–2009 and the pandemic, a similar phenomenon exists among nations, foreign entities, and wealthy individuals seeking a safe place in the US to store their wealth. It's called "lending at the discount rate," and it works like this at our current $2 trillion annual rate of deficit spending.

Each week, the US Treasury creates about $40 billion worth of net new $1,000 Treasury bills (popularly called "T-bills") that promise to pay the "bearer" $1,000 on a set date in fifty-two weeks.[6] While most T-bills are for $1,000, the Treasury can issue bonds in dominations up to $5 million, and for maturities between a few days to one year. The Treasury holds an auction to sell the $1,000 T-bills, for traditionally a discounted price of around $950 each, and the buyer (whom we'll call Lender A) returns to the US Treasury fifty-two weeks later to get their T-bill paid off for $1,000.

The fifty-dollar difference between what Lender A paid on Day 1 ($950) and the $1,000 Lender A receives at the end of Day 365 is called the "discount" and is effectively the interest paid by the US Treasury for borrowing $950 for 365 days—which works out to an annual interest rate in this case of 5.26 percent ($50 interest on $950 borrowed). Another way of looking at this transaction is that the US Treasury borrowed $950 at a 5.26 percent interest rate from Lender A, and then the US paid Lender A back $1,000; this represents $950 in principal and $50 in interest at the end of one year.

Now, assume that Lender A isn't alone in wanting to earn about 5 percent interest and requiring a safe place to store its money, especially during a major crisis like 9/11, the Great Recession, or the pandemic. Just when Lender A bid $950 for the $1,000 T-bill, another lender, whom we'll call Lender B, bids $960—offering the US Treasury a better opportunity to borrow $960 at a 4.17 percent effective interest rate ($40/$960) for one year. Before the Treasury auction ends, another lender, Lender C, shows up bidding $970 for the $1,000 T-bill—offering to loan the Treasury $970 for one year at a 3 percent interest rate ($30/$970). And so on, and so on, until down the line Lender Z offers to buy the $1,000 T-bill for $999.99—offering the US Treasury the opportunity to borrow $999.99 for one year at an interest rate of one penny, 1/1000th of a percent ($0.01/$999.99)—effectively 0 percent or 1/100 of a dollar in interest.

Why does a foreign person or entity want so dearly to own US debt, which is paying relatively low interest rates? There are many reasons, but let's focus on the two most important ones.

---

6   The Treasury actually creates enough T-bills to replace those reaching maturity, since almost all lenders roll over their maturing Treasury securities for new notes, plus about $40 billion a week in net new securities to cover the current $40 billion/week ($2 trillion/year) of deficit spending (new borrowing).

1. **US political stability** – Investors worldwide fear expropriation of their wealth more than anything else, either through confiscation, taxation, or communism. Even after the events of January 6, 2021, extreme partisan politics, mass shootings, and racial unrest, the US remains the most politically and economically stable major nation on earth. It is still the only large nation around today that has never defaulted on its debt.[7]

2. **US military strength** – If there is a major world war ever again, the United States would very likely come out as the last nation standing. It is the safest place to store wealth. In 2020, America spent $748 billion ($0.748 trillion) on the US military, which seems like almost nothing next to the $165 trillion in US assets that the military protects—$30 trillion in US debt + $135 trillion in US household assets (net of household debt), at a cost of less than one-half of 1 percent per year. I have often thought of the US military as the ultimate federal deposit insurance program protecting the wealth of the United States of America itself. I've also thought that the monies used to finance the US military, $748 billion or about three-quarters of a trillion dollars a year, should be directly charged pro rata to ultrawealthy individuals as a deposit insurance fee, since these individuals benefit the most from a strong US military.

In 1989, in Moscow, a Soviet economist disparagingly and inaccurately paraphrased the title of my book *Other People's Money* (Simon & Schuster, 1989). She criticized the United States military as the "poor slobs stuck with the job of protecting 'other people's money.'"

Unfortunately, she had a point, although not exactly the one she thought she was making. Hopefully, our volunteer military becomes increasingly high tech and its members become better financially compensated for their service. Perhaps one day Americans with extreme wealth, who disproportionately benefit from having the world's strongest military protect their

---

7   Technically, the US did default on repaying T-bills maturing April 26, 1979, for a few days due to operational, non-financial challenges.

wealth, will be taxed for the cost of US defense forces proportionate to their wealth. A 1 percent per-year defense tax on US household net worth would finance a $1.49 trillion annual military budget—a 200 percent increase over the current (2020) $748 billion military budget.

Whatever your opinion is of US political stability and of US economic policy, both are much better for investors than any other nation. The United States of America doesn't have to be perfect. It just has to be relatively number one in political stability and military strength to attract the world's capital and for the world's best and brightest individuals to want to live here.

As an economist and advisor on public policy, I've experienced negative interest rates three times in my career: during and after 9/11, during the Great Recession of 2007–2009, and during the pandemic. These three times were among the most impactful of my professional life because I realized how terrified foreign investors must be of their own nation collapsing—so terrified that they were willing to effectively pay the United States to take their money for zero or negative return.

Every US Treasury instrument purchased by a foreign entity, government, or person represents an enormous gift to the lives of ordinary Americans. This is compounded by the willingness to accept nominal and sometimes even negative interest rates.

As explained earlier, US debt is about $30 trillion with over one-third owned by foreign entities. This approximate $12 trillion is equivalent to a transfer of wealth from the citizens of these foreign nations to the citizens of the United States—since by definition this $30 trillion represents monies that have been spent. In chapter thirteen, "The China Challenge," I'll explain what many millionaire Chinese citizens, and other foreign nationals, really want from the United States—in most cases, legal US citizenship and US residency—and what this means to the US economy. The founders of Apple, Amazon, Google, Tesla, Facebook, and many more current billionaires were born in a foreign country or, like myself, are first-generation Americans.

In general, low interest rates benefit wealthy nations and investors to the detriment of those loaning their savings. While there is a view by many, including central bankers, that low interest rates benefit an economy, there is an inequality to be considered.

LET'S TALK ABOUT INFLATION

Inflation is on everyone's mind. Since World War II, the US has experienced three periods of prolonged double-digit inflations: 1946–1948, 1974–1975, and 1979–1981. There is a very real concern that we will experience an era like the 1970s when the inflation rate exceeded 7 percent for an entire decade while the economy stagnated.

The pandemic caused supply chain disruptions. The government stimulus packages increased consumer spending power. The Russian attack on Ukraine affected oil and wheat prices and supply.

It is my view that advancing technology and improved productivity will have more to do with slowing inflation than any actions taken by the Federal Reserve or the US government. Interestingly enough, incomes for the most part have kept up with price inflation. The biggest price increases have been for items that, by and large, represent a smaller share of consumption. Rice, for example, which feeds over half of the world's population is proportionately less as a share of income. Energy and food as a share of disposable income are also historically low. Advances in productivity and technology are reducing the overall bite of inflation, although not in ways readily discerned by consumers. This is not particularly comforting to those with lower incomes. Even small price increases can threaten their survival. While overall national income is up, wage gains have not kept up for those on a subsistence budget.

This suggests the solution of a universal basic income, discussed in chapter eight. It literally can be the difference between life or death for many Americans.

6) Remote Work

As a business owner and entrepreneur, I have found it useful to work remotely for many years. The locations of my companies are all over the place, and my responsibilities vary depending on the type of business and exigent circumstances.

The pandemic caused much traditional "office work" to be carried out from home or in a hybrid fashion. As the pandemic subsides, there is a gradual movement back to the office. Many employers and senior managers favor an office environment where they can build teamwork and synergy. That way they can manage "by walking around" and with motivational (in their view) meetings and synchronicity.

Employees have learned to love remote work. It eliminates the commute and facilitates childcare and other domestic responsibilities. Rather than employees working less, it has generally caused them to work extended hours.

It seems that the office is not going back to where it was. A hybrid remote and office system is developing. This has an impact on the commercial real estate market. There will not be the same demand for traditional office space. In particular, suburban and central business district office complexes with larger floor plans will be negatively affected. Companies will simply not need as much space or the same type of space.

In addition, remote workers may want a home that anticipates their office needs, both in design and location. It may now be possible to hold down a job in New York, while living and working in Park City, Utah, for instance.

THE SEVENTH UBER-REASON: THE TWELVE PILLARS

Our nation escaped falling into a pandemic recession or even depression by actions taken by our public and private sectors and the other reasons identified above. Let me emphasize, however, that these major actions pale by comparison to what has economically saved us from the pandemic: the economic potential of the twelve pillars and their positive, long-term impact on the US economy. Every entrepreneur and businessperson should endeavor to understand the rewards of these twelve pillars. They are bringing our economy into the new roaring twenties.

This does not mean that there won't be stock market declines and corrections. This also does not mean that there will be no recessions. Expect some of both during these upcoming volatile times. However, understanding the twelve pillars will help you survive and thrive.

The Six Economic Pillars

PART II

The economic promise of the new roaring twenties will be predicated in large part on six economic pillars. First and foremost, technology will drive wealth and impact our daily lives in ways we cannot yet readily perceive. The entire world is retooling for growth. This will be enhanced by an energy revolution the likes of which we have never experienced.

Structural unemployment is a sign of growth and progress, but its human toll is traumatic. Numerous and pervasive robotic applications will accelerate these concerns. Possible solutions include the growing gig economy and the important concept of universal basic income. There will be volatility and unique challenges during the new roaring twenties, but also amazing technological progress.

Chapter Three

TECHNOLOGY-DRIVEN WEALTH

*Most traditional economic theories are based on scarcity.
The theory of economic alchemy, based on abundance,
underlies the twelve pillars that will drive our economy
and our society in the new roaring twenties.*

I n this chapter, we will examine economic alchemy, which explains how we now have unlimited wealth due to the application of ever-expanding technology (i.e., human ingenuity) to our physical resources. In short:

W **(wealth) = P (physical resources) × T (technology)**
$$W = P \times T$$
Information technology has a multiplier effect (n)

$W = P \times T$ has been true throughout human history, except that technology (T) was often constant over the course of most people's lives. That's why the history of human civilization prior to the twenty-first century is mostly about the accumulation of more physical resources (P): land, minerals, fresh water, etc.

In order to acquire wealth (W), you can acquire more P or acquire more T. When you acquire more P, you use it up to create wealth. When you acquire more T, you don't use it up. Your acquired T becomes cumulative, until it is rendered obsolete by better T. That's how in my lifetime, the nation with the most P in the world, the former Soviet Union with the most land, minerals, and oil, economically collapsed. The nation with the least amount of land and natural resources but the most technology (in the 1980s), Japan, became the second wealthiest nation in the world (before China emerged).

Now consider, what if we viewed the world as providing unlimited resources that held the possibility of wealth for all? What if, like the ancient alchemists who tried to turn base metals into gold, we could use science and engineering to create great value where little existed before?

Today's alchemic world isn't just a promising model, a hypothetical theory, or an abstract dream. It is, in fact, the world in which we are living as we begin this new exciting decade of potential unlimited wealth.

In this chapter, we will summarize the three principles of economic alchemy and its central equation. We will also consider how you can apply this important concept to your life and business.

MY FIRST DAY AT WHARTON GRADUATE BUSINESS SCHOOL

I was attending my first class as an MBA student in January 1975 when I realized that I might have made a big mistake going to graduate business school. The class was macroeconomics, and the professor began his lecture as follows:

> *Economics is the study of scarcity. There is a limited supply out there of scarce resources—land, fresh water, oil, labor, and other raw materials. How we distribute our scarce resources for maximum efficiency, whether it be capitalism, communism, socialism, or any other "ism" you call it, is the science of economics.*

This was the moment I realized that I didn't want to be there.

Scarcity, I thought. *Really?* I thought I was going to Wharton to learn how to create unlimited wealth—food, housing, transportation, entertainment—that every person on the planet could afford. My professor's belief in scarcity didn't just contradict my beliefs as a student of science, it contradicted my religion. The God I loved and prayed to would not have created a world where humankind could multiply into the billions but be denied the ability to feed and shelter themselves.

In my next class, marketing, everyone seemed focused on beating the competition—getting a customer to switch to your brand of cigarettes or packaged food. This upset me almost as much as macroeconomics. To me, marketing should be about educating prospective customers about a new product or service that would improve their life or their health or both. To many of my fellow MBA students, marketing was about beating the competition by taking away someone else's customer.

Of course, back then I was a twenty-year-old graduate student who felt intimidated even being at Wharton Graduate Business School, let alone being up to challenging my professors, one of whom was awarded the Nobel Memorial Prize in Economics just five years later in 1980.[1] I didn't have a response then to courses based on scarcity rather than abundance—it would take me the next fifteen years to develop my own economic theory based on abundance. I called it the "theory of economic alchemy" in deference to the ancient alchemists who believed they could create gold through science and religious faith. This contrasted with then conventional wisdom that the only way to get more wealth, basically P, was to battle the people next door and take their land and gold.

THE THREE PRINCIPLES OF ECONOMIC ALCHEMY

Traditional economics holds that a society's wealth depends on its supply of physical resources such as land, labor, minerals, and water. The only way to get more of these resources is to take them from somebody else. In that model, one person's gain has to be someone else's loss, a depressing zero-sum game.

This view of the world has spawned wars, revolutions, political movements, government policies, business strategies, and maybe a religion or two.

Well, thanks to the technologies that enable the twelve pillars in the new roaring twenties, there are effectively unlimited resources out there from which we potentially can create unlimited wealth.

This is because, as you'll see in just a moment, the supposed scarcity of resources is merely an invention of the human mind. In addition, our minds are always inventing new resources before we run out of the resources that we have already defined.

Moreover, as you'll see in chapter twelve, "Gross National Happiness," we have a new benchmark for economic progress in the new roaring twenties, GNH versus GDP. GNH measures wealth we create once we take into account any physical resources we deplete—from clean air to fossil fuels.

Our technology makes it possible to turn the raw materials of nature into elegant and sophisticated devices that change our lives. We "make computers from dirt," as mathematician Mitchell Feigenbaum has said, referring to how silicon, which is used to make computer chips, comes from the world's most ubiquitous product (sand). Even "rare earths," such as lithium for batteries, are being extracted in new and exciting ways throughout the world.[1]

In measuring our wealth, it's not how many gallons of oil we have, it's how many miles per gallon we get when we drive—which can be unlimited when we drive all EVs powered by wind or solar power. It's not how many acres of farmland we have, it's how much food we can produce per acre—which can be unlimited when we use hydroponic farming techniques (without soil) and 100 percent solar-powered LED lighting, anywhere, even indoors or without land.

While a traditional economist looks for better ways to slice up the same old pie, an economic alchemist concentrates on baking a new pie that's big enough for all to share. In other words, an alchemist creates wealth; a traditional economist merely moves it around. The theory of economic alchemy makes the new roaring twenties a whole new ball game.

---

1   Mitchell Feigenbaum (1944–2019) was a mathematical physicist who developed deterministic chaos theory and the Feigenbaum constants.

The theory of economic alchemy explains how technology determines the nature and supply of our physical resources, what controls the speed with which technology advances, how technology determines the nature and level of consumer demand, and how we can use the technology gap to see what's ahead. Let's identify the three major principles of the theory of economic alchemy.

Principle One: Technology Is the Major Component of Wealth

With the exception of finding fresh water in lakes and rivers and some basic plants that grow in the wild, what we call physical resources or wealth are inventions of the human mind. From vessels to store and transport water, to agricultural produce, to minerals and fossil fuels, the definition and supply of all of our so-called "natural" resources are derived from technology. Moreover, once we have created and/or defined a resource as wealth, the supply of that resource is also determined by the technology with which we obtain it, process it, transport it, and use it.

As you'll see in chapter four, "An Energy Revolution," it is in the last category, usage of already-defined natural resources, where we will see some of the largest gains in the new roaring twenties. For example, simply switching from an incandescent to an LED light bulb can potentially reduce the ongoing cost of illumination by 1,000 percent, a 10x lift. This is equivalent in energy savings to switching from driving a car that was getting twenty miles per gallon to one getting two hundred miles per gallon. How would your life change if the $5,000 or so a year you spent on transportation dropped to $500 a year?

The World's First Energy Crisis

From approximately the thirteenth century until the beginning of the Industrial Revolution, a significant part of the world's economy rested on the whaling industry. The blubber was used to produce whale oil for lighting and heating homes, the spermaceti was used to make candles and lubricants, and the whalebones were used for numerous applications ranging from artistic carvings to the flexible stays in women's corsets. In fact, the economies of some of the earliest settlements in the United States were built entirely on the whaling business.

When America itself was less than one hundred years old, it had already come to dominate this six-hundred-year-old industry—by 1850 the US whaling fleet numbered approximately seven hundred of the world's largest 950 whaling vessels. While the ships of other countries caught whales and brought them back whole to their home ports for processing, ingenious Yankee whaling ships were entire floating factories in themselves—processing the raw whales into their useful products before they returned home. This allowed them to stay out longer at sea, bring back cargoes of much greater value, and reduce harbor pollution in their main port back home. This processing of the whale products at sea (mostly boiling down the blubber into whale oil) had the additional benefit of returning the unused products to the ecological chain.

The world's first major energy crisis struck in the middle of the nineteenth century when the worldwide supply of whales dwindled, mostly due to the Yankee efficiency in harvesting them. In 1859, over ten thousand whales were harvested from the North Atlantic alone, causing a worldwide shortage in whale products on both sides of the ocean.[2]

Then, in 1859, just as the doomsayers were predicting the end of their economies due the shortage of whale products, another burst of Yankee ingenuity came onto the scene with a lower-cost substitute for virtually all whale-based products. Col. Edwin L. Drake drilled the world's first successful oil well in Titusville, Pennsylvania, on August 27, 1859, ushering in the modern petroleum age.[3]

In England, which dominated much of the world's economy during the nineteenth century, the internal economy was primarily dependent on coal production. Coal, which was used both as a source of energy and as a

---

2   Peter Applebome, "They Used to Say Whale Oil Was Indispensable, Too," New York Times, August 3, 2008; Edward Butts, "The Cautionary Tale of Whale Oil," The Globe and Mail, October 4, 2019; Herman Melville, Moby-Dick or The Whale (1851).

3   While commercial production of oil from shallow reservoirs began in 1857 in Romania, Drake's well, which produced twenty-five barrels of crude oil per day, is generally credited to have begun the modern petroleum industry.

principal ingredient in steelmaking, formed the backbone of British industrial power.

"The Coal Panic," as the newspapers called it, struck in 1865 when William Stanley Jevons (1814–1891) wrote a book predicting the end of the British industrial era due to the exhaustion of British coal supplies by 1900.

Although Jevons was born into a well-to-do English family, he had considerable trouble in his personal life before he came to write his book in 1865. His mother died in 1845, his eldest brother became mentally ill in 1847, and his father, a Liverpool iron merchant, went bankrupt in 1848. This failure of the family finances led him to quit college, where he studied chemistry and mathematics. He accepted a post in Australia until 1859 when he returned to England to finish college.

In 1865, he published *The Coal Question: An Inquiry Concerning the Progress of the Nation, and the Probable Exhaustion of our Coal Mines*, a book not unlike the doomsayer books that often appear during our energy crises. Utilizing his knowledge of chemistry and mathematics, Jevons compiled graphs and parabolic curves showing that at the then current 3.5 percent annual rate of increase in coal consumption, "The conclusion is inevitable that our present happy progressive condition is a thing of limited duration." Jevons's theories were referred to as the "the Jevons paradox."

Jevons was a true pessimist. He was skeptical of finding substitutes for coal, and he discounted the possibility of reducing consumption through more efficient use. He argued that "cutting costs would simply stimulate industrial expansion and so ultimately lead to increased demand for coal."

He predicted the demise of prosperity and ended his book with the statement, in italics: *"We have to make the momentous choice between brief greatness and longer continued mediocrity."* He also suggested reducing the national debt in order to partially compensate posterity for the extravagance of the current generation.[4]

Jevons's book made him nationally famous and led to the appointment of a Royal Commission on Coal. This commission, which did not report until 1871, eventually produced reassuring estimates of coal reserves, and the

---

4   R. D. Collison Black, "William Stanley Jevons," *The New Palgrave: A Dictionary of Economics* (Macmillan Press, 1987).

public forgot its fears. Meanwhile, the rapidly developing petroleum industry displaced coal in the economy long before Jevons's prediction of coal
famine by the end of the century could have occurred.

Jevons abandoned the subject of coal shortages and began work on a
link between periods of economic activity and the then recently discovered
astronomical phenomenon of solar sunspot cycles.[5]

Principle Two: The Advance of Information Technology—the Speed That We Communicate, Process, and Store Information

Once we realize that technology defines what we call our physical resources
or wealth, and it determines how much of an already-defined resource or
type of wealth we have for our lives, the question becomes: How do we get
more technology? Since around 3000 BC, with the invention of writing in
biblical times, it has been the advance of information technology that determines the advancement of all other types of technology. To obtain more of
anything you want, improve the informational technology that you use to
define it, locate it, obtain it, process it, transport it, and use it.

The Apple iPhone—January 9, 2007

Our ability to communicate, process, and store information, more than anything
else, has been responsible for the enormous increase in GDP since 2007 and a
commensurate increase in US household wealth since WWII—US household
net worth rose from less than $1 trillion in 1945 to $60 trillion in 2007.

Since 2007, after falling $10 trillion during the Great Recession of
2007–2009, US household net worth has doubled, from $70 trillion in 2007
to $142 trillion in 2021.[6]

---

5   The eleven-year solar sunspot cycle was first identified (as a ten-year cycle) in 1843 by
     the German astronomer Samuel Heinrich Schwabe. Jevons, using statistics of fluctua-
     tions in grain prices, identified an eleven-year cycle, which he attempted to tie to new
     astronomical data that the sunspot cycle might be eleven (rather than ten years). This
     work is interesting in the context that at the time, the study of business cycles was in
     its infancy.
6   US Household net worth was $60 trillion in 2009 and $130 trillion at the beginning of
     2021. It rose to $150 trillion at the end of 2021.

This was in part due to Steve Jobs's introduction of the Apple iPhone on January 9, 2007. This device, and its smartphone competitors from Google and others, literally connected in real time almost half the people on the planet. There were 3.5 billion smartphones worldwide in 2021. Less than 10 percent (300 million) of them are in the US. As a result, there has been a massive increase in the world's level of information technology and communication capabilities.

Arguably, the smartphone in all of its incarnations has contributed to a $60 trillion increase in US household wealth. To put this $60 trillion increase in net worth in perspective, the US cost of all the wars fought since 2001 is $6 trillion, the projected total cost of the pandemic stimulus plans from 2020 to 2025 is $7 trillion, and the entire US federal debt in 2022, which includes these figures, is only $30 trillion.

Who says "we" can't afford the US federal debt? It depends on which "we" you are talking about. The top 10 percent of US households own 70 percent ($91 trillion) of the $130 trillion of total US household net worth. This top 10 percent could easily pay off the entire US federal debt if an emergency arose requiring such—which, by the way, I don't currently see on the horizon.

The Blockchain

The blockchain is an example of economic alchemy (i.e., unlimited wealth) and the expansion of information technology. As the rock group Dire Straits proclaimed in 1985, this is "Money for Nothing."

The blockchain technology is based on multiple ledgers of transactions managed by a decentralized computer network. This is potentially the infrastructure for Web3 or the metaverse, the next phase of the internet.

The metaverse, or a virtual reality universe, sounds like a Silicon Valley buzz word. However, today's hype sometimes becomes tomorrow's reality, even if it is virtual. Meta (Facebook) and others are spending billions and betting the future on the metaverse.

The term *metaverse* first appeared in Neal Stephenson's 1992 novel, *Snow Crash*, but the concept, often dystopian, has appeared in various science fiction works. It has come to mean a network of multidimensional worlds that share data and interact with one another. They can be simultaneously accessed by potentially millions of users. It is early days with respect to functionality and terminology as well as governmental regulation of the metaverse.

Crypto currencies like Bitcoin and Ethereum have been promoted as alternative stores of value. Perhaps, but the volatility and relatively close alignment with stock market equities belies this argument. Cryptocurrencies reflect a unit of exchange, a useful ledger. They are not reliable investments and do not have intrinsic value. As cryptocurrencies and the stock market decline, look for the "bezzle." John Maynard Keynes developed this term in 1929 to describe the "inventory of undiscovered embezzlement," when investors become ever more credulous and rising prices create the appearance that real wealth is being created. It is only when the tide goes out that we can see who is wearing no pants.

Further, the US government will take a hard look at regulation and even installing its own digital currency. Other countries, most notably China, take a dim view of digital currencies and perceive them as a threat to central planning and control.

Meanwhile, cryptocurrencies have spawned the market for non-fungible tokens (NFTs). This digital asset or collectible has much in common with baseball cards or rare first editions. Pop-culture trends are exactly that, trends, so values will change dramatically, depending on the current zeitgeist.

Principle Three: The Backlog of Unimplemented Technological Advances (the "Technology Gap") Is the True Predictor of Economic Growth

The technology gap can be as simple as a better way of doing something that, through ignorance or indolence, we haven't gotten around to making use of yet. For an individual, this can be as simple as a better shaver or smartphone that we know we should upgrade to but haven't yet found the time. For an organization, it could be as simple as moving weekly in-person sales meetings to virtual meetings. For a society, it could be changing our laws and attitudes on discrimination, which would bring tens of millions of additional productive employees, especially women and minorities, into our workforce.

Technology gaps create great opportunities, but they also pose formidable obstacles. We have wasted precious time and resources over and over again. Many manufacturing plants and service centers are outdated.

Mines and rare earth deposit sites in the US are not ready to process critical resources. There is work to be done.

In chapter five, "Structural Unemployment," I examine how by closing technology gaps, one can restructure many companies with one hundred employees to double their output or customers while keeping the one hundred employees, although not necessarily the same one hundred employees they had before restructuring.

In the past, the greatest predictor of a nation's wealth was its accumulated unused physical resources, whereas today the greatest predictor of a nation's wealth is the technology gap: this backlog of unimplemented technological advances that it has not yet utilized. As you'll see in chapter four, "An Energy Revolution," just switching to LED light bulbs is yielding a reduction in the amount of electricity used for lighting. Switching to EVs from internal combustion engines (ICE) is yielding a 5x (500 percent) reduction in the amount of energy used for transportation. The number of incandescent light bulbs waiting to be changed to LEDs, along with the number of ICE vehicles ready to be traded in for EVs, are just one part of our personal, or our nation's, technology gap.

ECONOMIC ALCHEMY AND TECHNOLOGY-DRIVEN WEALTH

The explosion of technology and wealth during the last twenty years is directly related to the theory of economic alchemy, which I wrote about in 1989.

Most importantly, the world has benefited from economic alchemy on many economic and social levels. The greatest application of economic alchemy is yet to come in the new roaring twenties. This is because the real growth in an economy today comes from exploiting undeveloped technological advances, just as centuries ago nations got rich by exploiting undeveloped natural resources.

Prior to the pandemic interrupting our economy in the first half of 2020, technology was already advancing faster than it could be utilized, causing a backlog of technological innovations. The business lockdown of 2020–2021 increased the pace of research and development dramatically, but it also stopped certain practical applications dead in their tracks, i.e., the technology gap. Never before in history has there been such a large backlog of unimplemented technological advances. As a result, despite everything else that is going on, we are positioned for economic growth during the new roaring twenties. The technology gap will do more to reduce inflation than the Federal Reserve or the US government.

By enabling us to make productive use of particular raw materials, technology determines what constitutes a physical resource. Virtually everything we consider of value is only of value because of the technology that allows us to define it, locate it, transport it, and use it—and it is in this last category, usage, where we will see the greatest improvements in the next decade, starting with energy and sharing.

Land wasn't considered a resource or anything of value until human beings learned how to farm it. No wonder Peter Minuet in 1626 was able to purchase Manhattan for the equivalent of twenty-four dollars. The Native Americans had already harvested the wild game and plants on the island that they thought had real value. Livestock wasn't a resource until humans developed the technology of domesticating animals. Oil, the black goo that (in ancient times) used to appear in pools and pollute the fresh water supply, wasn't a resource until humans developed the technology of refining and burning it. Technology determines our supply of existing, defined physical resources by determining both our ability to find, obtain, distribute and store them, and the efficiency with which we use resources. So let's revise $W = P \times T$ to $W = P \times T^n$.

$$W = P \times T^n$$

Where:

W stands for wealth,

P for physical resources (that is, the traditional measures of wealth such as land, labor, minerals, water, and so on),

T for technology, and

n for the exponential effect technological advances in information technology have on all technology.

Quantity technology – technology that determines the available quantity of already-defined physical resources.

Use technology – technology that determines the efficiency by which we use physical resources.

Supply technology – technology that determines our ability to find, obtain, distribute, and use physical resources.

You might be asking yourself, "This seems obvious, what is new about wealth being defined as the amount of our food, minerals, housing, transportation, etc.?"

What's "new" is that until relatively recently in human history, *T* was generally a constant. People were born into the Stone Age, the Bronze Age, the Iron Age, the agricultural revolution, etc.—all periods in time defined by their technology. Since $W = P \times T$, and *T* was a constant, the only way to get more *W*, wealth, was to get more *P*, physical resources. Technology was something invented or discovered in a lab or a university with a "look what we've found" and "how can we use this" attitude.

This changed during World War II when the entire process of invention was turned upside down. Scientists were literally ordered to discover or invent something that didn't yet exist. When cut off from rubber trees in Southeast Asia, scientists were ordered to make synthetic rubber. After the US fleet was decimated at Pearl Harbor, scientists were ordered to build the atomic bomb, incorporating hundreds of technologies that didn't yet exist. Later, in 1963, President Kennedy committed the US to putting a man on the moon by the end of the decade even though there was little technology at the time to accomplish this task.

A complete change in managing this advance of technological "needs first" took place in early 2020 when the pandemic was ravaging the world.

In early 2020, scientists were ordered to build, in twelve months' time or less, a vaccine for COVID-19—even though the vaccine technology that existed when they were given the mandate would only allow them to do so in five to ten years.

The genetic sequence of the novel coronavirus, which causes COVID-19, was discovered first by the Chinese authorities. This sequence was made available worldwide in January 2020 to hundreds of laboratories. At the same time, Jennifer Doudna and numerous other researchers, doctors, and scientists were adapting years of study and experimentation into possible solutions. Then, in the greatest scientific expansion of T of all time, hundreds of laboratories worldwide began sharing data to develop the first vaccines by summer 2020, and then hundreds more facilities worldwide began clinical trials of different vaccines while openly sharing their results. This is the magic of sharing and serving others.[7]

The first vaccines began to be administered worldwide in December 2020 and substantially reduced the mortality rate of those vaccinated and then infected. As new variants of the disease developed, scientists continued this expansion of T.

The rate at which a society's technology advances is determined by the relative level of its ability to communicate, process, and store information. This is critical because it is information technology that gives us the ability to distribute information. This is the most significant development from a multiplier standpoint.

By providing us with new products and processes that change the way in which we live, technology determines what constitutes a need and hence the nature of consumer demand.

Just as technology defines what constitutes wealth for a commodity on the supply side, technology defines, in our affluent society, what constitutes a need on the demand side. As described best by the economist John Kenneth Galbraith in 1958, "In the affluent society, no sharp distinction can be made between luxuries and necessaries."[8]

---

7   Walter Isaacson, *The Code Breaker* (Simon & Schuster, 2021).

8   John Kenneth Galbraith, *The Affluent Society* (Hughes Mifflin, 1958). Professor Galbraith (1908–2006) reviewed my first book, *Other People's Money* (Simon & Schuster, 1989), on the cover of the *New York Review of Books* and served as an important mentor.

Today's luxury item is tomorrow's necessity. Make a list of the items you recently purchased; probably 50 percent of them (cell phone service, online research, a foreign-defined meal, etc.) didn't exist when you were born and were created by advancements in technology.

Technology determines the level of consumer demand by establishing the price at which goods can be sold.

Alchemic demand – demand for goods and services in excess of basic physiological needs.

Quantity demand – demand for more quantity of an existing product.

Quality demand – demand for a different quality version of an existing product.

Technology defines the level of demand for each and every product by determining the price and how the product fits with other products and lifestyles.

We live in an era of zero marginal product cost for many of the things we buy. It costs literally nothing for the supplier of an unused movie ticket or SaaS (software as a service) product to give it away.[9] The empty movie theater seat patron may buy popcorn, and the SaaS toolmaker patron may later purchase an upgrade.

In chapter eleven, "Consumer Surplus," we'll examine how, for many businesses, selling below marginal product cost is mandatory if your strategy is to launch a long-term business like Amazon, where your most important asset is goodwill. Some technology businesses (spurred on by venture capital) buy customers for more than the quantified value in order to build size and a first-mover position. This is a common strategy in Silicon Valley, sometimes creating a great business, but often ending in failure.

The immediate economic potential for an individual, an industry, or a society can be explained by examining the technology gap—the best practices possible with current knowledge versus the practices in actual use. This leads naturally to a fully developed better product or method that is ready to

---

9   SaaS, or software as a service, is a means of providing applications over the internet. The applications are sometimes termed web-based software, hosted software, or on-demand software. The provider manages access, security, and performance. Usually this involves multiuser architecture and can be readily customized.

be put to use. This requires no additional skills or training than the product, method, or practice that it is meant to replace.

Economic alchemy and the technology gap are major drivers in the exciting prospect of the new roaring twenties. To the extent one can recognize technological gaps and act on them, one has the possibility of a real contribution to the economy and society.

ZERO-DAYS

As you will see throughout this book, technology will create massive opportunities and wealth in the new roaring twenties. However, technology also has its risks. Unfortunately, we have prehistoric emotions, ancient institutions, and mind-bending technology converging.

The US is an automated nation with virtually everything plugged into the internet. This creates natural vulnerability. While the US has tremendous offensive cyber-warfare capabilities, it is remarkably weak in cyber-security, i.e., defensive capabilities. We are 10–15 years behind in our data and device security.

A "zero-day" is a computer software vulnerability or bug affecting a vendor or user. Originally, it referred to the number of days a vendor has to fix a bug before its software is hacked. Once a vendor is aware, a repair or patch can be implemented. Often a zero-day will be undetected until a zero-day exploit creates a serious problem. This is called the window of vulnerability.

The US government has been stockpiling zero-days for decades, generally for national security reasons, i.e., spying. On September 11, 2001, the planes crashed into the World Trade Center. It became clear that this attack should have been identified and prevented. The US then dramatically expanded its financial support for cyber-intelligence. In 2010, a joint US-Israeli cyber-attack dubbed Operation Olympic Games, reportedly released the Stuxnet virus and caused major damage to the prototype Iranian nuclear facility at Natanz.[10]

---

10   *Zero-Days* (2016 Magnolia documentary, produced by Alex Gibney, Olga Kuchmenko, and Marc Shmuger, directed by Alex Gibney).

The Stuxnet virus escaped beyond its original use and became available worldwide in a number of variations. The mercenaries took over. The market became the Wild West, and east and north and south.

The biggest purchasers of zero-days include Russia, China, and Saudi Arabia. Independent and government sanctioned operators buy, sell, and exploit cyber-vulnerabilities, as a result, infiltrating millions of devices and software systems.

It has become increasingly difficult to determine if a microchip or line of code is secure or a problem, or both. Government sponsored and rogue hackers are well inside our infrastructure ranging from social media to the power grid. We are living on the edge of multiple disasters.

Just as technology has created the opportunity for unlimited wealth, technology has the capability (when combined with national awareness) to confront these critical security risks. In order to protect the promise of the new roaring twenties, action must be taken by our national leaders and our security experts.

Silicon Valley entrepreneurs race to get to market. If they move fast and break things, we as a society take unimaginable risks. Security should be the top priority from the beginning of each technology through its maturation.

Passwords are not really the answer. Much like airport security, they are theater—an illusion of safety.

There needs to be thoughtful and extensive regulation of open-source protocols and developers. Software and hardware products should meet detailed security requirements and a system of grading security protocols should be implemented. The US needs a national cyber-security commission, ideally at the cabinet level.[11]

Wake up, America! Your future depends on it.

---

11   Nicole Perloth, *This is How They Tell Me the World Ends*, (Bloomsbury, 2021).

TAKEAWAYS

1. The theory of economic alchemy (i.e., unlimited wealth) is the new landscape that has facilitated the development of the twelve pillars of our economy and our society.

2. Traditional economists and most politicians believe that there is a fixed, limited supply of raw materials, and the only way to get ahead is by taking (i.e., taxing) something from somebody else. No wonder they call economics the "dismal science."

3. Every person and business in the new roaring twenties has the potential to have unlimited wealth once they understand how technology (particularly information technology) defines both what constitutes a resource and the supply of already-defined existing resources.

4. There's no limit to the size of a national economy, or even your personal economy, because technology determines the level of demand by defining new products and services that people want or can now afford.

5. With great technology comes great risk, particularly from cyber-attacks. It is essential to deal with this threat and make it a priority in the new roaring twenties.

Chapter Four

AN ENERGY REVOLUTION

The price of energy affects everything from transportation to manufacturing products to agricultural produce!

Perhaps the best reason to move away from foreign fossil fuels is to interrupt the flow of cash to autocrats, oligarchs, and criminals. Taking control away from these powerful interests will not be easy. The energy revolution is rooted in world peace, climate change, and economic competitiveness.

In the new roaring twenties, the supply of energy from new and expanded sources—like fracking, ocean waves, better drilling techniques, wind, hydroelectric, hydrogen, nuclear, and solar power—could eventually double our total energy supply. This is a 2x lift, driving down the price of energy and virtually everything else. I believe real energy prices will actually fall on average beginning in 2033 for the first time in history.

Having said that, the US is woefully behind in approving the implementation of renewable energy projects and strategies. This keeps energy costs high and discourages investment.

Potential savings could come from applying better technology to our devices that use energy to massively reduce their consumption, devices like electric vehicles, intelligent heating and cooling systems, and home construction. This is especially true for illumination, which alone uses approximately 20 percent of world energy. Just switching from incandescent to LED lighting could eventually save the world 90 percent, $2 trillion on energy illumination costs alone. This is approximately half the total economy of Japan—enough to give an annual stipend of $250, about one thousand per family, to every one of the almost eight billion people on the planet.[1]

A logical and inevitable savings in energy will come from eliminating many of the things we do now that use energy, like in-person business meetings (versus Zoom meetings), in-store shopping trips (versus online), dining out versus takeout, self-driving EVs, and more. The ultimate 100 percent in energy savings comes from eliminating the task that was using the energy in the first place. Simply going to a four-day workweek is estimated to reduce energy consumption by 10–20 percent. All of these changes in energy supply and demand are happening now, fast, and creating business opportunities worldwide in the new roaring twenties.

For the 2030s and beyond, I'm suggesting something that could potentially make the whole energy industry practically obsolete—geothermal energy! This is renewable energy taken from the earth's molten rock core. It comes from the radioactive decay of materials created by the earth's formation. It's as if God created unlimited free energy billions of years ago, but then decided to withhold it from humanity until he/she felt we were responsible enough to be entrusted with it.

WHAT IS ENERGY?

Energy, in most of its original form, is a product that no one actually wants—what can you do with a lump of coal or a barrel of oil? However, energy is a product necessary to transport, power, and/or produce virtually everything that we do want—from cell phones (lithium-ion batteries) to heating our homes (fuel) to transportation (gasoline) to automobiles

---

1   Energy.gov; Electricchoice.com; Energystar.gov.

(electricity) to agriculture (fertilizer). No matter where we live, some form of energy is necessary 24/7 for us to exist.

About 10 percent ($9 trillion) of the world's $90 trillion in GDP goes to produce energy. This $9 trillion is about to get much cheaper. Today, worldwide, we get approximately 35 percent of our energy from oil, 30 percent from coal, 25 percent from natural gas, 5 percent from nuclear power, and 5 percent from all renewable sources combined such as wind turbines, hydroelectric dams, and solar panels.[2]

There are over 160 different types of crude oil alone traded on the market. Each type of oil has its own characteristics and, at a given point in time, is less or more desirable by refineries. Refineries turn the different types of crude into thousands of different products in tens of thousands of locations. That's why you may be surprised to read in the morning paper about a glut of West Texas Intermediate crude oil in Texas, while you're waiting hours in line for high-octane gasoline in Los Angeles at twice your normal price.

Let's examine the dynamics of oil production, storage, and consumption.

The world today produces and consumes about 4.17 million barrels an hour, or about 100 million barrels a day, of crude oil—that's 36.5 billion barrels a year. I've cited this figure per hour and per day because I want you to think about our supply of oil in a dynamic versus static manner. Almost all of the world's oil is constantly moving, or technically, flowing, from where it starts out in pools underground all the way to the gas tank of your car.[3]

For the most part, with the exception of biofuels, oil originates from drilling into dry ground or into land under the sea, from where it is then shipped to refineries to become gasoline, jet fuel, plastics, fertilizer, and many industrial chemicals. Again, it's constantly moving from place to place.

The US first entered the modern petroleum age on January 10, 1901, when the Spindletop oil field in Beaumont, Texas, came in and gushed oil 150 feet high, at a rate of 100,000 barrels per day. The original oil well at Spindletop was only 1,139 feet deep, and the pressure of the oil was low

2   Hannah Ritchie and Max Roser, "Energy," OurWorldinData.org; AmericanGeoSciences Institute.com; Lehigh.edu; TexasGateway.org; e-education.psu.edu; VisualCapitalist .com.

3   Statista.com; MarketWatch.com; USEnergyInformationAdministration.gov.

enough for the drillers to cap the well and regulate its flow with basic existing plumbing technology. Those were the good old days for the petroleum industry. During the next fifty years, the world discovered and harvested most of the earth's oil near the surface. Today the petroleum industry calls a "shallow oil well" an oil well drilled to a depth of ten thousand feet (about two miles) or less. The search and battle for oil has dominated global geopolitics for over a century. It has probably resulted in as many conflicts as religion and megalomania during that time.[4]

Most of the world's oil comes from deep-land or deepwater drilling using rigs like the ill-fated BP Deepwater Horizon in the Gulf of Mexico, which can drill up to 35,000 feet (about seven miles) below the surface. The world's deepest oil well, Sakhalin-1 in Russia, reaches more than 40,000 feet (about 7.5 miles) into the ground. On March 1, 2022, Exxon Mobil Corp announced that due to sanctions imposed on Russia, it would no longer manage the project. In addition, tanker owners became concerned about the implications of hauling oil from Russia and a lack of insurance coverage.

These deep-drilling rigs operate under incredible pressures and have this in common: once they are flowing with oil, they are very difficult and expensive to turn off and back on. To restart a single, large, deep-drilling rig that's been shut down could cost millions of dollars. Of course, with daily world oil consumption at 100 million barrels a day and increasing every day, why would anyone want a functioning oil rig to be turned off? Well, not until now.

DECLINING OIL PRICES IN THE NEW ROARING TWENTIES

During the next decade I'm expecting prices for some oil products to decline from time to time. You are reading correctly. Despite the Russian attack on Ukraine and $100-plus-per-barrel oil, I believe there may be such a glut of certain types of oil at certain times in the 2023–2033 period that some oil producers will pay oil consumers at times to take their oil away.

---

4   Daniel Yergin, *The Prize: The Epic Quest for Oil, Money and Power* (Simon & Schuster, 1991).

Oil prices can fall when supply exceeds demand and storage space is running out. This phenomenon also can apply to perishable commodities, software, and some manufactured goods that have a low marginal product cost. During the pandemic, farmers sometimes gave away their produce for free on a first-come, first-grab basis rather than let it rot in the fields.

The price of oil is highly elastic; this means the price fluctuates widely with small changes in supply or demand. No one wants to get stuck with too much oil when supply increases and no one want to experience too little oil when demand increases.

I became fascinated with the elasticity of oil prices on September 24, 1990, when Iraq invaded Kuwait, and the Middle East began preparing for the Persian Gulf War. In just a few weeks, the price of oil doubled to $78.31 per barrel, adjusted for inflation.

In February 1991, I was asked on the *Larry King Live* television show when oil would reach $100 a barrel. Much to the surprise of my host, I replied that the price of oil would fall to $40 a barrel if and when a shooting war started in the Middle East. I explained that with the price of oil rising almost daily the last few months, everyone with oil in the ground, in a storage facility or out on a tanker at sea, had slowed down production or deliveries as much as they could, hoping to get a better price for their oil "tomorrow." Now the tide had turned. Many producers, shippers, and refineries panicked that they would soon, figuratively and literally, be drowning in a sea of oil.

"You can see the filled tankers piled up outside the refineries from Long Beach, California, to Elizabeth, New Jersey, holding out for a better price," I explained to Mr. King. "But now their suppliers in the Gulf region like Saudi Arabia are panicking. They can't effectively shut off their wells, their storage facilities are at capacity, and they are terrified at the thought of having no place to put their ever-flowing oil."

Even though the shooting war did not start for a few more months, the following week, the price of oil halved to $37 a barrel because no one wanted to get stuck with unsold flowing oil and no place to put it.

Today, the world has an estimated storage capacity of 6.8 billion barrels of oil, a figure that includes vessels of all sizes, from two-million-barrel super-tankers to the twenty-gallon gas tank in your SUV. While 6.8 billion barrels may sound like a lot, it's only 2.2 months' worth of annual world supply or demand, and much of that storage capacity is needed just to maintain inventory on certain oil products for specific customers' ordinary operations.

Over the long term, most experts expect oil to be replaced by renewable, clean sources— but that's not anticipated to fully happen for decades, giving the oil industry time to convert from fossil fuels.

What would happen today if the demand for, or supply of, oil stopped? Period. The world found out on April 20, 2020, forty days after the World Health Organization (WHO) officially declared the coronavirus outbreak a pandemic on March 11, 2020.

APRIL 20, 2020 – THE DAY THE (PETROLEUM) WORLD STOOD STILL

On April 20, 2020, more than half the world's population was under lockdown in ninety countries—people were ordered for the most part to stay at home. In the US and much of the developed world, highways were empty, planes stopped flying, and public transportation operated on a limited schedule. Needless to say, consumption of gasoline and jet fuel, the two main products produced from crude oil, plummeted to near zero. Refineries shut down. Soon the world's 6.8-billion-barrel storage capacity in many locations became full.

Panic set in when trading began that morning and the futures price for West Texas Intermediate, a benchmark product in the oil market on which other products are based, tumbled to zero. That's when traders and refiners who had purchased oil months earlier for May 2020 delivery realized the extent of their problem. There were no buyers and no storage facilities. Soon the price for May delivery of West Texas Intermediate crude oil dropped to negative $37.63 a barrel.[5] There were, of course, some oil consumers who still needed oil, but these user demands were relatively small compared to the supply. Soon, a downward trending price war broke out between OPEC, Russian, and US producers for many types of oils. Everyone was determined to limit their exposure.

---

5   "Oil for Less Than Nothing? Here's How That Happened," Bloomberg News, April 21, 2020.

ENERGY SUPPLIERS AND CONSUMERS IN THE 2020S

Rapidly advancing technology is now allowing some consumers of energy to switch between different energy products on a moment's notice—to and from solar, wind, different types of oil, natural gas, and electricity—mostly based on the price. Many homes today are built to utilize renewable sources like sun and wind only when it's sunny or windy.

Some homes have added a new source while leaving intact their old source. The house my parents bought for $35,000 in 1954 had an oil-burning furnace. My mother switched to natural gas in 1974 but kept the old furnace in place in case she ever wanted to take advantage of a favorable price advantage for oil instead of natural gas.

The vast majority of electric cars today are plug-in hybrid vehicles capable of running 100 percent on gasoline, 100 percent on batteries for a short distance, or some combination of both. Users can choose between their best source at the flick of a switch. Six million hybrid vehicles were sold in the US as of December 2020—there have been a lot more since. EVs were less than 4 percent of new car sales in 2020. However, more than 50 percent of new car buyers are now willing to consider an EV.[6]

As I write this, the bestselling US hybrid is the Toyota Prius, which has sold more than two million vehicles. Hybrids have two principal advantages over traditional all-electric EVs. They are much less expensive to produce because they have much smaller batteries. They don't cause "range anxiety" for consumers worried about getting stuck without a charger nearby. One would only need to watch the 2022 Super Bowl advertisements to see the major automobile companies proudly featuring their EVs and hybrids. The major problem in this regard may well be the lack of charging stations. This is, of course, both a problem and a business opportunity for the right entrepreneurs.

---

6   Hyunjoo Jin, "US Hybrid Electric Car Sales Hit Record Highs," Reuters, January 6, 2022; Alexandra Kelley, "56 Percent of Car Owners Likely to Buy an EV or Hybrid Car Next: Poll," The Hill, September 15, 2021.

In the 2020s, advancing technology will make more vehicles capable of running on multiple energy sources—from diesel to gasoline to batteries to liquid hydrogen to natural gas to—the list goes on and on. This will alleviate "spot shortages" in one or another type of energy source while allowing consumers to greatly reduce their overall energy expenditures.

AUTOMOBILE FUEL ECONOMY MOVES BACKWARD

Sadly, even though most of our energy comes from oil, in the US, until recently, we have been moving backward when it comes to more efficiently using oil. In the original Roaring Twenties (1920–1929), the average US automobile got about 25 miles per gallon (mpg), including the Ford Model T (1908–1927), which got 21 mpg. Gasoline cost $0.30 a gallon, equivalent to about $4.00 a gallon today. Then, fuel economy fell 40 percent to 15 mpg by 1975, mainly because oil was so cheap and drivers were not charged a fair price for the real cost to society (i.e., pollution) of driving an ICE (internal combustion engine) vehicle. As explained in chapter twelve, "Gross National Happiness," most economists agree that society should be charging drivers of ICE vehicles approximately $4 per gallon surcharge in addition to the cost of gasoline at the pump for using up clean air.

In 1975, the average car in the United States got 15 mpg and gasoline cost $0.57 a gallon, about $2.85 a gallon in today's dollars. Spurred by the memory of long gas lines during the fuel crisis in the early 1970s and the government-imposed Corporate Average Fuel Economy standards (CAFE), which began in 1975, our engineers went to work.[7] In just ten years, by 1985, the consumption of an average US car had almost doubled to 27 mpg— but many consumers didn't notice because the average price per gallon also doubled to $1.14. It still cost the same amount of money to drive to work.

---

7   The Corporate Average Fuel Economy standards were enacted in 1975. "Corporate Average" refers to the production-weighted average of mileage ratings across each auto manufacturer fleet. These calculations are not based on data from actual performances on the road. The objective is to compel auto manufacturers to improve fuel efficiency by producing and selling more fuel-efficient vehicles, including EVs.

This doubling of fuel economy happened primarily because automakers learned how to replace three-hundred-dollar mechanical carburetors with twenty-five-dollar electronic computerized fuel injectors. If your car only used half the amount of fuel to get somewhere, it also produced only roughly half the pollution from more efficiently burning your gasoline.

SEAMLESSLY CHANGING FROM USING MORE OIL TO USING LESS OIL

Up until now, most of the world's reduction in energy costs have come on the supply side by reducing the cost of obtaining, refining, and transporting energy. This has been accomplished by using less expensive energy production techniques like strip-mining, offshore deepwater drilling, cheaper transportation techniques like supertankers and pipelines, as well as switching energy sources to natural gas, wind, solar, and hydropower.

In the new roaring twenties, we will see meaningful increased efficiencies in the devices that use energy. Already, today's non-polluting EVs make the energy we use for transportation about 400 percent more efficient than today's gasoline-powered 25 mpg vehicles. This is the equivalent of 100–125 mpg vehicles. All EVs today basically use the electric energy equivalent of one-fifth the amount of gasoline, getting the environmental equivalent of 125 mpg vehicles. However, pure EVs today are very expensive to produce because of the high cost of batteries.

Adding a small electric motor/generator and relatively inexpensive smaller batteries to traditional ICE vehicles, so-called plug-in hybrids, can massively boost their fuel efficiency while greatly reducing pollution. Hybrids like the Toyota Prius have already doubled fuel economy to 50 mpg or more, and experts expect such vehicles to achieve 100 mpg in the next decade. Hybrids can operate fully on their batteries until they run out of battery power, at which point they switch over to ICE power. They are an interim solution until we find a way to make more affordable batteries for all-EV automobiles and expand the availability of charging stations.

The Environmental Protection Agency (EPA) began testing the fuel economy of gasoline cars in 1971—"mpg" is the largest item you see on the

MSRP sticker that comes with every new automobile. Today the EPA also calculates the equivalent mpg for all-electric and hybrid vehicles, which they call MPGe for "miles per gallon of gasoline equivalent." To calculate MPGe, the EPA first measures the amount of electric energy equal to the amount of energy in one gallon of gasoline and then figures the vehicle's consumption of this amount of electric energy to go a specific distance—producing a roughly equivalent MPGe figure for an EV or hybrid.

Today, for a typical ICE car that gets, say, 25 mpg, the hybrid model gets 30 MPGe, and the all-electric EV model gets 125 MPGe. It's easy to see why EVs are so efficient. An ICE vehicle uses less than 40 percent of the energy burned for turning the wheels and wastes more than 60 percent in heat loss from the engine—whereas an EV (or a hybrid in all-electric mode) sends close to 100 percent of the power burned to the wheels. This 500 percent efficiency of EVs over ICE vehicles doesn't take into account the many intangible benefits of EVs, starting with virtually no air pollution.

Critics of EVs sometimes point out the effect on the environment of producing the additional electricity to power the vehicle. As a practical matter, this is minimal because most EVs and plug-in hybrids today charge in the middle of the night using surplus electricity that probably couldn't be stored anyway.

The small city I live in is bisected by a twelve-mile-long, slightly downward sloping, 55 mph highway with five major traffic signals that are not synchronized—we used to have no traffic signals at all when I moved here forty years ago. It has often seemed foolish to me each time the signal changes to green to watch all the vehicles accelerate from zero to 55 mph—as any high school physics student will tell you, accelerating to a faster speed uses much more energy than maintaining a fixed speed. Then, when the next signal turns red, all the cars going 55 mph brake to zero by pushing the brake pad against a metal disc—releasing tremendous amounts of polluting heat energy into the atmosphere. Then, all the mostly ICE vehicles idle at the next red light for a few more minutes, and then accelerate back up to 55 mph—repeating this cycle five times over just a single twelve-mile segment of highway. This process always seemed incredibly foolish and wasteful. Then I bought my first EV in 2014.

Assume I'm waiting in my all-battery-powered EV at the first traffic signal for the red light to change to green—my vehicle is not wasting energy idling since my electric motor turns on instantly when I push the accelerator. Then I accelerate much quicker to 55 mph and see the next traffic signal turning yellow and then red. As I decelerate to zero, the energy screen in the car shows that the car's propulsion motors have turned themselves into generators. Although I'm pushing on the brake pedal, the brakes haven't yet engaged. The motors-turned-generators are slowing down the car and putting back into the batteries much of the energy I just used to accelerate.

In fact, our family lives at the end of the six-mile-long sloping highway. When I typically leave my home, I might have 290 miles of range. When I get to the end of the downhill sloping highway, I usually have 300 miles of range left.

The EPA rates my 2018 Tesla Model 3 EV at 125 MPGe, a figure that basically says the monetary fuel cost of driving is one-fifth the cost of an equivalent 25 mpg ICE vehicle (a 500 percent or 5x lift). That's where the savings to my wallet and to the environment begin. My EV is expected to last much, much longer than an equivalent ICE vehicle because the components don't run out—the motor in my Tesla Model 3 has an expected one-million-mile range with no maintenance. There's no lubricating oil to change every five thousand miles, no spark plugs to replace. In fact, while the manufacturer says I should come in for a checkup every 100,000 miles, my local service center tells me they don't know what they might do every 100,000 miles since most components are rated for one million miles.

It's no wonder that every major car manufacturer announced plans to sell EV and hybrid versions of their cars in 2022 and to convert their entire fleet to EVs by 2035. Getting 125 MPGe versus 25 mpg is equivalent to buying five-dollar-per-gallon gasoline today for one dollar a gallon.

In chapter six, "The Robots are Coming," you'll learn how an AI-powered robot, Waze, can also improve your car mileage, up to 50 percent, by routing your driving onto the least crowded streets. Furthermore, you'll see that autonomous driving by robots can be safer, less stressful, and add extra time to your day.

THE NEED FOR LITHIUM

Lithium is a critical component of rechargeable batteries, enabling them to be lighter and to last longer. This is essential for EVs and other applications. The US government plans to invest over $3 billion to improve the battery supply chain and domestic lithium sources. The Defense Protection Act has been invoked to increase battery material production. More is needed.

Historically, lithium has been found in hard rock or salty brine ponds. This extraction process is expensive and takes years. It also is damaging to the environment and ends up extracting only 40 percent to 50 percent of the available lithium.

New methods, generally called direct lithium extraction (DLE) are being developed to significantly accelerate the time frames and potentially extract 75 percent to 90 percent. They typically use a chemical process or membranes combined with robots.

These initiatives often work well in a laboratory, but it is difficult to apply them on a large scale. China is well ahead of the US in acquiring lithium deposits and applying new technology.

The Salton Sea in the California desert has been an environmental disaster for years. Now DLE is prompting some hope that this area will experience industrial renewal because of the potential of environmentally friendly lithium extraction possibilities.

The 2020s will be known as the decade of technology implementation, when thousands of new technologies, from clean energy to Zoom meetings, made the jump from the laboratory to the home and workplace—closing the technology gap and laying the foundation for decades of prosperity. One shining (no pun intended) example is bright-white LED lighting, which was developed in the 1990s but not rolled out until the 2000s—a feat that earned its renegade inventor the 2014 Nobel Prize in Physics.

THE LIGHT BULB SHINES

Human beings have worshipped the sun since the beginning of time, mostly for providing light.

Light gives us the ability to see, to live inside, to read, to grow crops, to raise animals. Light is necessary for almost everything that defines our existence. What would your life be like in a world of total darkness?

New artificial sources of illumination—from campfires to candles to whale-oil lamps to gas lamps to Edison's incandescent light bulb—have always been an important part of human history. Natural illumination (e.g., solar) adds incredible value to our lives. Artificial illumination extends the length of our days, transforming nighttime into daytime.

Today, world GDP is $90 trillion. Critically, $9 trillion (10 percent) of that goes toward the production of energy. More than 85 percent of this $9 trillion is produced from pollution-causing, nonrenewable gas, oil, and coal. Everyone benefits when we can reduce the amount of energy used for this or any other purpose.

Of the $9 trillion of GDP used for energy production, 25 percent, $2.25 trillion, is used for illumination.

A Japanese-American scientist's discovery in 1994 is about to give us effectively free illumination in the new roaring twenties by cutting the annual cost of our $2.25 trillion spent on artificial illumination to $250 billion—saving the world from using about $2 trillion per year in mostly pollution-causing, fossil-fuel energy sources. To put this in perspective, the entire GDP of Japan in 2020 was $5 trillion.

The phenomenon of an LED (light-emitting diode) being able to produce light from electricity was known throughout the twentieth century and especially noticed in the 1960s when LEDs became commercially viable as low-intensity indicator lamps. However, the light produced by LEDs was not suitable for general lighting and was colored deep red or green. Beginning in the early 1960s, physicists and engineers worked diligently to produce a bright-white LED bulb, which is technically called a blue LED.

SHUJI NAKAMURA – INVENTOR OF
PRACTICAL LED LIGHTING[8]

Shuji Nakamura was born on May 22, 1954, in a small fishing village off the coast of Shikoku, the smallest of Japan's four main islands. He was a poor student and his father worked in maintenance for the local power company. His father taught him how to create and build toys, and he fostered a belief that his son could create anything through trial and error, versus the scientific method he was taught in school. In college, Shuji split his time between mostly playing competitive volleyball and studying physics and building practical electronic devices—which eventually led him to a nondescript job with Nichia, a local chemical firm.

At Nichia, Nakamura was instructed to create commercially viable gallium phosphide, a material used in making green and red low-intensity LEDs. He succeeded, but due to Nichia's late entry in the market, the product was not a commercial success, nor were other similar "me too" products that he produced. Nakamura realized that the company needed to lead the market in illumination technology. He convinced his boss to allow him to spend $4 million on the development of new technology that ultimately led, through trial and error, to his developing in 1993 the first bright-blue-light LED—the forerunner of today's modern white-light LED bulb.

Nakamura immigrated to America in 2000 and received the 2014 Nobel Prize in Physics for his 1993 accomplishment, along with Isamu Akasaki and Hiroshi Amano. Although there were many physicists over the prior decades who worked on bright-white LED technology, Nakamura today is recognized as the leading pioneer in white-light emitters based on the wide-ban-gap semiconductor

---

8   The research on Shuji Nakamura for this chapter was led by my son, Mark Avi Pilzer, currently a freshman at Caltech.

gallium nitride (GaN). This same technology was also used by
Nakamura to develop Blue-ray DVDs in 1999.[9]

Starting in the 2000s, but not really taking hold until 2020,
Nakamura's first LED discoveries, bright-white blue LEDs, took the
original equipment manufacturer (OEM) and replacement lighting
markets by storm, mostly because they could be manufactured as
R-I-Ts (ready-to-be implemented technological advances), which
were direct replacements for existing incandescent and fluorescent fixtures.

LED white-light bulbs are still very new and constantly improving.
Practically speaking, they are less than ten years old. Here are just a few of
the benefits of white-light LEDs we already enjoy today.

1. **20x lift in original cost** – Simple LED bulbs generally cost
    somewhat more than incandescents, although the cost is
    continuing to come down. They potentially last as much as twenty
    times longer, driving their true cost down to five cents each,
    one-twentieth of the bulb they replace—and even much less if you
    factor in the labor cost of replacing bulbs annually versus only once
    every twenty years.

2. **10x lift in energy cost** – The electricity used by an LED bulb
    today is typically one-tenth of an equivalent-lumens incandescent
    bulb. Physicists expect that this electricity usage will drop to
    one-twentieth over the next few years, making the electricity usage
    of a LED bulb almost irrelevant at 5 percent of a comparable
    incandescent bulb.

3. **Lower operating temperature** – LED bulbs produce one-tenth
    or less of the heat produced by an equivalent-lumens incandescent

---

9   Shuji Nakamura, Gerhard Fasol, and Stephen Pearton, *The Blue Laser Diode: The Com-
     plete Story* (Springer, 2000); Robert Johnstone, *Brilliant! Shuji Nakamura and the Revolu-
     tion in Lighting Technology* (Prometheus, 2007).

bulb, greatly reducing the need for air-conditioning and sprinkler systems along with many other engineering benefits.

4. **Quality of life** – Two billion people, more than one-fourth of the world's population, live off the grid without access to electricity. LEDs consume so little power that they can run all night and fully recharge the next day from the sun with a small solar panel—vastly improving the quality of life for more than 25 percent of our planet. This benefit alone for our poorest brethren could have merited that Nakamura be awarded the Nobel Prize for Peace in addition to the Nobel Prize for Physics.

5. **Agriculture** – LEDs today are already ubiquitous in indoor growing farms for high-value crops—like cannabis, specialty vegetables, and pharmaceutical plants. Their cost per lumen is so low that they should soon be used for general agriculture, making affordable, healthy, "farm to table" food grown in the attic or basement of the restaurant a reality in the new roaring twenties.

6. **Directional lighting** – All of these benefits are further compounded by what was once considered a negative aspect of LED lighting—LEDs shine only in one direction. In contrast, light from all other sources (fluorescent, incandescent, fire) shines 360 degrees (3D) in all directions and must be inefficiently reflected to where it is needed.

7. **Vastly improved lighting** – LED lighting allows you to select on the Kelvin scale the color temperature of your white light, from 2200K (candlelight) to 2700K (incandescent) to 4000K (solar). Some of the newest bulbs allow you to control each bulb's color temperature in real time.

8. **Benefits you didn't ask for** – The LED smart bulbs in my teenagers' bedrooms today cost less than ten dollars each, are controlled by their smartphones, change color with their moods, and can do many more things that my children are just beginning to understand. Best of all, they require no new wiring to install and greatly reduce the wiring cost of new and replacement construction because they use so much less power.

On Monday, April 25, 2022, the Department of Energy finalized two rules requiring manufacturers to sell energy-efficient light bulbs only. This effectively bans the sale of bulbs that produce less than 45 lumens per watt. The rules will be phased in over time but eventually will prohibit most incandescent and halogen light bulbs.

LEDs, with their 10x power-savings benefits and 20x installation-cost benefits, are representative of the kinds of technological improvements I expect to see in many areas of our economy and society in the new roaring twenties! From EVs that pay you to own them by autonomous self-driving ride-sharing (i.e., Uber, Lyft), to virtual reality classrooms that affordably bring the best teachers of every subject to every student, it is going to be the most exciting decade in history, starting with dramatic reductions in our cost of energy.

GEOTHERMAL ENERGY

In the course of writing this chapter, I met with scientists and engineers to discuss what could happen to energy sources in the 2020s. During some of these meetings, I felt that I was missing something even bigger than the price of certain types of petroleum falling to negative numbers. As explained earlier, on April 20, 2020, the price for future delivery of West Texas Intermediate crude oil dropped to negative $37.63 a barrel.

One of the world's most well-regarded astrophysicists confided in me that it isn't just what's going to happen to solar, wind, nuclear, or any other mainstream energy form in the next decade that matters. Rather, it's what's going to happen in the decades after that. He explained how "as a result of astronomical accident, the earth is well set up for geothermal energy. The earth is a large enough planet, a giant nuclear heater, and its core contains enough radioactive elements with long half-lives, that it remains molten."[10]

---

10 I first met this then-future astrophysicist, Antony Stark (yes, that's his real name) when we were both twelve years old—we were chess-playing and star-trek-watching classmates in Port Washington, New York. Antony was and still is known as the most intelligent student in our class. He graduated with honors in physics and astronomy from Caltech, received his PhD in astrophysical sciences from Princeton, has authored more than 100 academic articles, and has a ridge in the Churchill Range in Antarctica named

That molten rock is far more accessible on the surface of the earth than it would be on a planet (like Venus) that did not undergo the unlikely moon formation that left our earth with a molten core of lava. Our earth may be one of the few planets that has a molten, red-hot lava core, comprised of elements with a half-life such that they will effectively never expire. Moreover, earth may be the only planet that has thousands of places where hot lava (liquid rocks and metals) naturally rises to the surface.

Coincidentally, as I write this text, my wife, Lisa, and two of our four children are exploring active volcanoes in Iceland, a northern cold country where 90 percent of the population heats their homes and buildings entirely with geothermal energy—mostly from hot water and steam fissures formed from hot lava. Iceland also generates 30 percent of its electricity from geothermal energy.

The Two Places We Find Geothermal Energy – Core and Crust

There are currently two primary places we find geothermal energy: in the earth's core and from the sun striking the earth's crust.

Heat energy comes from the molten core of the earth, which transfers by conduction to the surface and occasionally breaks through fissures in the crust as molten lava or steam. There are currently forty-seven terawatts of renewable energy flowing through the earth's crust into space. This is miniscule compared to the millions of terawatts of renewable molten lava located in the core, which is the size of our moon, left over from creation. At the surface, this forty-seven terawatts of energy from the core is dwarfed by an additional 173,000 terawatts the earth receives from the sun. Practically speaking, when it comes to the millions of terawatts in the earth's core flowing to us at forty-seven terawatts, plus the 173,000 terawatts from the sun, we have, for all intents and purposes, unlimited geothermal energy to power anything we could currently contemplate, including future planetary exploration and development.

---

after him in recognition of his services to Antarctic science. Coincidentally, he is friends with another one of our classmates, Robert Hahn, the Oxford economist who led the research team on Consumer Surplus at Uber described in Chapter Eleven—Robert also received a PhD in economics from Caltech, the same college where my youngest son enrolled as a sixteen-year-old freshman.

What we don't have, yet, is the harvesting technology to locate it, process it, ship it, store it, and convert it into electricity or heat. We don't have tools to handle or vessels to store molten lava. This is changing in the new roaring twenties.

Along with solar panels harvesting sun-based geothermal energy on our crust, our world has made great strides recently in harvesting core-based geothermal steam and heat. Twenty-four nations generate more than 15 percent of their total electricity from geothermal energy, including Kenya (38 percent), Iceland (30 percent), Philippines (27 percent), El Salvador (25 percent), and New Zealand (25 percent). The US leads the world in total geothermal electricity generated—about 4,000 megawatts—but the US generates only 0.3 percent of its total electricity from geothermal electricity.

This will change in the 2020s as our world switches from fossil fuels to renewable fuels—not just because of the monetary cost of fossil fuels, but because of what nonrenewable fossil fuels do to our environment and global climate change.

The Geothermal Gradient

Physicists speak in terms of the geothermal gradient, the temperature of the earth below the surface, which surprisingly doesn't vary that much by location. Basically, if you dig a hole almost anywhere on Earth, once you get past the local ground soil and pools of water, the temperature of the earth rises about one degree Fahrenheit per seventy-seven feet or about sixty-eight degrees per mile (twenty-five degrees Centigrade per kilometer). In the near future, every home or neighborhood (thanks to the sharing revolution) may have its own vertical "heat sink" of polyethylene piping going down thousands of feet—enough to heat, cool, and even generate electricity—making the housing unit or entire neighborhood energy self-sufficient, with enough leftover capacity (depending on the "thermocouple") to power the family EV.

There's even a much more affordable alternative available today based on your location. In most latitudes of the United States and Europe, the ground temperature just a few meters below the surface is a relatively constant 54 +/-3 degrees Fahrenheit regardless of the temperature on the surface. An inexpensive heat pump can pump a refrigerant into the ground through a closed-loop polyethylene tubing—creating a "heat sink"—transferring the now 54 degrees Fahrenheit refrigerant to the surface. Depending on whether you're heating or cooling, a heat pump can reduce your fuel consumption by up to 50 percent by allowing your furnace or air-conditioning systems to start out with their refrigerant at 54 degrees Fahrenheit. If you're cooling air from, say 95 degrees Fahrenheit to 72 degrees Fahrenheit, or heating air or water from, say 20 degrees Fahrenheit to 72 degrees Fahrenheit, it doesn't take as much conventional fuel if you start out at 54 degrees Fahrenheit, for free. This is why heat pumps are rapidly becoming standard equipment in new homes and are easily retrofitted onto existing air-conditioning compressors and home furnaces.

Even though the installation price of a geothermal system can be several times that of an air-source system of the same heating and cooling capacity, the additional costs are returned to you in energy savings in five to ten years. System life is estimated at up to twenty-four years for the inside components and fifty-plus years for the ground loop. There are approximately 50,000 geothermal heat pumps installed in the United States each year. For more information, visit the International Ground Source Heat Pump Association.

Every new home may soon include a heat sink with either one hundred feet or more of horizontal tubing located next to or under the foundation or vertical tubing going straight down one hundred feet or more before turning back up. According to the US Department of Energy, a complete water-based, three-ton heat pump system for a two-thousand-square-foot home costs between $2,500 and $5,000 installed. This system will be cash-flow positive for the homeowner. The monthly savings in fuel cost should be one to two times the additional monthly cost of the mortgage payment calculated at a 6 percent interest rate. It may be even less if financed as part of your initial home purchase or new construction.

I live in a ski town where the need for snow and ice removal is constant for six months of the year. Most luxury homes have had heat-sink driveways powered by gas furnaces for decades. Until recently, heating one's driveway with fossil fuels was considered expensive and environmentally reckless. This is no longer the case with such snow-melt systems powered in full or part by direct geothermal energy. This same technology is starting to be used by cities to keep their streets and sidewalks clear of snow and ice.

EVs Can Allow Geothermal and Solar Power to Replace Petroleum

Until recently, the most practical thing you could do with geothermal energy was heat or cool, which was of limited benefit since two-thirds of the petroleum we produce is used for transportation. This changes overnight with electric vehicles. Solar, wind, and geothermal-produced energy can now be harvested anywhere and readily converted to electricity, which can be used by EVs for transportation, replacing petroleum.

The bestselling vehicle in the US is the Ford F-150 pickup truck, which in 2021 became available in a 150 kWh-battery all-electric version. The enormous 150 kWh battery in this vehicle can store your own solar or geothermal-produced electricity and then serve it back to power your home when the sun isn't shining, the wind isn't blowing, or the current season isn't optimal for your own electrical production on demand. Your Ford F-150 EV could power an entire home for days or more while you wait for sunshine or more wind.

Closing More Technology Gaps in Geothermal Technology

Today, a $2,500–$5,000 heat pump addition can close one of your home's technology gaps, halving your home's HVAC fuel cost. This is just the beginning. For those readers wanting to capitalize on technology gaps in geothermal energy, the device to watch in the 2020s is the thermocouple: a solid-state (no moving parts) device that can convert a temperature difference between two sources into an electric current and vice versa. This device, when fully developed for electricity generation, which I expect will happen in our current decade, will make any home self-sufficient when it comes to producing its own electricity. The most desired new appliance when making a home purchase may soon be its built-in electrical power station.

I expect that during the new roaring twenties, every home can have its own built-in source for unlimited electricity, along with unlimited sources for direct heating or cooling. This will allow single-family home and multi-family apartment construction to occur anywhere, on or off the grid. Human beings occupy only 10 percent of the land on earth. Geothermal energy will allow us to occupy the other 90 percent without destroying the environment.

Self-generated, renewable, clean electricity could be used for heating, cooling, transportation, and waste disposal.

Although most geothermic systems are cash-flow positive from day one—they save more in fuel costs than they cost to install, especially with today's low interest rates—the three youngest population group generations, Generation X, Generation Y (millennials), and Generation Z, have demonstrated a willingness to pay more for clean geothermic power regardless of the economic benefits.

Robots, and especially robots with AI, have significant roles to play in geothermal development. Some technologies have traditionally required a human being to manage their geothermic devices. Now geothermic devices can be made autonomous with AI robots.

ENERGY IN THE NEW ROARING TWENTIES

In the next decade, the economy worldwide will benefit just from energy savings alone. These savings will come from a potential doubling by 2033 of the amount of energy produced from all existing and new sources, a 2x lift. In addition, the potential halving of the amount of energy consumed by devices that use energy results in another 2x lift for a total 4x lift.

Too good to be true? Illumination uses approximately 20 percent, $2 trillion, of the $9+ trillion of energy produced worldwide. Just the conversion of incandescent lighting to LEDs alone saves 90 percent of the energy cost, a 10x lift—plus many other intangible benefits like twenty-year life, cool-running bulbs. Transportation by ICE vehicles today costs their owners about $10,000 a year with $5,000 spent on fuel. Switching to EVs saves $2,000 to $5,000 on fuel and potentially a similar amount on maintenance. Geothermal has the potential to change everything, particularly in the years following the new roaring twenties.

The best reason to move away from fossil fuels from non-US sources is to interrupt the flow of cash to bad actors including autocrats, despots, oligarchs, and criminals. Elon Musk has suggested this is the reason he founded Tesla. On some level, alternative energy is an attempt to foster world peace.

Certainly, the Russian attack on Ukraine has caused supply chain and energy pain, but it also has focused Europe on its dependency on Russian oil and gas. A move to alternative energy sources (which need to become primary energy sources) is not only economic, but also strategic.

Please take a look at your own use of energy and how it might become more efficient. Also consider whether you might find a business opportunity by correcting or improving one small part of the energy paradigm.

TAKEAWAYS

1. Prior to 2020, most of the world's savings in energy costs have come from finding better methods to obtain and distribute fossil fuels. Starting in the 2020s, these savings will be compounded from windfall efficiencies in the devices that use energy—like 100 mpg cars (or EV equivalents) or almost-free-electricity LED light bulbs. In addition, significant advances will be made in the 2020s and 2030s towards harnessing the earth's own energy, geothermal.

2. For the first time in world history, energy for heat, light, transportation, manufacturing, and mostly everything else will be effectively free. This will have enormous repercussions throughout the economy, as well as political repercussions for oil-producing nations like the United States and Russia. This becomes very important in times of political crisis such as the Russian attack on Ukraine.

3. As illustrated by the negative oil prices that occurred on April 22, 2020, at the height of the pandemic, some sources of energy that no one wants, like oil, will be less than free—at certain times producers may pay users to take their energy away for free rather than shut down production.

4. The strategic need to cut off fossil-fuel revenue going to bad actors is yet another reason that alternative energy sources will flourish in the new roaring twenties.

Chapter Five

STRUCTURAL UNEMPLOYMENT

Unemployment due to technological change is the first sign of economic growth. The challenge and opportunity for society is to get the unemployed retooled and reemployed so society enjoys the output of their new and old job.

O ur modern economy grows when a machine or better method takes away a person's job and the displaced employee finds a new job—allowing society to enjoy the work output from his former job (now done by machine) plus the new job. In this chapter, we explore this phenomenon and how it will drive economic growth in the next decade, as well as how it will also create massive disruption for societies worldwide.

PILZER'S ISLAND

Imagine a desert island, what my students often call Pilzer's Island, a self-sufficient tropical island that is home to ten men and their families, where all ten men make a subsistence living by fishing with poles and lines from a communal boat. I will use men for this example, but women could be appropriate as well. Along comes a missionary who shows the men a new and better way of fishing. Instead of using individual poles and lines, this method uses a large casting net.

Now, only two people are required in the boat to catch the same amount of fish: one to pilot the boat and the other to mind the net. Once the islanders adopt this fishing technique, you could say unemployment on the island immediately went from 0 to 80 percent, since eight of the ten fishermen are no longer needed on the boat.

Yet, the island as a whole is still just as wealthy, because the two fishermen using the net catch as many fish as all ten men using the lines had before. This is one of the most misunderstood things about unemployment caused by changes in technology or better methods. Economists call this "structural unemployment," meaning that the "structure" of something in the economy has changed, causing people to be out of work—versus unemployment caused by lower demand due to economic depression, war, or pandemic.

When a machine or better method takes away a job, the wages of the displaced worker are transferred to either the owners of the machine, the owners of the business, the other remaining workers, or to some combination of all three. True economic growth occurs when the displaced worker finds a new job, often producing a new good or service that didn't exist before. Then, society benefits from receiving the additional GDP generated by the worker's new job or employer, plus the (same) GDP generated by the worker's former employer.

This process has been going on since the dawn of human existence. Until recently, changes caused by structural unemployment typically occurred over generations. Now they occur over single lifetimes.

In the past, blue-collar workers could learn a trade and perform that trade for their entire lives. Some even passed their trade along to their children in their last names (e.g., Miller, Baker, Smith) or in the form of a family business.

I wrote about this phenomenon almost thirty years ago in *God Wants You to Be Rich* (Simon & Schuster, 1993):

> *There is nothing new about the unemployment we are experiencing today except for the increased speed with which it is occurring. Changes that used*

to take fifty years now occur in five or ten years, causing us to deal with the problems of retraining existing employees within single lifetimes as opposed to passively waiting for their descendants to choose other, more productive, occupations.

Now, I must adjust that statement because changes that used to take five or ten years are often occurring in five or ten months, ten times as fast. These days, a new technology, a more efficient supply chain source, or less expensive source material can lead to massive layoffs in short order. We are seeing global companies announce deep staffing cuts on one continent even as they recruit thousands of new employees on another continent. This is especially true in companies using flexible manufacturing systems (FMS) as described in chapter six, "The Robots are Coming," where manufacturers build identical assembly lines so they easily switch production between venues.

Despite my positive view of the upcoming technologies, the underside is the devastating effect of structural unemployment. The massive disruptions in family and political life from these types of rapid employment changes threaten to tear our world apart!

Often, changes in employment locations affecting tens of thousands of families are unknown to companies outsourcing their production from multiple sources around the globe. For example, Apple typically has several unrelated plants on multiple continents making finished iPhones of the same model and many more plants worldwide making standalone subcomponents like screens or batteries for a new model. Some of these plants are owned and managed by Apple corporate. Some are wholly independent companies working for Apple on a contract basis. When one supplier, either wholly owned by Apple or an independent company, cannot provide the needed product or can offer the product at a lower price, Apple seamlessly shifts production orders from or to that supplier. There's no warning or negotiation. A similar plant manager in Taiwan just looks at their next three months' production orders and clicks on a screen telling schedulers to hire eight thousand new workers. A similar plant manager in Vietnam lays off ten thousand workers who were formerly making the component now being made in Taiwan.

Prior to February 2020, most of these decisions were made by computer algorithms (instructions or procedures for specific actions in either hardware or software routines) based on delivery time and price. That was before the pandemic added two new factors to the algorithms—country risk and pandemic risk. When the pandemic shut down virtually all production in China in early 2020, supply-chain managers outside China were left stranded, and plants were idled worldwide making, say, $1,000 iPhones—often for want of a one-dollar subcomponent like a memory chip or a ten-dollar battery. In just sixty days, Chinese plants and subcontracting companies lost hundreds of their major customers worldwide. Moreover, when the Chinese plants reopened, they faced new competition. Western customers recognized the need to have multiple independent sources for every critical component. They have been told by their customers to never again rely on critical components coming from one country, or subject to the same local risks, like pandemics. These supply-chain issues are changing the way business is facilitated and supplied.

Let's return to our ten-man island experiencing 80 percent unemployment in its fishing industry. The island society must decide how to feed and house the eight unemployed fishermen. They have three options:

1. They can outlaw the use of the net, returning to the old ways.
2. They can tax the two working fishermen 80 percent of their earnings and redistribute the money to the unemployed.
3. They can train the eight unemployed fishermen for new occupations producing new goods and services that will add to the wealth of the island. These will likely be occupations that didn't exist before, when all of the ten men were fully occupied fishing with their lines and poles. We'll examine some of these new occupations in chapter sixteen, "Business-Opportunity Businesses."

Let's further examine these three options.

Option One

The return to the old ways was embraced in the early 1800s by some in the United Kingdom. Violent gangs called "Luddites" destroyed newly mechanized clothing factories that increased unemployment, cutting jobs traditionally held by hand-loom weavers and framework knitters. In response, the

British government passed the Frame-Breaking Act of 1812, which made the destruction of factory machines a capital felony. Seventy of the Luddites were executed. In fact, the dispute was more about disruption of society and distribution of wealth caused by industrialization and structural unemployment than the machines themselves.[1]

Option Two

Taxing productive employees seems just as ludicrous. What society would increase the income tax rate to 80 percent or more for productive workers using the latest technologies?

Yet, during the first half of the last century, this was the world's primary response to structural unemployment that resulted from technological advances, which made certain people far richer than their neighbors. Between 1913 and 1960, the United States and Western Europe instituted highly progressive income taxes. In 1959, the top US federal income tax rate was 91 percent for individuals earning more than $131,000 per annum!

From 1917–1991, Eastern Europe and about half the world chose communism, which is effectively 100 percent taxation, removing the individual's incentive to implement new technological methods. This resulted in a long-term economic spiral that Eastern Europe is still struggling with today.

Option Three

Retraining displaced workers has been the approach talked about in much of the world with the exception of China—and that's only because the Chinese economy has been growing so much over the past fifty years that they seem to always have a new job for everyone. The issue for China is whether displaced workers (particularly young ones) want to do the new job. Every nation agrees that retraining is the most desirable approach, but no country has figured out how to successfully accomplish this task or which jobs to retrain displaced workers for that may soon similarly become obsolete.

---

1   Richard Conniff, "What the Luddites Really Fought Against," *Smithsonian Magazine*, March 2011; Christopher Klein, "The Original Luddites Raged Against the Machine of the Industrial Revolution," History.com, January 4, 2019.

It's easy to see why. Our educational institutions are trapped in the twentieth century. Students are still asked, "What do you want to be when you grow up?" as if they could study a profession once and then practice that one profession without more education for the rest of their lives. Fortunately, as you'll see in chapter seven, "The Gig Economy," and in chapter sixteen, "Business-Opportunities Businesses," this may be a moot point. Our free enterprise system is attempting to take care of itself by finding employment for those who want or need it.

CAPITALISM, SOCIALISM, AND DEMOCRACY – JOSEPH SCHUMPETER

"Creative destruction" is the term economists use to describe how capitalism leads to rapid economic growth. Each new invention or better method, such as fishing with a net, creatively destroys the existing method because the new method is so much more productive. Each act of creative destruction, of course, leads to more structural unemployment.

The founder of the concept of creative destruction was the great Austrian economist Joseph Schumpeter (1888–1950).[2] Over an incredibly prolific lifetime, he wrote hundreds of technical books and articles explaining how technology advances due to a new method can destroy the status quo.

His famous work, *Capitalism, Socialism, and Democracy* (1942),[3] dealt with the social turmoil and destruction that occurs in a rapidly advancing capitalist society as individuals are displaced from their jobs due to the implementation of better technological

---

2   Schumpeter claimed that he had set himself three goals in life: to be the greatest economist in the world, to be the best horseman in all of Austria, and the greatest lover in all of Vienna. He said he had reached two of his goals, but he never said which two. Today he is best known for his theories on business cycles and entrepreneurship.

3   Joseph Schumpeter, *Capitalism, Socialism, and Democracy* (Impact Books, 2014, originally published in 1942).

methods. While the book praised such technological advance-ment for increasing the size of the total economic pie, Schumpeter predicted that capitalism would eventually self-destruct as the people displaced by advancing technology would democratically vote in favor of a socialist form of government, killing the goose (technology) that had laid the golden eggs (productivity). He fur-ther predicted that after many years of socialism and the resultant economic decay that socialism would cause, the same people (or their children) would turn vehemently capitalist and start the cycle all over again.

Schumpeter's prediction that the socialist eastern bloc of nations would turn capitalist came true in the 1990s, but his pre-diction that the western capitalist nations would turn socialist has not really come true. Schumpeter distinguished true socialism from democratic socialism found in a number of European countries.

However, time will tell. Many countries, like Russia, have turned away from democratic institutions towards autocracy or rule by a dictator or oligarchs. Candidates for higher office in the United States have openly called themselves socialists and embraced policies challenging capitalism. Others have espoused doctrines tilting towards autocracy and totalitarianism. Socialism and nationalism each taken to extremes merge into national socialism, the government of Nazi Germany.

Five years after writing *Capitalism, Socialism, and Democracy*, in another one of his influential works, *Can Capitalism Survive?* (1947), Schumpeter wrote that he did not expect capitalism to be able to politically survive.[4] Asked if this meant he supported com-munism, Schumpeter wrote: "If a doctor predicts that his patient will die presently, this does not mean that he desires it."

---

4 Joseph Schumpeter, *Can Capitalism Survive?* (Harper Perennial Modern Thought, 2011, originally published in 1947).

In the late 1980s and early 1990s, I advised officials in the Soviet Union and their republics on how to reorganize their economies from a large-government employer system to a more open system that promoted individual entrepreneurship. It was a very difficult task to reorganize everything while still providing critical services. Organized (and disorganized) crime was rampant. Well-intentioned foreign advisors and businessmen were threatened and sometimes killed.

This resulted in billion-dollar windfalls to many individuals (the oligarchs) who got there first, mostly unfairly due to connections with high-ranking officials. It also resulted in many Russian entrepreneurs being incarcerated by political opponents who manipulated a fluid, emerging income tax code for leverage against their competitors.

In the 2000s and 2010s, I advised government and private entities in the People's Republic of China (PRC) on the same issues. China did much better than the former USSR in privatizing much of its economy, primarily because when China sold, say, a $100 billion state enterprise to an entrepreneur, it typically sold only 10–20 percent and kept the majority $80–$90 billion for itself—"itself" being the 1.4 billion people of the People's Republic of China. When the enterprise was modernized and ready for a $300 billion exit, the Chinese people ended up with 80–90 percent ($240–270 billion) of the profits, and the entrepreneur was still highly incentivized, earning $30–60 billion on his or her $10–20 billion investment.

Let's look in again once more on our ten-fisherman island, now with eight unemployed. Our fishermen have several employment options for their eight unemployed citizens. These include:

1. **Farming** – Producing healthy fruits and vegetables and trading their produce for fish caught by the two islanders still working as fishermen.
2. **Teaching** – Opening a school for all the children on the island and trading the education of the children for fish, fruits, and vegetables.
3. **Shelter building and repair** – Constructing, maintaining, and fixing the huts.
4. **Caregiving** – Tending to the sick and infirm in exchange for food, shelter, and clothing.
5. **Tool and gear rental and repair** – Providing and servicing essential tools for other islanders.
6. **Entertainment** – What would an island be without its own Jimmy Buffett or Bob Marley?
7. **Distributing or Retailing** – Keeping up with the latest and greatest products and services and making sure they get to the people who can best put them to use. Like Jeff Bezos of Amazon, this person would likely become the richest person on the island because of the value provided by distributors in a zero-marginal-cost economy (see chapter eleven, "Consumer Surplus").
8. **Public safety** – Operating a combination firehouse and police station to safeguard the island.

In what time period would you like to be living or visiting the desert island? Would you want to be on the original island, where the only thing to do day and night was catching and eating fish? Or would you like to live on the newly reengineered island, where you could still have all the fish you wanted—along with fresh fruits and vegetables, education services, shelter construction, caregiving, tools and gear, entertainment, and safety?

Finally, before we leave our desert island, remember that none of the new products or services produced by the eight displaced fishermen existed at the time the original job displacement from the net took place, nor did any of the jobs producing these things.

The most important thing needed by the displaced fishermen is faith in their ability to adapt and succeed, perhaps with the help of a higher power.

GOVERNMENT REACTION TO
STRUCTURAL UNEMPLOYMENT

Traditionally, most governments have had the wrong reaction to structural unemployment. Like Luddites in old England, US local and state governments have focused on slowing down the pace of structural unemployment by charging employers who lay off workers even higher unemployment insurance premiums. Instead, they should be helping out the displaced unemployed with what they really need: education and retraining to return to work. Rather than fighting structural unemployment, government should be encouraging the substitution of technology for labor and designing unemployment benefits programs that encourage displaced employees to return to the workforce and/or accept part-time work.

For example, every state in the US offers its citizens unemployment benefits that generally pay you about two-thirds of your former paycheck up to, say, $235 a week in Mississippi and $783 a week in Massachusetts, if you are unemployed through no fault of your own. These benefits end after a period of time, when you accept a job for almost any kind of full or part-time work, or when you are offered suitable work that you turn down. Each state is different as to its precise rules and requirements.

These depression-era programs are designed for traditional unemployment caused by a cyclical downturn in the economy. They assume that the unemployed person will be called back to an old job when the economy recovers. Unfortunately, while these programs do provide needed emergency payments to the families of the unemployed, these programs typically do not address the fact that the majority of the unemployed today are unemployed due to a technology mismatch between their skills and the skills now needed by their former, or any, employer.

I've argued for years that an unemployed person's benefits package should include a mandatory training allowance that the unemployed person must spend, somewhere, on approved programs designed to teach whatever skills they are missing to get a job. Moreover, employers should be able to offer training and education programs paid for by the state to those receiving unemployment benefits. When a person receiving unemployment benefits is hired, both employer and the new hire should be paid a hiring bonus based on what they save the state in unemployment benefits.

An example of both a correctly and an incorrectly designed employment benefits program was the CARES (Coronavirus Aid, Relief, and Economic Security) Act passed by Congress on March 31, 2020, in response to the pandemic. This act gave the states billions of dollars to extend by thirteen weeks the limited number of weeks offered in state unemployment benefits. However, this act gave an additional $600 per week in federal unemployment benefits until July 31, 2020, to anyone receiving state unemployment benefits. Once the economic recovery began, as described in chapter two, "The Great Recovery," this $600 per week feature made it much more lucrative for tens of millions of unemployed to stay home on unemployment rather than return to work—significantly slowing down the economic recovery from the pandemic.

The largest group of people furloughed in March 2020 were in low-paying service jobs ranging from $7.25 to $10 per hour. A person working forty hours per week at $7.25 to $10 per hour has gross weekly earnings before payroll deductions of $290 to $400 per week. Typical unemployment benefits for this salary range would be about $260 to $320 per week depending on the state. Now, when this person went on unemployment, they received an additional $600 per week in federal benefits, for a total of $860 to $920 per week! No wonder when social distancing restrictions began to lift in 2021, millions of restaurants, gyms, spas, retailers, dry cleaners, and other small employers couldn't get their employees to come back to work. They were receiving three times their weekly pay for staying home. There is a requirement in most states that unemployment benefits terminate when you are offered back your old job, but many states relaxed this regulation because they didn't want employees still concerned about the pandemic to feel forced to return to work.

What are your personal thoughts on unemployment, structural or otherwise, and the governmental attempts to deal with it? What has been your personal experience? Has there been a satisfactory solution for you and your family?

TAKEAWAYS

1. When technological change takes away a job, our society is just as rich because the wages of the displaced worker are transferred to either the owners of the technology, the owners of the business, the other remaining workers, or to some combination of all three.
2. True economic growth occurs when the displaced worker finds a new job, often producing a new good or service that didn't exist before.
3. Unemployment caused by technological change is called "structural unemployment" and often is the beginning of economic growth.
4. Structural unemployment does not apply to unemployment caused by war, pandemic, or other third-party noneconomic phenomenon.
5. It is important for investors and entrepreneurs to be able to distinguish between unemployment caused by a pandemic versus unemployment caused by technological change.

Chapter Six

THE ROBOTS ARE COMING

The greatest economic opportunities of the new roaring twenties may lie in designing, building, programming, selling, and maintaining robots.

In this chapter, we define what a robot is, what it does, and why it is only a matter of time before virtually all work is done by robots. Robots, by themselves, aren't that scary—they are simply tools that help humans complete tasks. Robots with artificial intelligence (AI) change everything in the new roaring twenties.

As I write this, labor is scarce—there are not enough skilled workers for the new economy. Technology and robots are now more critical than ever for future economic growth.

WHAT IS A ROBOT?

A robot is anything that replaces effort formerly done by a human—it can be a mechanical machine, an electronic device, a computer program, or even a simple tool. Robots are designed by humans to take work away from humans—that's their purpose! That's why it's only a matter of time before a great deal of human effort as we know it today is replaced by robots.

The US economy is roughly divided into three major sectors: industrial (18 percent), agricultural (5 percent), and service (77 percent). It sometimes seems like there is a battle going on between humans and robots over who gets the jobs in each sector.

In the industrial sector the robots have already won. Entire manufacturing plants are now designed from scratch around robot versus human labor. Some new plants don't even have enough bathrooms and HVAC systems to accommodate human workers.

In the agricultural sector, the robots are winning—self-driving autonomous tractors, directed by autonomous agricultural drones, now map fields, sow seeds, irrigate soil, and harvest produce.

In the important service sector that dominates our economy, robots already are everywhere in our cars, homes, and offices. They are just now getting ready to come after the jobs of the rest of us. It's fascinating to watch robotic pizzaiolos at Costco make each pizza from scratch with your chosen toppings. This pizza technology took off during the pandemic because the robot pizzaiolos were consider safer and cleaner than human pizza makers.

The competition between robots and humans may already be a moot issue because if robot effort is not superior to human effort in any one area, it's only a matter of time before humans improve the robot effort enough to be superior to human effort. Ultimately, of course, the humans always win because humans own all the robots, although often not the same humans who lost their jobs to robots. On a macroeconomic scale, as explained in chapter five, "Structural Unemployment," each time a human loses their job to a robot, society is still as wealthy because the wages of the displaced human are transferred to the owners of the robot, the owners of the business, the other remaining human workers, or to some combination of all three of these parties. This is, of course, cold comfort to the human workers who are replaced.

Take a moment and think about the following interrelated definitions, which help us understand how robots are changing our lives. Consider the human effort expended in your work experiences and the technology gap that exists between such efforts if done today by a robot instead of a human. The difference between each of these work efforts is you or your employer's technology gap—a gap one can make a lot of money closing if one gets there first.

ROBOT TERMINOLOGY

Robot – A machine or device, or combination thereof, that replaces human effort. A robot may or may not physically resemble the part of a human being whose function it replaces—a robot to sort and load boxes may resemble a mechanical arm, a conveyor belt, or something completely different. A robot may or may not do physical labor—computerized personal information managers (PIMs) from Microsoft Outlook, Siri from Apple, and Alexa from Amazon are examples of robots that only exist as code in the cloud and have no earthly physical existence.

Machine – Anything that multiplies human effort to make work easier, from a simple lever to an electric screwdriver to a complex kidney dialysis machine.

Cloud computing – A network of remote servers hosted on the internet to store and manage data, rather than a local server or personal computer. A mainframe without the mainframe.

Device – A mechanical, electrical, or digital tool that manages all or part of a machine, turning it into a robot. A cell phone can be just a device for communicating via video, voice, or text, or part of a more complex robot when it is used to control a machine.

Labor – Human effort to make or do something.

Capital – Anything used to make something else.

Semi-autonomous robot – A robot that does things but requires constant human intervention. My 2018 semi-autonomous Tesla EV will drive itself on and off a freeway ramp, change lanes, parallel park, and accelerate with traffic—but it's programmed to pull over and shut down if it detects I'm not holding on to the steering wheel or paying attention to the road with my eyes.

Autonomous robot – A robot that does things with a high degree of autonomy, eventually enough autonomy to completely mimic the human effort it replaces. By the time you are reading this book, Tesla and others expect to be offering "full autonomous" mode on their EVs, where you just speak a name or address and the car completely drives itself to your destination: navigating through car traffic, traffic signals, and even accidents, equal to or better than the safest human driver. Soon all of this may happen without a human driver in the car.

Artificial intelligence (AI) – The simulation of human intelligence in robots, especially doing tasks from which the AI system learns and shares information with other robots. With AI in the new roaring twenties, my Tesla might drive me to work and then go into autonomous Uber mode: answering third-party ride-hailing requests and driving strangers around all day for compensation, until it's time to come get me at the office and drive me home.

ROBOTS HELP YOU LIVE LIKE A MILLIONAIRE

Thanks to robots, life in the 2020s for many of us already resembles what life was like in the 1920s for a wealthy few. This is and has always been the case with new technologies. Automobiles started out around 1900 as play toys for the very rich. Thanks to Henry Ford's 1907 Model T, automobiles soon became affordable tools for the masses that changed everything about how we lived and worked.

Let's examine what life might have been like in the morning for a wealthy person in the 1920s, without robots, and then we'll examine how much better off that person, or you, are today in the 2020s with robots.

First, one hundred years ago, you wake up and take a bath or shower, using linens and towels that had been hand washed, dried, and folded by your maid the night before.

Second, you go to your dressing room, where your maid or butler would have laid out your clothes for the day. In those days, shirts had detachable collars and cuffs (the parts that got dirty), and working executives needed a full-time employee at home just to keep themselves and their family properly clothed.

Third, you go to the dining room where your cook would have prepared for you a hot breakfast to your liking.

Fourth, you walk outside, where your chauffeur would be waiting to drive you to your plant or office. Your chauffeur would probably then return home to drive your children to school and perform other family errands.

Fifth, you arrive at the office. The first person you interface with is your secretary, your most trusted employee, who manages your calendar, communications, and your work schedule for the day.

Robots have taken over so many functions that were formerly performed by secretaries that some readers may need an explanation here of what a secretary used to do. These functions included all of your communications, scheduling, record keeping, filing, and various other tasks.

Let's think about what your life might be like on a typical morning in the new roaring twenties.

First, after taking a bath or shower, you'd use linens and towels that you had washed and dried yourself using a robot washer and a robot dryer, or a combination thereof, so you didn't have to transfer your clothes from the washer to the dryer. If your home was recently built, it may already have a small washer/dryer in your master bedroom closet. In the earliest years of the twentieth century, washers and dryers, and later dishwashers, were some of the first robots invited into the home. They've been in our homes so long that most people don't even realize they're robots. The first electric-powered washing machine was made by the Hurley Machine Company in 1908. These common appliances started out as machines to "multiply human effort" but quickly became semi- and fully autonomous robots controlled by a constant evolution of mechanical, electrical, and digital devices.

Second, instead of going to your dressing room to get dressed in something that might be out of fashion, if you are a female executive, you might go to your closet where there would be several designer outfits from Rent the Runway—a company that rents and delivers fashionable clothing outfits for four- to eight-day periods. This company began in 2009, and by 2021 was already a billion-dollar-valued business with eight million customers. Using Rent the Runway or one of its competitors, it is much easier and more affordable to stay fashionably dressed.

Instead of having a butler available 24/7 to facilitate deliveries and pick-ups of your new wardrobe, you have put a hanging rod for Rent the Runway and other virtual clothiers in your garage, or in a locked "deliveries room" near your building's front door, managed by multiple robots who have replaced your butler. When your UPS or FedEx delivery arrives, their presence is noted by a thirty-dollar robot called a Chamberlain MyQ Smart Garage Door Opener. This robot opens and closes your garage or delivery room door for the delivery person and sends a picture notification to your cell phone of what is being delivered or picked up. I installed this robot myself and liked it so much I purchased one for each garage door—mainly because it has the added side benefit of sending me a picture notification each time one of my teenage children departs or arrives home. They don't seem as pleased by this technology as I am.

Third, before heading to your kitchen for breakfast, you will ask your iPhone, "Siri, what's happening for breakfast?"

In seconds your robot iPhone will reply: "Good morning, Paul. In thirty-two minutes at 7:43 AM, your breakfast from Zabar's of Nova Scotia salmon on a toasted sesame bagel will arrive at 104 Woodhill Lane. Please confirm this is correct or say 'change' to modify the menu selection, delivery time, or delivery address." If you're running late, you can easily redirect your breakfast to be delivered to your office.

Fourth, when you walk outside, waiting in the driveway will be your fully autonomous Tesla X ready to drive you to work. As you approach the vehicle, the automatic rear gull-wing doors will open, and the vehicle will say, "Welcome, Mr. Pilzer" or "Mrs. Pilzer" using a built-in facial-recognition robot. "Based on current traffic and weather conditions, we should arrive at your office at 234 Sunset Avenue in thirty-eight minutes at 7:57 AM. Please let me know if I should wait at your office today or go answer ride-hailing calls from Uber or Lyft for payment—they have 'surge pricing' because of the inclement weather so 'we' should be paid twice as much." (We'll discuss surge pricing in chapter eleven, "Consumer Surplus.")

Fifth, and most important, when you arrive at your office, there won't be an expensive human secretary waiting for you. Instead, starting with your calendar robot, or a collection of robots, depending on your profession, will respond to your voice commands—confirming appointments, arranging transportation, turning on the climate control in your vehicle in enough time to be comfortable when you enter, and making sure you have online the materials you need for each meeting. All the intellectual work functions of your former human secretary are now performed by a collection of robots built into your smartphone or laptop personal computer.

HOW TO BECOME A ROBOT ENTREPRENEUR

Assuming you're the entrepreneur or intrapreneur (an entrepreneur within a large company) I expect to be reading this book, by now you've probably figured out one of the many ways you can use robotics to succeed:

1. Identify each human effort completed from dawn to dusk by people whose time is invaluable;
2. Figure out how you can replace or reduce this human effort using one or more robots;
3. Stay focused on every human effort already being accomplished that could be taken over by a robot. The nature and dynamics of your new business will begin to fall into place.

ROBOT ASSEMBLY LINES

Most people today get their perception of robots from science-fiction movies. They think of robots as humanoid-like machines that resemble human beings, having one head, two eyes, two ears, a mouth, two arms, and two legs.

This perception is far from the truth. The appearance of each of the millions of industrial robots that exist today follows the function they were engineered to do. This typically means a modern robot used in manufacturing has ten to fifty cameras (eyes), one to seven arms, one to twenty-four hands that can articulate many directions, multiple cameras inside their hands, and zero to six legs or wheels for locomotion.

Up until the 2020s, robots were used mostly in manufacturing and consisted of large stationary single-arm machines. Today's new generation of robots is smart enough to walk (or roll) upright like a Segway transporter or scooter.[1]

Picture a rudimentary moving assembly line, where the relatively simple function of the line is to open a box, mount and screw ten subassemblies onto a chassis, and then repack the chassis into the original shipping box. The line has ten stationary robots that are each ten feet long. Each fixed-in-place robot has a single arm and five hands with cameras located in each hand and at each articulating point on its single ten-foot-long arm. The robot chassis is this brightly colored ten-foot-long "arm." Ten of these robots are situated sequentially next to the assembly line. Here's how the assembly line functions:

1. The first robot, using its cameras and hands, opens the shipping box, picks up a subassembly, and places it in an exact spot on the chassis on the moving assembly line, followed by the empty box.

2. The second robot places the second subassembly onto the chassis and mounts it through twenty-five screws that are preloaded on a moving paper strip inside its arm—eliminating the need for

---

1   Segway is a homophone of the word "segue," to transition from one place to another. Segway has had limited success transporting humans, but its concept has found extensive application in transporting robots.

someone to hold the screws in place, someone to tighten the screws with a torque wrench, and someone to record the level of tightness applied on the particular chassis. If you've ever worked around your house and "needed an extra hand," each of these robots has five of them—plus there are nine identical robots each standing five feet away if one needs more help.

3. The third robot does the same function as the second robot for a different subassembly.

4. And so on and so on, until all ten subassemblies are mounted to the chassis and the last robot packs the finished chassis back into the shipping box.

The unique part of this assembly line is its flexibility, which is why it's called a flexible manufacturing system (FMS). If something changes with any component or subassembly, or if the business wants to build something entirely different, the only thing they have to change is the programming for each of the ten robots. A given robot manufacturer may have hundreds of identical assembly-line installations of their robots around the world, making it very easy for a manufacturing plant ten thousand miles away to retool for production of a different item or to make some replacement parts.

The Impact of FMS on Unemployment

Just as many people incorrectly think industrial robots look like humanoids, many people think an FMS has robots and humans working side by side together, with the robots taking over the human's jobs one by one. This is a misconception. The reality is much worse for the human workers due to global supply-chain management.[2]

"Global supply-change management" refers to the manufacturing and distribution of products worldwide from potentially hundreds of different plants to potentially millions of individual customers around the globe.

---

2   Jack Kelly, "US Lost Over 60 Million Jobs," *Forbes*, October 27, 2020; *World Economic Forum*, "Annual Report 2020–2021," September 29, 2021; *World Economic Forum*, "The Future of Jobs Report 2020," October 20, 2020.

During the pandemic, disruption of the supply chain affected virtually all manufacturing and service industries.

Picture between fifty and one hundred almost-identical industrial installations of a specific industrial robot FMS around the world. Before robotics and recent technological advances, manufacturers of finished products, in order to maintain product quality, had the work done in one or as few locations as possible. Now, there are many identical industrial robot installations worldwide. An FMS is ready to close, or open, many more facilities in real time.

This means that regardless of how well or how poorly a particular human or robot manufacturing team is performing, a decision maker eight thousand miles away in Hong Kong or in New York can potentially choose to retool an existing FMS plant. The plant owner today doesn't just lay off a human for lower performance relative to another human or robot. The plant owner is constantly retooling their FMS locations around the world, laying off everyone at once to shift production to different venues. The robots are recycled immediately to another task and/or another location—the humans aren't usually so lucky. Clearly this has significant supply chain and societal impact.

ARTIFICIAL INTELLIGENCE

Artificial intelligence or AI is where robots get really interesting and somewhat scary. When robots can learn new tasks all by themselves, potentially for the purpose of improving life on the planet for human beings, the pace of change dramatically accelerates. Robots equipped with AI are machines capable of learning from every transaction and from each other.

Here's a simple example of AI. The first time you dictated an instruction on Apple's Siri, like "find a book by Paul Zane Pilzer," your iPhone probably spelled my last name as "Pilsner," like the popular beer, and probably told you there were no books available by "Pilsner." If it was a recent-model smartphone, it might have suggested similar misspellings of my name like "Pilser."

But after you corrected its misspelling, the Siri robot inside your phone "learned" the correct spelling, forever, and not just for my name but for other

Pilzers—from my Grammy-winning, music producer cousin Charlie Pilzer, to the violinist Max Pilzer, no relation, who made his US debut at Carnegie Hall in 1917.

The ability to learn, and share with other robots what it has learned, is the best and scariest thing about AI robots.

Think about a human amputee pitcher with a robot prosthetic arm designed to throw a ball. In addition to throwing the ball toward the batter, the robot arm automatically collects and returns data to all the other robot arms on all other amputee pitchers worldwide. That information might include the ball's weight; data on its leather surface; the effects of air temperature, humidity, and wind on the ball's flight; and the flight pattern variances depending on the spin of the ball. Consider that the robotic arm prosthesis can also use all of this data to perform calculations that improve the pitcher's effectiveness in real time, pitch by pitch—from hundreds if not thousands of similar amputee pitcher robot arms.

Now apply this example of a robot arm to a robot white-collar manager—say, a robot manager at McDonalds whose job is to project demand and schedule labor, ordering (just enough) food and supplies for the next day. The previous manager likely was a real person, maybe two real people, each working a day or a night shift to keep the store running.

The new robot manager works both shifts, twenty-four hours a day, doesn't get tired, and shares its experiences in real time with up to thirty-eight thousand other McDonald's robot store managers worldwide. Think how much more accurate and efficient this new cloud-based "manager" will be. That's before you factor in no sick leave, no maternity leave, no sexual harassment issues, no complaining, and no asking for a raise. Ever.

If you owned this McDonald's franchised store, which type of manager would you like to hire to run your franchise business?

ROBOTS IN MEDICINE

Ultimately, everything a robot does, by replacing human effort with a better or cheaper method, is designed to serve humanity. This is especially true in medicine.

Robots as replacements for missing or poorly functioning human body parts are one of the most exciting applications of AI-equipped robots today. It's a great place to build a career in robotics and a field that's just getting started.

The Americans with Disabilities Act of 1990 dramatically improved life for millions of disabled people by requiring building owners to make their premises accessible—starting with wheelchair ramps and braille-labeled elevator buttons. Today, what we've learned over the past thirty years designing systems for paraplegics is being used to design specific robotic body parts for the disabled and elderly. It's only a question of time as people age before they will one day need a robotic internal prosthesis or external exoskeleton to breathe, read, or just walk unassisted up a flight of stairs. Exoskeletons are AI-equipped robots that you wear over an arm or leg to maintain strength, but which can also make you into the next Tony Stark (Iron Man) if you want to take on a superhuman task at work or sports.

There are many thousands of different robots working in medicine today. Two that fascinate me are da Vinci robot surgeons and nanobots.

Da Vinci surgical robots allow a surgeon with a particular surgical specialty, who is located in, say, Los Angeles, to operate remotely on a patient in London—just as if the surgeon was operating in the same room as the patient. Moreover, since the robot records every movement of the specialty surgeon, a less experienced surgeon (or even a robot) can use the da Vinci robot to perform that same operation without the specialty surgeon being present in either location.

Nanobots are just what they sound like: very (very) small robots (at or near a nanometer, 10^{-9} meters in size—that's one billionth of a meter!) that are used to enter the human body and perform functions like destroying cancer cells or counting (bad) molecules. Nanomedicine, led by nanobots, is one of the most exciting fields of robotics today, holding the eventual promise of curing disease and extending human life span. Nanorobots are robots at or near a nanometer, 10^{-9} meters in size—that's one billionth of a meter!

Approximately forty million Americans currently work as caregivers, although many of them are unpaid volunteers. Aside from the emotional rewards that come from taking care of a loved one, most caregivers would welcome the opportunity to transfer the physical responsibilities of caregiving to a robot—and they are about to get the chance. Japan has had for decades an extreme shortage of available caregivers due to aging demographics. This has forced the Japanese to develop affordable robots that assist their elderly population with the basic needs of living. The products range from walk-in bathtubs to robot food preparers to automatic wiping toilet seats. I suspect importing Japanese robots for assisted living to the US could soon become a multibillion-dollar industry.

WAZE – EVERYONE WINS BY SHARING

One of my favorite crowdsourcing applications for AI robots is Waze, the online GPS navigation system now owned by Google. Waze shares motion data in real time from your smartphone with the smartphones of millions of other Waze users as you drive. Its story is truly inspirational and illustrates the unlimited wealth that can be created when users and suppliers blend together in the sharing economy.

In the 1960s, at age thirteen, I lived in the suburbs of New York City and was a ham radio operator. I often took my mobile radio gear with me when my father drove us to visit relatives in Brooklyn. As the traffic built up and slowed to a crawl on the Long Island Expressway, my father would sometimes ask me which route we should take that would have the least traffic. I loved raising other mobile ham radio operators located between our home and our destination and asking them how fast traffic was moving in their area. I fantasized back then how one day we would collect the speed and direction of cars on every artery in New York City and publish the data in real time for drivers wishing to avoid heinous traffic jams. I assumed this could never happen because of the enormous amount of capital it would cost to build and maintain a traffic monitoring station on every road and highway in New York.

In 2006, Ehud Shabtai, an Israeli programmer, founded a community project to create a digital real-time map of cars in Israel and its overcrowded roads—showing how fast each individual automobile was moving on every artery—using the built in GPS tracking chip in their cell phones. He figured out algorithms that turned your smartphone into a tracking robot and facilitated potential users of the data instantly becoming suppliers of this data to each other. His hyperlocal revenue model allowed businesspeople to send advertising messages to drivers on a specific street.

In June 2013, Google bought Waze for almost $1 billion, and Waze's one hundred employees received, on average, $1.2 million each.

Using the data from every user's cell phone, Waze knows, and shows you, how fast traffic is currently moving on every road by providing color-coded street maps. It automatically makes intelligent decisions to route and reroute your trip. Its built in AI algorithms even know the future—when rush hour will increase or decrease on every road.

Not only does Waze help Waze users, it helps nonusers by smoothing out the traffic bottlenecks that affect us all. During peak traffic times and ski season, and especially during the annual Sundance Film Festival, traffic becomes so crowded in my ski town that emergency responders can't get through. To alleviate this situation and to create a safe passageway through town, the police ask Waze (now used by Uber and Lyft) to broadcast false data—routing traffic away from certain arteries needed during an emergency.

Each time I use Waze, I feel a beautiful theological connection to the other millions of Waze users worldwide. We are all helping each other out by freely sharing our information.

CUSTOMER SERVICE ROBOTS

Customer service is a challenging area for both humans and robots. It is difficult for a customer service representative to understand the needs of a customer and the context in which a customer appears and to coherently address questions and solve problems. While customer service is often not highly paid, it is the front line of the customer experience. A brilliantly handled customer service exchange can be the difference between success and failure of an entire business. Employers would do well to appreciate and pay higher wages to their human representatives.

In the meantime, robots are taking over virtually all aspects of customer service, sometimes successfully and often not. All you have to do is remember the last several telephone interactions you had with a robot as you sought to gain a straightforward answer or actually pay a bill. And don't get me started on spam or robot calls.

Despite these frustrations, customer service robots are here to stay, and we will need to adapt to them. Companies find them efficient and cost-effective. Gradually, more stores are implementing robot cashiers or at least a hybrid version of human and robot stations. We are the subjects of these grand experiments.

Walmart Experiments with Robot Cashiers

Walmart is the largest employer in the United States, with about 1.6 million people on their US payroll and 2.3 million worldwide. It is the third largest employer in the world, after the US and Chinese armies. With the largest private labor force, Walmart stands to gain the most if it can reduce some of its human positions by using robots.

One of the main jobs at Walmart, occupying about a third of their labor force, is checkout cashier. Walmart is constantly experimenting with different models of self-checkout based on robots replacing human cashiers.

In the first model, which they are testing in almost every US store, Walmart has customers do self-checkout on robot cash registers that seem almost identical in function to their live-person cash registers. Customers enter a designated checkout area with their filled shopping cart, scan each of the items in their cart onto a robot cash register—similar to what a human cashier would do—pay with cash or credit, and bag their purchases before leaving the store. I estimate that one human checkout person is required in the designated checkout area for about every eight self-checkout robot cashiers to help customers when they get stuck—which seems to happen frequently with items like unmarked produce; "Is that an organic tomato or regular tomato?"

Frankly, today when I shop at Walmart, I prefer the human cashiers to scanning each item myself—but that may change when Walmart switches from using optical barcodes on all merchandise to RFID-type chips built into every item. With RFID, I just fill my shopping cart and walk out past an RFID-reader robot cashier. All at once, the RFID scanner shows a picture and price of everything in my cart and asks me if I want a paper, SMS text, or email receipt showing each item.

A second model being tested at some Walmart stores has customers install Walmart robot cashier apps on their smartphones, scan each item as they take it off the shelves, and simply walk out of the store following simple directions on their phone. This also creates a permanent list of what they bought on each trip for later reference or reordering online—and helps shoppers stay within their budget while shopping.

A third model is to teach their customers to shop online with online robots called "bots"—eliminating the Walmart retail store entirely and thus eliminating the need for most of their retail employees, along with the jobs of the traditional cashiers. In this model, customers order online and have their purchases either home delivered or waiting in a box for pickup outside their local store. Of course, at this moment in time, the delivered goods invariably contain a mistake—something is left out or erroneously added to the order.

All of these models and more to come have the added benefit of creating a priceless permanent shopping list—which will serve consumers and allow Walmart to build an online product review and info center for each item—similar to what Amazon has now with their reviews. In an age where consumer surplus is king, manufacturers will pay dearly to be put in touch with a consumer that has switched brands after being disappointed. See chapter eleven, "Consumer Surplus."

Soon, most consumers will demand a hybrid online/live shopping experience everywhere. Customers will go to the store and learn about new items in person while robots collect all their staples and repeat items—leaving them more time to physically shop in the store or do things other than shopping.

You may be thinking: "What about people who steal merchandise?" Every self-checkout model tried by Walmart has proven better at reducing "shrinkage" than the traditional live employee at the checkout register. AI high-resolution cameras capable of reading barcodes from one hundred feet away, and invisible RFID scanners, ensure that any item leaving the store is paid for by the customer. In similar models tried by Amazon's Whole Foods Market, customers were dared to try to steal merchandise and told: "You can keep any item if you can get it out of the store without being detected, and we won't penalize you for trying."

HOW DO I GET STARTED IN ROBOTICS?

At this point you're probably asking yourself, "How do I and my children learn about robots?"

First and foremost, entrepreneurs don't have to technically understand how to design and build robots. The robot manufacturers already have the motivation to teach you everything you need. Rather, ask yourself what industry you already know about and/or have contacts in, and how you can use robots to change that industry. What are you intrigued by and passionate about?

Robots are changing everything for entrepreneurs because in many cases they will allow them to scale their businesses without being dependent on human labor.

Let's say you have been a customer of a ride-hailing company like Uber or Lyft—you already understand most of their business model. Today, the idea of owning a single Uber vehicle and driving it yourself may not excite you. What about when ride-hailing vehicles become autonomous in the late 2020s—meaning they can completely drive themselves for Uber or Lyft without a human driver present. If you understand how their business model works, in the new roaring twenties you could be one of the first local entrepreneurs operating a fleet of autonomous ride-hailing vehicles that you send out each day to make you money. Each night, the vehicles return home for a cleaning and to charge their batteries. Not only can you expand without hiring more human labor, the cost of maintaining an EV is a fraction of maintaining a traditional ICE vehicle.

Robotics Is the New Football

If you have K–12-age children, you are in luck when it comes to learning about robotics. Here's how my family got started in FIRST Robotics and how it changed the lives of two of my children.

Dean Kamen founded FIRST (For Inspiration and Recognition of Science and Technology) in 1989 to teach STEM (science, technology, engineering, and mathematics) to K–12 students. In 1992, Kamen, along with MIT professor Woodie Flowers, created the FIRST Robotics Competition.

In 2020, FIRST hosted robotics competitions worldwide involving 3,647 teams and 91,000 students.

In 1992, Kamen was a forty-one-year-old college dropout but a highly successful inventor. He had already invented the Segway Human Transporter and numerous medical devices such as the AutoSyringe (infusion pump for diabetics) and iBOT all-terrain electric wheelchair. These products changed the world for millions of disabled persons.

Two of my children joined the FIRST-affiliated robotics clubs at their public middle school and high school, and they quickly became captivated by—some might say addicted to—building robots 24/7 to compete worldwide. My wife, Lisa, became a tournament director for FIRST, and our family spent much of the next four years traveling to regional, state, and national competitions.

Frankly, I didn't realize back then what a big thing robotics is in schools today until I was giving a speech at my alma mater and took along my tenth-grade, fifteen-year-old daughter to see the school. We were having lunch with the university president and the dean of engineering when my daughter excused herself to use the bathroom. As she walked away from our table, the president grabbed my arm and said: "Paul, you and your daughter have got to help us: We're getting killed by Carnegie Mellon and other great schools in robotics competitions, and we've got to start recruiting high school and even middle school robotics students at an early age. Today, when it comes to getting our engineering students great jobs and helping us in fundraising, robotics is the new 'football.'"

My children's grades did suffer in high school and, being an academic, I worried about their futures. I shouldn't have. Robotics competitions gave them a purpose in life and incredibly challenging experiences at an early age. These experiences inspired my son to accelerate his education and become a sixteen-year-old college freshman at Caltech and enabled my daughter to skip college entirely and begin a full-time tech career with a $100 billion company directly after high school.

Robots Put Creative Destruction on Steroids

The Russians Are Coming, the Russians Are Coming is the name of a 1966 comedy film taking its title from what most Americans then perceived as the greatest threat to the American way of life: the Soviet Union. In the 2020s, robots are the greatest threat to the world's way of life, especially in developed nations. While robots do take tasks away from human beings, until recently, in many cases these often were tasks that humans simply couldn't or wouldn't do. So up until now, we've been saying "good riddance" to some of the jobs that have gone robotic, like disposing of hazardous waste or flying drones (versus humans) ten thousand miles away to kill terrorists.

In the previous chapter, we examined the Schumpeter-predicted cycle that the western nations would turn socialist and the eastern nations would turn capitalist, ad infinitum, as their democratically elected leaders dealt with the advantages and disadvantages of each system. The latter prediction happened in the early 1990s. The former prediction has not happened, and one reason may be that the early robots that took our jobs did so at a relatively slow pace. These were jobs like assembly-line workers, telephone-switchboard operators, bowling-pin spotters, elevator/lift operators, and highway toll collectors—jobs readily changed from people to robots. More significantly, the rapidly expanding labor-driven service sector created many more jobs at a much faster pace.

This relatively slow pace of technological change is no longer our world. Schumpeter never met a robot, let alone a robot with AI. Today, whole factories are designed and built for robot employees. When these factories are turned on, thousands of jobs are often eliminated on a single day, as are entire plants with thousands of employees potentially located thousands of miles away.

Moreover, most of the significant changes coming from robotics have been in the shrinking manufacturing/industrial sector, which is only responsible for 18 percent of the US economy versus 77 percent for the service sector. Robots are now about to do to the service sector what robots have already done to manufacturing.

ALGORITHMS AMOK

There is a growing point of view that a real threat to democracy in America does not arise from partisan bickering and obstruction, but rather from the behavior of a small group of large technology companies utilizing robotic algorithms to track and manipulate consumer behavior. These companies are larger and have more power than many nations. They have the capability to both enhance our lives and to do great harm. They reflect the ultimate dilemma regarding the present and future of robots.

The phenomenon is sometimes referred to as the "technostate" or the surveillance economy. The large social media companies don't necessarily have a strong political point of view. Their focus is on generating revenue from advertising.

An algorithm is a process used to solve a problem or make a calculation. Algorithms typically incorporate a linear sequence or progression of tasks and then make decisions regarding alternative courses of action.

The objective is to generate "clicks" and "watch time" by any means possible because this is what sells advertising. What upsets us is often the most effective at creating activity. The result can be outrage, on the internet and in society. The algorithms and recommendation engines inevitably show one side of a situation or idea over and over again. This enhances commitment, addictiveness, and disinformation.[3]

Facebook (Instagram), Google (YouTube), Twitter, and TikTok are problematic in this regard. Amazon and Apple make their revenue from selling things, not as much from advertising. Apple recently interrupted the ability of Facebook to track click behavior on Apple devices. This has negatively impacted advertising revenue garnered by Facebook and many publishers who used Facebook to track their customers.

Few technologists, humanists, and entrepreneurs really want outrage, disinformation, and toxicity from robots. Algorithms should not be in charge of free speech.

ROBOT SECURITY AMOK

As robots take over more and more of our work, cybersecurity issues become increasingly important. Some cyber-attacks come from governmental or

---

3   "Rabbit Hole" (*New York Times* podcast); "Your Undivided Attention" (Center for Humane Technology, humantech.com); *The Social Dilemma* (2020 Netflix documentary produced by Larissa Rhodes, directed by Jeff Orlowski).

quasi-governmental units, others simply want to ransom or blackmail for financial gain. Still others want to disrupt, emanating from envy, desperation, or maliciousness.

The United States and its companies are very vulnerable in this regard. Key robotic networks like the power grid, airport controls, and national security agencies can be attacked successfully. The ability to withstand these potentially catastrophic attacks is critical. It requires more resources and focus from both companies and the US government. We need to do better.

THE NEW ROBOT REALITY

In 2020, the World Economic Forum concluded that "a new generation of smart machines will supplant eighty-five million jobs by 2025."[4] The same report concluded that the tech driven economy will create ninety-seven million new jobs by 2025—and that while the balance of work done by robots versus humans is now 30/70, by 2025 the balance will be 50/50. The future is now.

I hope that this book helps you consider business opportunities created by robots and technology. I also hope that it helps you to understand the social challenges coming from putting creative destruction on steroids, and to consider what we as a society and individually can do to help potentially billions of people through the transition to a robot-driven economy.

TAKEAWAYS

1. Robots, and especially robots with AI, don't just do things faster or cheaper, they do things much better. Aside from the important social impact of unemployment, we all benefit from things getting done better—from faster and safer traffic on highways to cheaper and better products and services.

2. Robots do labor formerly done by human beings, that's why they exist—that's why it's only a question of time until robots do virtually all labor.

3. While structural unemployment and creative destruction have not yet led to full-blown socialism or communism in the West, this could change due to the extreme acceleration of change and loss of human jobs caused by robots with artificial intelligence.

4. The toxicity and addictiveness of social media driven by algorithms and the potential for aggressive cyberattacks pose real risks to our democracy and economy.

Chapter Seven

THE GIG ECONOMY

*A gig is any temporary job where you're paid for completing
a set task, versus by the hour, month, or year.
Everyone who has a marketable skill or who has ever had a
job is able to participate as a provider in the gig economy.
The greatest rewards in the gig economy await people who start
businesses, like TaskEasy, Uber, Angi, and Airbnb. They make
their money matching up gig providers with gig customers.*

Approximately one-third of working Americans (sixty million people) participate in the gig economy, which will dominate the US and world labor markets by the end of the 2020s.[1]

In this chapter, we will examine how and why the gig economy is growing so fast, its historical roots from prerevolutionary times to the Industrial Revolution of the nineteenth century, its impact on US immigration, and why it works so well today for the gig employer and the gig employee.

---

1   Statista.com (February 21, 2021); Ryan Pendell and Shane McFeely, "What Workplace Leaders Can Learn from the Real Gig Economy," *Gallup.com*, August 16, 2018; James Woodcock, *The Gig Economy: A Critical Introduction* (Polity Press, 2019).

There are two primary reasons you should understand the gig economy. You are either soon going to be a gig worker yourself, or you are going to be hiring gig labor for an increasing number of tasks.

The restructuring of some of America's largest industries under the gig economy pillar is underway, creating enormous entrepreneurial opportunities and societal challenges.

As of 2021, Airbnb had six million listings in the US alone, more than the six largest hotel groups combined. Airbnb was founded in 2009 and is today worth more than $70 billion. In contrast, Marriott hotels was founded in 1927, has 1.3 million rooms, and is today worth $50 billion.

Uber has more than one million drivers in the US and four million worldwide, compared to 233,000 US taxi and chauffeur drivers. Uber is just getting started with Uber Eats, UberX Share, Uber Freight, Uber Health, and more! See chapter sixteen, "Business Opportunities Businesses (BOBs)."

MY FIRST ENCOUNTER WITH THE GIG ECONOMY

At age twelve, I played electric guitar in a neighborhood rock band that was always looking for gigs. The term "gig" was coined by jazz musicians around 1905. Back then, and for our band, a gig was a chance for a musician to perform in public—sometimes for pay and sometimes to get exposure and the opportunity to get paying gigs.

A few years later, when I became a computer nerd, a gig was an abbreviation for "gigabyte," which back then was an enormous amount of digital memory—1,024 megabytes or roughly one million bytes.

Today, in our "gig economy," a gig is any temporary paid job where you're compensated for completing a set task, versus paid by the hour or by the year for just showing up. The gig economy today also refers to employers using social media to locate and hire specialized contract workers who receive no benefits and no guarantee of long-term employment.

Despite these shortcomings when it comes to benefits, the gig economy has taken off as the employment model of choice for workers, employers, and governments. State and local governments hate the lack of benefits but relish getting displaced employees back to work.

In order to best understand the gig economy taking us by storm in the new roaring twenties, we need to first understand the traditional large-employer model that the gig economy is now displacing.

THE ECONOMIES BEFORE THE GIG ECONOMY (1750–1899 AND 1900–2000)

From around 1900 through 2000, industries became organized around a traditional model in which big companies recruited young employees without skills and gave them training and lifetime employment. Before this model existed, around 1750 through 1899, a model similar to the modern gig economy existed; it was called the "apprentice craft system." Workers learned their own trade, supplied their own tools, and only worked on specific jobs where they were paid upon completion. Management's job was merely to divide the work among the skilled and unskilled workers and see that they did it, rather than to provide guidance or training to improve their labors. That's why most business leaders were called "managers."

In the eighteenth and nineteenth centuries, having a skill was more than having the ability to earn a living—it was a way of life. In addition to current income, it provided social status and, most importantly, a legacy to pass on to one's children.

Then, starting with textile and steel production, the technology and efficiencies of mass production changed to favor the large organization staffed by unskilled employees, paid by the hour or day versus for completion of specific tasks. By 1920, the majority of Americans lived in cities rather than on farms. Most then wanted an exciting job working for a prestigious large organization—like being a newspaper reporter, a hotel chef, a doctor in a hospital, or a lawyer with a large firm. These jobs became their identity. We'll examine this more in chapter twelve, "Gross National Happiness."

Frederick W. Taylor (1856–1915), an American inventor and engineer, developed a new system where management took an active role in training and developing the skills of its unskilled workers, rather than merely coordinating their activities. Taylor called this new system "scientific management." Under Taylor's system, managers had to do more than merely hire the best skilled workers they could find and schedule their work. It was incumbent upon managers to develop job techniques and teach them, thereby enabling each worker to better perform their job. This philosophy fit well with what was happening to the American labor supply beginning in the late 1800s.[2]

UNSKILLED IMMIGRANTS FOREVER CHANGED US EMPLOYMENT

Newcomers are often the fastest to learn new methods. Before the Civil War, most of the immigrants coming to America were either skilled laborers or professionals, self-motivated to come to the New World to try their fortunes. This changed after Abraham Lincoln became president of the United States.

On July 4, 1864, President Lincoln signed the Act to Encourage Immigration. This act allowed private companies to pay an immigrant's transportation expenses to the United States in return for a legally binding pledge of the worker's wages for up to twelve months (as repayment for the cost of his or her passage). It also exempted the workers imported under this program from compulsory military service.

Under this new law, which became known as the "alien contract labor law," private recruiters were paid fees for inducing foreign workers to come to the United States. Recruiting and transporting new immigrants quickly became a major business in the US—by 1880 one of the largest companies in America was the American Emigrant Company, whose sole business was to recruit

---

2   Frederick Taylor lived and worked between my two alma maters, Lehigh University and University of Pennsylvania. His efficiency techniques are summarized in his book *The Principles of Scientific Management* (1911), and he is generally regarded as the father of industrial engineering.

immigrants in Europe on behalf of American corporations and towns desirous of skilled laborers.

The efforts of these recruiting businesses were the scourge of European nationalists who feared the economic loss of their skilled professionals. In England, the press disparaged the US recruiters, with one manufacturer protesting in 1865 that "the emigration of one spinner involves the stoppage of probably ten additional hands." In France the same year, the government denied the US consul at Marseille permission to circulate copies of the Act to Encourage Immigration. In Germany, the press accused the US government of "swindling" in passing the act.[3]

However, ironically, while the emphasis of most of these programs was on skilled labor, the majority of people recruited were unskilled workers. Anxious potential immigrants often lied to the recruiters about their skills, and in some cases were encouraged to do so by their mercenary recruiters. Recruiting immigrants was a very lucrative business, with the recruiter paid on arrival for bringing over "skilled" workers—even if their skills didn't turn out to be as promised.

Ironically, in many cases these "unskilled" workers turned out to be more productive than truly skilled workers because the new arrivals were much more receptive to using the newest methods and tools in their work. For example, in the steel industry, at every step of production involving technological change after 1880, managers discovered that it was easier to teach new methods to completely unskilled workers than to retrain skilled workers from related crafts and industries. By using almost exclusively unskilled immigrant labor and training them in the newest methods, the US steel industry became the world's largest almost overnight. Total

3   Charlotte Erickson, *American Industry and the European Immigrant* (1860–1885) (Harvard University Press, 2014).

US steel production rose from twenty-two thousand tons in 1867 to eleven million tons in 1900.

The steelmaker and industrialist Andrew Carnegie (1835–1919) was fanatic about continually training unskilled immigrants in the newest production methods. He became famous for his "scrap and build" policies, which consisted of utterly destroying his own steel plants and then starting over with new workers utilizing the latest technology. Complacent British steelmakers once criticized Carnegie's scrap-and-build policies, boasting that they (the British) were using the same methods and equipment for twenty years. "That," Carnegie replied, "is what is the matter with the British steel trade."[4]

Some commentators wish that the events of the 1800s could be happening again in the new roaring twenties. Innovative American entrepreneurs are turning some of the world's least-skilled people into the world's most productive, setting the United States economy on course to becoming the greatest in the world. Unfortunately, this is not how things are perceived by many existing Americans, who see the continued waves of new immigrants as a threat to their economic security.

Today, the founders of Apple, Amazon, Google, Tesla, Facebook, and thousands more great American companies were either born in a foreign country or are first-generation Americans. Many of our best scientists, engineers, and medical practitioners come from overseas. Many service jobs from lawn care to housekeeping are staffed by immigrants, eager to get a foothold in the American dream.

We'll cover this more in chapter eight, "Universal Basic Income," where we'll look at potential economic opportunities from retooling some of America's most disadvantaged and least productive citizens.

---

4   David Nasew, *Andrew Carnegie* (Penguin Group, 2006).

WHAT'S SO NEW ABOUT THE GIG ECONOMY?

Growing up in New York City as the son of an immigrant, I never knew there was anything except the gig economy, which, to me back then, meant getting paid only for work you completed rather than an hourly or monthly salary. From 1919 through 1977, my father and his brothers had a family business making bedspreads with most of the employees paid for "piecework," which is just what it sounds like. Each employee had a specific title—like cutter, sewer, folder, bagger, packer—which described what they did. Employees were paid for each item they worked on, e.g., twenty-five cents for sewing a pillow cover, or eight dollars for cutting one hundred yards of fabric into bedspread pieces, and so on. Sometimes these would be a guaranteed daily minimum stipend in case we didn't have enough work for a specific employee. Everyone worked every day in the same factory, which was open six days a week from 6:00 AM until 5 PM. When I worked for my father on weekends and during the summers, it would have been unthinkable for me to ask to be paid for anything except what I had actually produced on the floor of the factory.

The gig economy as we know it today is much more advanced than my family business, starting with its sheer size. More than one-third of US workers (36 percent of the employed) or fifty-nine million people now participate. It took off during the Great Recession between 2007–2009, when tens of millions of people lost their regular jobs and needed to find work—anywhere at any price—since the government back then did not provide the trillions of dollars in stimulus payments.

Thus, when I first heard the term "gig economy" during the Great Recession in the late 2000s, I couldn't understand what all the fuss was about—the gig economy seemed to merely describe the business world that was all around me growing up. I soon learned there was more to the gig economy than just paying employees for piecework, but even today there is no universal definition because this pillar of our economy is so new.

CONSTRUCTION: ANOTHER PREDECESSOR OF THE GIG ECONOMY

I experienced a predecessor of the gig economy in the 1970s when I was involved part-time in building and renovating luxury beach houses in Westhampton, New York, often one at a time. Some days we'd need workers who were skilled in digging and pouring a foundation, then some days we'd need carpenters to frame a building, then some days we needed workers skilled at electrical or plumbing, and so on.

Occasionally, just past dawn, I'd accompany my general contractor, Ed Turner, to the local Home Depot parking lot in Riverhead, New York, twenty miles away. I'd watch him interview crew managers, speaking with them in Spanish, until he found the specific teams we needed that day, which would be different than the teams we had hired the day before or would need in a few more days. While such outside labor bazaars were highly efficient compared to hiring full-time employees with limited general skills, I remember thinking how efficient these labor bazaars could be if all the buyers and sellers were somehow connected electronically and able to share their résumés and availability. Of course, this was before the internet, let alone the World Wide Web.

While other employers would simply hire raw labor at an hourly wage, Ed defined each task we wanted to accomplish in writing and then hired crew managers who selected their own laborers, to be paid on completion of the job to a pre-set specification. Today, construction is a prime example of the gig economy, as is motion picture production. Skilled workers are hired for a job, and once finished, they go away to other work.

THE MODERN GIG ECONOMY

The following are the main characteristics of the modern gig economy:

1. In business, the word "brand" is a five-letter synonym for trust. Most gig workers typically use a heavily "branded" platform (e.g., Airbnb, Uber, Lyft), which collects and holds payment until the gig is completed to the satisfaction of both parties.

2. Most branded platforms completely manage payment issues.
3. Unbranded gig workers are paid seamlessly via Venmo, PayPal, Zelle, Google Pay, and many more effortless payment mechanisms.
4. The payment mechanisms automatically account for and issue regular reports.
5. The internet locates work for gig workers on numerous specialized overlapping gig platforms—like quality retailers selling the same branded product.
6. Gig workers are reviewed online by employers who have the ultimate upper hand (social media) if and when work is incomplete or inferior.
7. Gig employers get to rate gig workers and vice versa, both as individuals and entire branded platforms, and give them opportunities to resolve conflicts.
8. Each gig worker is given a defined task for their gig.
9. Gig workers are given a timetable for completion.
10. Gig workers are paid upon completion with some monies often withheld by the parent (e.g., Airbnb) until all parties are satisfied.
11. Gig workers report to a different place to work for each gig, although many work virtually from home using teleconferencing apps.
12. Gig workers receive no guarantees of future work after a gig is complete.
13. Gig workers are legally independent contractors rather than employees. They receive no health insurance, no retirement benefits, no maternity pay, no social security contribution—basically none of the employee benefits most developed nations mandate employers provide their employees.
14. There is a significant business opportunity for gig workers to organize trade-type associations to provide the workers with employer-type health and retirement benefits.
15. Gig workers have no obligation to work unless they want to, leaving them free to schedule whatever they want in their lives.
16. Gig workers can negotiate a different price for each gig.

17. Millennials dominate the gig worker market, comprising 37 percent of all full-time gig workers. Millennials have embraced gig work—mainly for the independence it gives them.
18. Baby boomers comprise 35 percent of all full-time gig workers.
19. Gig worker compensation is often far above minimum wage. Some of the higher-paying gig work includes, although actual rates depend on particular circumstances:[5]

Artificial Intelligence – $115 per hour
Blockchain architecture – $90 per hour
Robotics – $80 per hour
Ethical hacking – $65 per hour
Cryptocurrency – $65 per hour
Lambda coding for Amazon – $50 per hour
Virtual reality – $50 per hour
Reach.js development – $40 per hour
Final Cut editing – $40 per hour
Instagram marketing – $30 per hour

WHY THE MODERN GIG ECONOMY COULD EVENTUALLY BE THE MAJOR ECONOMY FOR LABOR

The gig economy has taken off—although less than fifteen years old, the modern gig economy is already responsible for employing about 40 percent of the US labor force: sixty-five million people.

There are three parties involved in every gig, and all three benefit.

1. **Gig workers** – These include quality-branded workers like Lyft and Uber drivers, to highly paid professionals who are full-time independent contractors like architects and hoteliers. The

---

5   Fortunly.com; Glassdoor.com; Indeed.com. One of these jobs, ethical hacking, consists of detecting vulnerabilities in computer systems.

millennials among them all desire the same thing when it comes to employment: flexibility. As we'll examine in chapter nine, "The Millennials Step Up," millennials comprise the majority working group in our economy and are ready to forego consistent income for flexibility and work/life balance.

2. **Gig businesses** – Businesses in our gig economy are consumers themselves of gig workers on an organized basis, like Airbnb and Uber, or end-use consumers themselves of gig labor and services. The alternative for businesses to hiring gig labor is unacceptable and unaffordable for many employers. Many companies can no longer afford to hire full-time employees with ongoing, uncontrollable benefit obligations.

3. **Gig consumers** – Consumers in our gig economy benefit the most. Anything a consumer wants can be purchased economically on the internet, where the consumer knows in advance exactly who, or what, they are getting. This comes with quality reviews provided up front, along with enormous bargaining power (reputation and nonpayment) for the consumer if they are unsatisfied.

WHY THE GIG ECONOMY IS SO EFFICIENT FOR CONSUMERS

Assume in a given city that one hundred refrigerators in homes need repair. If you've ever had this happen to you, with a refrigerator full of fresh food and medicine for an older parent or young child, you know how urgently you need a technician right away. Before the gig economy, each consumer might have to phone ten (or more) appliance repair businesses trying to locate one with an available technician who knew how to repair their model and brand of appliance. Now, the consumer just signs on to the appropriate gig economy website, puts in information about their model and brand and what time they want the technician to arrive, and connects with the right technician who often brings parts with him or her to fix the appliance that day. The main reason this works statistically is that the consumer has theoretical access to one hundred (versus ten or less) technicians, which include a couple like:

a. Technician A, whose wife needs him available on two hours or less notice for childcare. He can only accept calls he estimates will take less than one hour and that are less than thirty minutes away—before the gig economy, he would have had to take the entire day off and not be available at all.

a. Technician B, who needs to make more money this week and is willing to accept calls that start at 7:00 AM and end up to 9:00 PM—something he could never do while working for someone else on a flat salary, subject to local and state labor laws.

CROWDSOURCING IN THE GIG ECONOMY

Crowdsourcing is one of the hottest new areas today of the gig economy—there's a debate over who may have first used the term around 2005–2006. Many give credit to *Wired* magazine's Jeff Howe and Mark Robinson who wrote, in 2005, about how businesses were using the internet to "outsource work to the crowd."

Crowdsourcing refers to a model in the gig economy where people obtain goods and services from a large group of providers.

I first saw the power of the modern gig economy, along with crowdsourcing, in 2010, when my colleagues and I were seeking a graphic designer to create a logo for my retail business startup, Zaniac. Our chief technology officer, Sid, suggested that we invite designers to submit their ideas by posting a description of our product and our intended customer, and offering $1,000 for the winning design.

The goal was to have graphic designers worldwide submit logo designs with no compensation unless they were chosen to create the final product.

I wasn't sure any designer would be willing to submit work under those circumstances, but more than three hundred designers from around the world responded with logos.

We narrowed down the three hundred–plus logos submitted to our ten top choices, and then sent out a query to all three hundred who had entered, asking if they would help us choose the best design. I was even more surprised when over half offered opinions and suggestions on their competitors' designs. They had become vested in our success, and they wanted to learn from the eventual winner, even if it wasn't them. Their opinions and suggestions proved invaluable. We chose a winner, paid them $1,000, and had an online virtual party celebrating their success.[6]

The key for success with this program, as I later learned, was transparency. Most of the participants were millennials, who pride themselves on playing fair as much as they do on playing to win.

TASKEASY

One of my favorite facilitators in the gig economy is TaskEasy, a company I invested in through Kickstart Seed Fund, a Utah venture capital firm. TaskEasy allows homeowners who need landscaping work to get real-time bids from local contractors via a proprietary application based on Google Earth. Then, after the work is completed, using only their smartphone, the homeowner is asked to confirm completion, point out anything still needed, and release payment to the contractor.

I recently heard that the company had sixty new employees in Venezuela. I asked Ken Davis, the CEO and founder, what we were doing in Venezuela. He replied, "We don't have any customers down there. Many of the landscape contractors who wanted to use TaskEasy in America were one-man operators who didn't

---

6   Ultimately, we ended up changing months later to a new design that was developed by an outside advertising agency. We had learned so much about logos and branding that we were instantly able to choose our final design when we first saw it.

speak English. So, we opened a sixty-person, Spanish-speaking call center in Venezuela to help these potential contractors in the US set up their business page on the web and compete for gigs in their neighborhood."

I get a great feeling knowing that my investment is helping provide people on the lowest end of the economic scale—those who may not speak English but have access to a lawnmower—the ability to become entrepreneurs and compete online with companies hundreds of times their size. Plus, we are employing sixty people in a war-torn nation that desperately needs employment.

REWARDS AND CHALLENGES IN THE GIG ECONOMY

Everyone who has a marketable skill, or who has ever had a job, is able to participate as a provider in the gig economy. Gig work pays off quite well for many. People are quitting full-time jobs for contract work and often making six figures. Perhaps the greatest rewards await people who start businesses, like TaskEasy, that make their money matching up providers with customers.[7]

1. Entrepreneurs whose companies create gig opportunities for displaced employees will be the most successful in the 2020s. We already see this in the valuations of companies like Uber, Lyft, Airbnb, and TaskEasy. All of these are facilitators that help you connect with services you need for your home or your business.

2. The second greatest gig challenge facing governments in the 2020s will be what to do with an additional 25 to 40 percent of our

7   Kathryn Dill, "People are Quitting Full-time Jobs for Contract Work – and Making Six Figures," *Wall Street Journal,* March 17, 2022; Julia Carpenter, Kathryn Dill, and Veronica Dagher, "The Post-Paycheck Economy," *Wall Street Journal,* March 12–13, 2022.

population, those who will be structurally displaced before we have safety nets in place like universal basic income (UBI). On the one hand, governments today dislike gig entrepreneurs like Airbnb hosts who displace hundreds of thousands of hotel employees. On the other hand, governments are grateful for gig entrepreneurs who provide employment—and sometimes better employment—for displaced employees.

3. The greatest immediate gig economy challenge facing governments in this decade is that gig employees are not subject to withholding for federal taxes, state taxes, retirement funds, health insurance premiums, and much more. When it comes to structural displacement, the greatest shift may be for government entities whose functions and funding sources may disappear.

The gig economy is here to stay. During the pandemic, small companies (fewer than ten employees) grew, often with a substantial online component to their success. Americans created almost three million more online businesses in 2020 than 2019. The number of unincorporated, self-employed Americans reached over ten million in 2022. This has been driven by the pandemic layoffs, stimulus checks, more widely available broadband, greater digital fluency, and a more mature e-commerce marketplace.[8]

TAKEAWAYS

1. The gig economy is causing the complete restructuring of our economy from a nation of large companies to a nation of entrepreneurs.

2. Ahead to the past: this is actually a return to the very founding of the United States. Our founding fathers were entrepreneurs first and politicians later, who rebelled against laws and regulations that impeded their pursuit of commerce.

---

8   Jeffrey Hartman and Joseph Parilla, "Microbusinesses Flourished During the Pandemic," Brookings (January 4, 2022).

3. It takes relatively little capital today for a gig economy entrepreneur to get started, provided he or she has some meaningful link to future customers. Many if not all of the providers you need for a pop-up business are themselves pop-up businesses, ready to help you serve your customers.

4. Three examples of gig economy businesses ready to get you started today in your own gig economy business tailored to your talents include Airbnb, Uber, and Amazon. There are many more if you think creatively and clearly understand your own interests and abilities. See chapter sixteen, "Business-Opportunities Businesses (BOBs)."

Chapter Eight

UNIVERSAL BASIC INCOME

Universal basic income (UBI) was something I thought I'd never see in my lifetime, until it became ubiquitous in early 2020 as the first remedy tried by Washington, DC, to rescue the US economy from the ravages of the pandemic—with fairly good initial results!

U niversal basic income could be a major factor in making the new roaring twenties actually roar. It will stabilize society like a safety net, ameliorating the cruel impact of structural unemployment and creative destruction, and, most of all, providing the employment and location buffer that people will need when they strike out in a new job or new locale. If the new roaring twenties becomes the turbocharged engine for the economy, UBI will be its lubricant.

This chapter explains what UBI is and how UBI saves money by replacing existing wasteful entitlements with efficient cash payments. Most importantly, UBI can provide displaced employees with a safe buffer while they retool their professional skills or switch employers.

This concept was advanced during the 2020 Democratic presidential primaries by candidate and entrepreneur Andrew Yang. He took a lot of flak over UBI before dropping out of the race, and then in April 2020, a one-time version of UBI, called "stimulus," was approved bilaterally by Congress in response to the pandemic.

Other vocal proponents of UBI have included Tesla CEO Elon Musk and Facebook CEO Mark Zuckerberg. Both contend that UBI would assist the estimated thirty-five million American workers in the 2020s expected to lose their jobs to robots, providing a wider safety net.

The concept of UBI has been around for a long time. In the sixteenth century, Sir Thomas More (1478–1535) wrote his masterpiece *Utopia*, which depicted a society in which every person receives a guaranteed income.[1] In the twentieth century, UBI proponents included Martin Luther King Jr., former president Richard M. Nixon, and conservative economist Milton Friedman.

I've been an enthusiastic proponent of UBI for decades, much to the surprise of many of my conservative colleagues in economics.

However, unlike many UBI supporters who are ready to add as much as $250 billion a month, $3 trillion a year, to the US annual federal deficit, I want to pay for $1.5 trillion a year in UBI payments by cancelling $1.5 trillion of existing entitlements that provide mostly noncash services like housing, food stamps, medical services, disability payments, and federal education grants.

UNEMPLOYMENT BENEFITS AND UBI SHOULD NOT CONFLICT WITH THE LABOR MARKET

Traditional entitlements end when beneficiaries go back to work or increase their income. This gives beneficiaries disincentives to return to work because their tax-free entitlement benefits often exceed in value their taxable wages and/or medical benefits. I have lobbied unsuccessfully for years to allow beneficiaries to keep receiving all or part of their entitlements when they reenter the labor force or start earning more income.

---

1   Sir Thomas More is recognized as a saint by the Catholic Church. He was beheaded for refusing to acknowledge Henry VIII as the head of the Church of England.

As explained in chapter one, "The End of the World as We Knew It," in its haste to get emergency cash in March 2020 into people's hands, the federal government tried to piggyback onto existing government programs, like state-run unemployment insurance—adding a federal $600-per-week ($31,200 per year) stimulus unemployment payment to every US worker's unemployment check. This resulted in a formerly employed $10-per-hour employee, normally receiving $400 per week in gross wages (about $300/week take-home pay), receiving about $300 per week in unemployment benefits plus an additional $600 per week in federal stimulus benefits—a total of $900 per week while being on unemployment. No wonder some of these workers weren't interested in rushing back to work—they'd be taking a two-thirds pay cut (from $900 per week back to $300 per week in take-home pay).

This is exactly what the government should never have done—interfering with the economics and homeostasis of the labor market.

UNEMPLOYMENT BENEFITS AND UBI SHOULD ENHANCE THE LABOR MARKET, NOT FIGHT IT

In 2021, as the business lockdown ended and workers were called back to their jobs, many didn't want to return. Technically, in most states, they should not have been given that option—states are supposed to stop paying unemployment benefits when a worker is either called back to work or offered something else by another employer. Few states had the manpower or the willpower to hold back any unemployment benefits after the pandemic.

Moreover, economically, as long as the federal government kept renewing the $600-a-week federal stimulus subsidy to state unemployment benefits, $600 a week, $7,200 per year, represented a free enormous transfer of wealth to the states themselves from the federal government. No wonder states were not in a hurry to cut or reduce unemployment benefits! The benefit appeared to be coming from a beneficiary's state-run unemployment fund, but most of it was actually coming from the federal treasury.

What the states should have done was to tie unemployment benefits to employment rather than unemployment—providing proper incentives for unemployed people to return or work, as you'll see in a moment with something I call "reverse withholding."

Someone working forty hours per week should receive a living wage—but this should be the responsibility of all of us instead of our small business owners. We need to eventually balance our budget, but not on the backs of small business.

UNCONDITIONAL UBI FOR EVERYONE (WHETHER THEY NEED IT OR NOT)

Here are a few of the many reasons I want to see unconditional UBI for all Americans over age eighteen, independent of their economic or job status.

Responsibilities to Working-Class Americans

Approximately seventy-five million hardworking Americans work full-time but earn just above the poverty level, earning too much to qualify for entitlements like food stamps or health insurance, yet too little to make ends meet.

Even if they can balance their monthly budget, they are often just one layoff or automobile fender bender away from financial catastrophe. These working-class Americans serve in our military, work as volunteer first responders, and pay taxes on everything from their food to their gasoline. Moreover, as explained in chapter two, "The Great Recovery of 2020," about negative interest rates, the work many of these seventy-five million Americans do is directly responsible for the US's extremely low interest rates and low mortgage payments that disproportionately benefit middle- and upper-class citizens.

The difference that a $1,000-a-month per couple UBI bonus would add to the quality of their lives is beyond measure.

The Alternative to Raising the Minimum Wage

UBI is much different than simply raising the minimum wage. I want to live in a nation where every person with a full-time job earns enough to live a decent life, but I don't want to see this achieved by simply increasing the minimum wage. This would devastate millions of small employers and be a regressive tax on their retail prices paid by their mostly lower-income customers. Giving people the opportunity to earn a living wage is a responsibility for our society, not just the responsibility of small business owners. All taxpayers, not just small employers and their customers, should contribute to helping working-class Americans make ends meet. UBI makes this happen.

One solution for which I have lobbied for years is "reverse withholding." Let's say an employer has fifty employees ranging in compensation from starting-wage employees earning $10 per hour to experienced employees earning $40 per hour. Assuming the federal government deems $15 per hour a living wage in their area, the employer would add up to $5 an hour to everyone with a gross wage below $15 per hour, so that no employee receives a gross wage below $15 an hour. The employer would be reimbursed immediately for this up-to-$5-per-hour subsidy—taking the subsidy money from the payroll withholding taxes collected on the higher-wage employees. Employers support this because they get help recruiting and hiring employees with an effective wage of $15 per hour, but these employees only cost the employer $10 to $14.99 per hour. Anyone working forty hours per week should receive a living wage—but this should be the responsibility of society, not small business owners and their customers.

Poor Americans Deserve Choices

Approximately forty-five million Americans live in poverty. They are typically unable to work, and they survive by receiving entitlements such as food stamps, public housing, and medical care.

Instead of giving these Americans money to choose for themselves what *they* think they need, we give them mostly vouchers on specific products and services that *we* think they need—vouchers controlled by government bureaucrats.

For housing, they are forced to live with other low-income families in designated public projects. For food, they get food stamps that they can only use to purchase items on a list developed by lobbyists for the food suppliers. For their medical needs, they can only see certain providers and receive medical services on a list preapproved by bureaucrats. Incredibly, thanks to successful lobbying by big pharma regarding Medicaid recipients, in most cases a Medicaid recipient pays less co-pay for name-brand drugs than for generic drugs—even though the state and federal governments pay many times more when Medicaid recipients choose name-brand over generic drugs.

If these low-income households were allowed to make their own decisions on how to spend their $1,000 a month UBI, some might use a portion for training programs to lift them out of poverty. Some might encourage more efficient supermarkets to locate in their neighborhoods, and some might make financial mistakes and learn from them—like we all have done. Entrepreneurs, churches, food banks, and homeless shelters everywhere would develop programs to help the poor. We don't know how much the free market might develop programs to help the poor because we've never had potentially forty-five million poor Americans with $1,000 a month each in discretionary spending power. Retraining and coaching these poor could become an overnight $540 billion industry, figuring forty-five million couples times $12,000 a year!

Replace Subsidized Housing with Cash or Rent Coupons

In the 1950s, the president of a major labor union based in California campaigned for both Republican and Democratic candidates. This union president said that we need to demolish public-housing projects everywhere, starting with Cabrini-Green, the infamous crime-ridden slum in Chicago, and simply give the former residents cash or universal rent vouchers that any landlord could accept. He argued that by grouping all these unfortunate matriarchal families together, we are sending the wrong signal to poor, young males: a signal that their family responsibilities end, versus begin, upon the birth of a child. This is the main reason, he argued, that we now have multigenerational poverty. I came across his work on low-income housing subsidies while I was still a teenager. His name was Ronald Reagan, the former president of the Screen Actors Guild, governor of California, and president of the United States.

End Disability Benefits

Roughly ten million working-age Americans receive disability, ranging from 9.9 percent of the working population in Utah to 15 percent in Texas and to 20.1 percent in West Virginia. Median benefits are $22,000 a year, about two-thirds of the earnings of people without disabilities (or about the same when you consider that disability benefits are tax free).[2]

This $220 billion system is ripe with fraud perpetrated by thousands of lawyers continually advertising how much more they can get for their "injured" clients. *CBS News* estimates that 50 percent of the disability benefits paid out in some states are fraudulent.[3] And once on disability, it's often economically impossible to get off, since starting salaries typically pay much less than disability benefits. Assuming that this 50 percent fraud figure is true, that still leaves five million legitimately disabled Americans who need monthly subsidies to live. They would be better served receiving $1,000 per month, or perhaps slightly more, with no questions asked, paid even after they rehabilitated themselves and returned to full or part-time work.

Curb Medicaid and Medicare Waste

If you're getting upset thinking we're losing $110 billion on disability fraud, don't get me started on the fraud and waste built into our Medicaid ($616 billion) and Medicare ($660 billion) systems. I estimate we lose to fraud and waste $300 billion (25 percent) of the $1.3 trillion we spend on these entitlements and another $300 billion on inefficient delivery systems. Not to mention the complexity of signing up for Medicare and supplemental insurance coverage. And, oh yes, the administrative nightmare if you are seriously ill and inserted into the byzantine healthcare systems. It is exhausting and dysfunctional.

For example, for ten years I've asked my medical providers if I could have virtual video doctor visits using Zoom meetings versus expensive live appointments. They've refused, claiming that the government and insurance companies won't pay for them or allow virtual visits to qualify to renew prescriptions. My medical providers were forced to offer such virtual visits in

---

2   The federal government pays disability benefits through two programs: the Social Security Disability Insurance (SSDI) program and the Supplemental Security Income (SSI) program. Each state has its own scheme, and state health and human services agencies do the reviews for eligibility.

3   *CBS Evening News Special Reports* (2021) Disability fraud includes failure to report changes in employment status or recipient's death/health, as well as false statements on an application or medical record.

2020–2022 during the pandemic lockdown, because they had no choice, and it looks today like virtual telemedicine will continue into the new roaring twenties—saving billions in medical costs and making billions more available for entrepreneurial medical providers who want to retool our medical delivery systems.

Provide a Fighting Chance After Incarceration

Every year the US releases 650,000 prisoners. Two-thirds of them end up returning to prison in short order. Duh! What do we expect them to do when few employers are willing to hire a convicted felon? UBI paid to former prisoners would give them a fighting chance to develop a trade or their own employment in the emerging gig economy.

Help the Underemployed and Discouraged

Twenty million Americans work at a job below their ability. Many have given up looking for work entirely. UBI would allow this population to wait longer until a more suitable job is found or live out their lives in dignity receiving the same UBI monthly payment received by every other American.

Build Community Support

Every community has organizations to help the homeless, the disabled, and the elderly. The problem is that these organizations don't have funding to provide much more than a onetime quick fix with little follow-up.

If every potential beneficiary had an incoming $500 a month UBI payment, or in some spendthrift cases $125 per week so they can't spend it all at once, these organizations could develop long-term programs to help the disadvantaged on an ongoing basis. A benevolent church could do more than just pray for an economically lost soul. They could offer weekly programs to teach the same soul a better way of managing their UBI.

There are obviously many details to be worked out for UBI to succeed. However, the more I analyze entitlements and their destructive power over the poor and working class, the more motivated I become to help get some form of UBI replacement for entitlements out into our society.

MY BROTHER STEVEN

Full disclosure: My late brother, Steven, had a heart of gold and a contagious smile. He finished high school and bounced between jobs for ten years until 1973, at age thirty, when he landed a job in property maintenance at $7.50 an hour, $1,200 a month. This was more than twice the minimum wage back then of $3.35 an hour and we, his family, were proud of him.

Then his employer laid him off, and his union got involved to negotiate severance. The union lawyer representing Steven was thrilled when the attorney made the following deal with the opposing lawyer representing the employer. Instead of the employer paying severance, each party would certify and document that Steven had "back pain," entitling him to a lifetime, tax-free disability payment of $2,400 a month—twice his former wage—paid for by the state and federal government at no cost to the employer.

During the next thirty-five years, we all tried to help Steven get back to work, but we couldn't because starting salaries everywhere were far less than the $2,400 payment he received from disability—a monthly payment that would terminate the day he took any job at any salary. Steven passed away more than ten years ago, and thus, only now am I comfortable telling this story.

As an economist, each time I work on unemployment issues, I think of Steven and his contagious smile. Unemployed people aren't just "millions of people without jobs"; they are millions of "Stevens" who have baby brothers like me who love them very much and who wish they could help their big brother return to a productive life instead of being economically disincentivized to stay at home, unemployed.

Many people, upon first hearing about UBI, jump to a story of someone irresponsible they know who will squander their UBI stipend. The opposite is more true. UBI will give tens of millions of Americans who currently live off their friends and families the opportunity to learn how to manage their money and become financially independent—even if they fail at being prudent one month, they will get to start over with another learning experience the following month.

I'm not advocating UBI just for the benefit of the thirty to fifty million Americans living in poverty. I'm advocating UBI mostly for the 50 percent of 160 million Americans, eighty million, living paycheck to paycheck—terrified of the slightest disruption to their precarious financial situation. A simple fender bender might take away their transportation, leading to being unable to get to work. A minor illness or staying home to care for a loved one might lead to bankruptcy.

We can do better. This is America. It's time to move away from giving people entitlements of stuff and towards universal basic income for everyone.

TAKEAWAYS

1. UBI actually saves society money because poor people purchase exactly, and only, what they want, versus what some third-party bureaucrat says they should receive.
2. UBI can be paid for partially by replacing existing bureaucratic housing, goods, and services entitlements with simple cash subsidies transferred weekly or monthly to debit cards.
3. A key part of UBI is the *U* for "universal"—everyone, rich and poor, receives their monthly UBI stipend whether they need it or not—just like Social Security. This removes the stigma often associated with government payments and lets all Americans embrace the program.
4. UBI provides the funding mechanism for so many things that benefit us all. For example, my family and your family are safer if every person released from prison receives a monthly stipend

instead of being put back on the streets, desperate and unable to fend for themselves.

5. UBI will spawn a whole new industry of helping the economically disadvantaged half of America, 175 million people, manage their funds and focus individually on what they each need the most to improve their personal economy.

The Six Social Pillars

PART III

N ow we look at the six social pillars impacting the promise and volatility of the new roaring twenties. First, there are the millennials and
their successors, Generation Z, the largest populations in the United
States. They will be the dominant force in determining the evolution and
ultimate fate of society.

The sharing revolution is already remaking how life is lived and relationships develop. Consumers are demanding that consumer surplus, offering
more than what is merely sufficient, be a part of transactional society.

The pandemic has caused us to consider our lives amid ethical concepts like gross national happiness. We are looking at success as more than economics.

Then we have two critical geopolitical concerns: the China challenge and the Russian wild card. Both will affect the nature of our world and whether in fact we have a world worth keeping.

Chapter Nine

THE MILLENNIALS STEP UP

The baby boomers (born 1946–1964), in terms of economic output, are the generation that made the world a much bigger place to live (gross domestic product).The millennials (born 1980–1998) are the generation that is making the world a much nicer place to live (gross national happiness). Generation Z (born 1999–2012) is accelerating the millennial impact. Soon Generation Z will be the largest demographic.

Americans born from 1980 through 1998, who became adults in the beginning of the twentieth century and are today (2022) age twenty-four to forty-two, are generally referred to as millennials. There are about eighty-three million of them, which makes them currently, and for some time to come, the largest US generation, outnumbering the seventy-two million in the baby boom generation of their parents. Millennials will be entering their most productive years in the new roaring twenties. Baby boomers are gradually retiring and eventually will be dwindling in numbers.

Millennials represent 25 percent of the US population, 30 percent of the voters, and 40 percent of the workforce. Millennials are the first generation to come of age in the "information economy" and the explosion of social media. They are masters of the wired universe, from online gaming to online dating and 24/7 communication. Information technology is their natural habitat. Baby boomers are immigrants to this world.

This generation has entered adulthood without many of the safety nets their parents took for granted, including a welcoming job market offering long-term security and employers that provided health insurance and pensions.

Millennials are confronted with pressures ranging from the pandemic, social media, and expensive education and housing costs. They have been bombarded by illegal drugs and opioids. The foundation of the world has changed, and there are no longer standard formulas for a career or "success." It is not easy being young.

Just as the baby boomers defined most of society in their postwar time period, millennials will define the majority point of view for society as they come of age. They are your suppliers, your customers, your employees (and often your employers), and your neighbors. Understanding how millennials think is the key to understanding your economy in the new roaring twenties. So let's get started learning about millennials.

When I speak of millennials, or any other age-defined group, there is no specific behavior or thought process that defines everyone in that age group. There is certain general behavior, like having a large social conscience for millennials, that we assign to people of a particular age. Precise age definitions for generations vary, but here is what we will use for this purpose.[1]

The greatest generation	born 1901–1927
The silent generation	born 1928–1945
Baby boomers	born 1946–1964
Generation X	born 1965–1979
Generation Y (millennials)	born 1980–1998
Generation Z	born 1999–2012

---

1   US Census Bureau, FRED, St. Louis Reserve Bank; Michael Dimock, "Defining Generations: Where Millennials End and Generation Z Begins," Pew Research (January 17, 2019).

CUTTING IN LINE

One evening, sometime in December 2016, I decided, last minute and without a reservation, to take my daughter out for a special dinner at her favorite restaurant at 6 PM before we had to meet the rest of the family for a movie at 7:15 PM. It was peak ski season, the busiest time of the year in our ski town, and restaurants were overcrowded with tourists.

When my daughter and I arrived at six o'clock, the restaurant was packed, and there was a line out the door. We needed to eat and be ready to leave for the theater by seven, but the hostess said it would be about an hour-and-fifteen-minute wait to be seated, and she added that the kitchen was running slow.

My daughter wanted to turn around and leave, but I told her to wait a moment.

I walked outside and I took out my smartphone.

"Dad, what are you doing?" my daughter wanted to know.

"Getting a table," I replied as I sent a text message to the manager of the restaurant, explaining our dilemma.

I'd been to this restaurant often and even rented out the entire place a few times for company events. I'd entertained business clients there, taken my family there, and had developed a relationship with the manager of the restaurant. So it didn't come as a surprise when, just moments later, the hostess came outside to find me, calling out loudly, "Mr. Pilzer, Mr. Pilzer, your table is ready!"

My daughter looked embarrassed as we followed the hostess through the filled-to-capacity restaurant and to an empty, waiting table. The hostess smiled as she handed us our menus and told us she would send our server over right away because she knew we were in a hurry.

As soon as she was gone, my daughter turned to me. "Dad, you cut in line! All these other people are standing out there, waiting their turn because they want to eat here. You cut right in front of them! We took the seats of people who have been waiting one hour and fifteen minutes! I want to go home!"

I couldn't believe my ears—her explanation went right through me. At that moment, I realized I've been cutting in line my whole life. It's what

I'd learned to do in business, and life, to get ahead, from as early as I can remember. Whether I wanted tickets to an oversold Broadway show, or a reservation at a popular restaurant, I was a master at getting, legally, to the front of the line.

When I was a nineteen-year-old undergraduate, I applied to Wharton Graduate Business School for my MBA—I got rejected. Instead of asking if there was a waiting list—there was—I requested a meeting with the director of admissions and got accepted a week later. When my children read this story in one of my previous books, they accused me of taking a coveted spot on the waiting list away from another applicant. Honestly, until they accused me of "cutting the line" for admissions, I had never thought that my acceptance meant that someone else, probably someone on the waiting list, had been denied a spot in the class because of my actions.

When my wife was pregnant with our fourth child and began having complications with her pregnancy, we didn't go to the doctor's office and wait our turn. I drove quickly to the hospital and used my connections to make sure her doctors were waiting at the emergency room when we arrived.

I did the same thing once when my mother was dying of a stroke. It was the evening of Yom Kippur, she was in the North Shore Hospital run by New York University (NYU) in New York, and her surgeon couldn't get the surgical team he needed to stay late at the hospital to help her. As an adjunct professor at New York University, I had an NYU ID badge, so I pulled out my badge and implied I was a professor in the med school at NYU (not merely a professor of economics). I got them to keep the team members in the hospital to care for my mother. She had a subdural hematoma, and she survived, thanks to the trauma team leaving their families that night to take care of her.

None of these things ever seemed wrong. I was just using my resources to get the service my family and I needed. That's not how my daughter saw it. She pushed the menu aside and said she wasn't going to eat. Anything.

"Of course you are," I said. "We're here, we're seated—your not eating is not going to change anything for the people who are still waiting outside."

I then explained that, from the perspective of the restaurant manager and the owner, it made good business sense for them to get me a table. We live in Park City, a ski town, and eat there all the time. Most of the people who were at the restaurant that night were tourists here on vacation. That meant the odds of them coming back to Park City—let alone coming back to this particular restaurant—were quite low.

"As an entrepreneur, the best thing you can do is take care of your existing customers," I told her. "Because when I have a good meal and a good experience here, I'm going to keep bringing people back. I'm going to give him more business. Moreover, if they didn't seat us right away, we might go to another restaurant and start taking our business to one of their competitors."

Our server appeared but my daughter refused to order. I ordered for both of us, choosing her favorite dish on the menu and figured she would give in once it arrived at the table. After all, she was an athletic teenage girl—and a hungry one, at that.

When the food arrived, she pushed it aside and wouldn't touch anything on the table. We continued our debate about cutting in line. I pointed out that the restaurant manager rewarding us for having eaten there before was no different than when Delta rewarded us last month with free upgraded first-class seats based on my being a frequent flyer.

"That's completely different!" she said. "Delta is transparent. Everyone knows about frequent flyer miles. Everyone can choose whether or not to fly on Delta or pay more for first class and get those rewards. That's not what you did here. You cheated!"

I realized then that we were coming from two very different places, and I couldn't say whether either of us was wrong. The world that I was raised in was all about working hard, going to college, learning skills, making contacts, and getting ahead by using every legal advantage at your disposal. We maintained friendships and business contacts not for the purpose of gaining an advantage over others, but to improve our relationships and better serve our customers. Many of my close friendships had started as business contacts.

In my daughter's eyes, however, I had used influence to gain an unfair advantage. I realized that, from a millennial standpoint, cutting in line was breaking an unspoken code. The world of a millennial is about waiting your turn and earning your place—about social equity and making sure everyone has the same opportunities. If you work hard to get ahead, everyone else had the same opportunity and everything is transparent, then there was nothing wrong with being more successful than someone else. That changes when one person has an advantage, especially an undisclosed advantage not available to all.

MILLENNIALS CHANGE HOW WE DO BUSINESS

That conversation with my daughter was eye-opening, because it made me realize that this generation of millennials is already changing the way we do business. They're changing the way we approach the work/life balance and disrupting some of the old, tried-and-true principles of the business world.

Millennials now exceed baby boomers in actual numbers, and they will soon exceed boomers in purchasing power. Generation Z, which shares many of the same values as millennials, will soon pass them in size. The incident at the restaurant with my daughter made me realize that ethics are not necessarily absolute, but rather a moving target. I was raised in a world with a clear-cut view of the Judeo-Christian, I now find myself in a world where ethics are more fluid. What's right and what's wrong depends largely on what lens something is being viewed through.

If you're around my age, you probably remember tipping a maître d' or hostess to get a nice table or rewarding them after your meal so they'd remember you next time. When I had a great meal, I used to even ask for their business card and have my secretary write them a personalized thank you on Citibank letterhead. My millennial children would possibly view this today as building advantage to cheat other patrons who had been waiting months for a reservation. Millennials working in service jobs, however, do accept tips.

Whether or not you are one now, and whether or not you agree with their philosophies, soon most of your customers are going to be millennials and Generation Z. The sooner you understand how millennials and Generation Z think, the better it will be for your business and your continued success.

The millennial generation is sometimes criticized for being disengaged and entitled but admired for being generous and grounded. As the largest generation, they will dominate the workforce, the economy, and politics in the new roaring twenties.

THE STUDENT LOAN GENERATION

In 2021, US student loan borrowers, mostly millennials, had about $1.7 trillion in outstanding student loan debt representing forty-five million borrowers, an average of around $37,777 for each borrower. This burden can harm long-term financial security and well-being. It also can finance attendance at poor-quality institutions, like fraudulent for-profits, or encourage pursuit of programs and degrees without realistic occupational opportunities.[2]

However, I believe that ultimately the ability to borrow for higher education is a good thing for our society and especially for millennials. Just think of it: forty-five million millennials whose parents couldn't, or didn't, save enough for their college educations were allowed to borrow, with no credit, $1.7 trillion to attend college. My father arrived in the United States in 1914 at age eleven and had to quit high school to help support his family. Sometimes I consider how my father's life might have been if they had student loans back then and he could have gone to college.

That said, many entrepreneurs do not go to or finish college. This is an important decision for millennials, and the right answer is not always the obvious one.

The previous two generations before the millennials, Generation X and the baby boomers, saw student loans as an opportunity to jump their economic class, not as a burden. To be fair, these generations came of age during the inflationary 1960s–1990s, which means that unlike the millennials, these generations only had to effectively pay back in "real" money one-fifth to one-half of what they borrowed. Here's how borrowing in an inflationary environment works.

Let's say you borrowed $100,000 in 1970 for a college or professional school education—you got an education worth $500,000 in 2000 dollars. When you were finishing paying off your $100,000 in 2000 dollars, you were effectively paying off only one-fifth of the value you received since one dollar

---

2   Abigail Johnson Hess, "The US has a record-breaking $1.73 Trillion in Student Debt," CNBC, September 9, 2021; Ayelet Sheffey, "4 Reasons why the $1.7 trillion student debt crisis is so bad for 45 million Americans," *Business Insider*, November 11, 2021 (referencing Bipartisan Policy Center report analyzing how policy decisions affect the student debt crisis).

in 1970 was worth five dollars in 2000 due to inflation—effectively an 80 percent discount on your school loan.

Conversely, there has been low inflation since 2001: One dollar in 2001 was worth only $1.46 in 2020 dollars due to inflation. A baby boomer borrowing $100,000 for education in 1970 effectively only needed to pay back 20 percent of this amount ($20,000) adjusted for inflation, while a millennial borrowing $100,000 for education in 2000 effectively needed to pay back $1.00/$1.46 (68 percent) or $68,000 adjusted for inflation—almost three and a half times as much as $20,000 in real dollars after inflation.

Inflation is making its way back into the US economy. This could reduce the effective amount being paid back by millennials on these student loans. In addition, certain federal loans are being forgiven, either in whole or in part.[3]

Moreover, you'd have been hard pressed in 1970 to spend $100,000 for a college education. My undergraduate alma mater, Lehigh University in Bethlehem, Pennsylvania, cost $3,000 a year for tuition, room, and board to attend in 1970 and in 2022 costs $75,000 a year. Now that's inflation!

Unfortunately, a good deal of college tuition inflation is attributable to higher administration and fundraising costs rather than being used to enhance faculty and student experience. Please don't get me started on this topic. We'll be here all night.

Millennials consider themselves "working class," much more than previous generations. They tend to stay single and childless longer than their parents did. More than half of millennials do not plan to have children, according to a series of studies conducted at the Wharton School of the University of Pennsylvania.[4]

Virtually all millennials witnessed, and remember, where they were on 9/11. That event marked arguably the most significant traumatic and violent event any American generation has experienced since the World War II experience of the "greatest generation." This trauma has created a permanent sense of instability and anxiety.

---

3   On August 24, 2022 President Biden announced a Student Debt Relief Plan providing up to $20,000 in forgiveness if certain criteria are met.

4   Pension Research Council Archives of the Wharton School of the University of Pennsylvania: Millennials (2019–2022).

What the millennials experienced during 9/11 at an early age pales by comparison to what they personally experienced nineteen years later, in 2020. The pandemic hit them at more economically impressionable ages. Millions could not attend college for advanced studies or got laid off from their very first job even before they even had a chance to get started. Moreover, the fallout from the 2020 election and January 6, as well as recent Supreme Court decisions, may well have undermined the younger generation's faith in the stability and fairness of our democracy.

Millennials receive a lot of criticism. Feel free to blame their parents. They do! They've been disparaged as "Generation Me," after a 2006 book of the same name by psychologist Jean Twenge. According to Ms. Twenge, they grew up being rewarded for just showing up, versus winning.

However, there is much to admire about millennials. They are often very close to their parents and siblings. Anecdotally, I'm told by friends that their average millennial college student speaks to their parents once a day. When I went to college in the 1970s, we typically didn't speak to our parents more than once a month, and that was often to make sure we had a family car to borrow during an upcoming semester break.

When it comes to the economy, to a greater extent than any prior generation, millennials are characterized by certain characteristics. Please also keep in mind that these are generalizations. They by no means apply to every millennial. People are complex and have multiple experiences and unique identities.

1. Millennials often don't want to own homes, they prefer to rent, and to be ready to move whenever and to wherever they want, on relatively short notice. The "American Dream"—homeownership—may not exist for them costwise, but often because they may no longer want it.

2. Millennials don't need to own cars; they prefer mass transit, Zipcars, and Uber-type ride-hailing.

3. Millennials don't want to own things in general. They prefer various life experiences and don't want material possessions to limit their mobility.

4. Millennials have a social conscience not really seen since the greatest generation during World War II or the baby boomers

during the civil rights and Vietnam War protests of the 1960s. They are willing to sacrifice their careers and finances for the greater good. This was evident during the unprecedented Google walkouts of 2018 when twenty thousand Google employees worldwide walked out on their jobs to protest how the company dealt with sexual harassment. Other millennials working at the best jobs on the planet (e.g., Facebook, Apple, Disney, Microsoft) similarly walked off their jobs over social programs of their employer that had no direct effect on most of them.

5. Millennials are politically active in greater numbers than any generation since the baby boomer generation in the 1960s—their activism speaks to their sense of fairness.

6. Every nation from China to Europe has a different term for millennials, but those born anywhere after 1980 seem to have similar characteristics. Millennials are a worldwide phenomenon.

The first three characteristics alone, in the sectors of housing, transportation, and leisure, will have a meaningful impact on monetary GDP because these items traditionally represent the bulk of US consumer spending. As we'll see in chapter twelve, "Gross National Happiness," they may have a positive effect on GNH since millennials will still have the benefit of housing and transportation at less cost due to their decreased consumption. As a result, millennials may have much more disposable income.

John Maynard Keynes said that consumption is the sole objective of all economic activity. Today, a modern day Keynes might say that happiness is an additional important objective. If a millennial with a two-thousand-square-foot home is as happy as a baby boomer with a four-thousand-square-foot home, is the millennial twice as rich as the baby boomer if both have the same size home? At four thousand square feet, probably no—since the millennial doesn't want a home that large. At two thousand square feet, probably yes, since the two generations seem to equally value home sizes below this amount.

Either way, the millennials have already changed our values and will challenge them much more in the next decade by redefining what we consider to be economic output in every category. As a society driven by millennial values, we already find that we receive much more value from fewer physical possessions—driving a new definition of "prosperity" in the new roaring twenties. Baby boomers are similarly experiencing an urge to "downsize." As a baby boomer, you spent the first part of your life accumulating things and now the latter part trying to get rid of them.

GENERATION Z: YOU AIN'T SEEN NOTHIN' YET

Generation Z is coming on fast and they may well be millennials on steroids. Once again, please indulge some generalizations.

As a group, Generation Z is industrious and career oriented. They are risk adverse and cautious, but still entrepreneurial. They embrace technology and the gig economy.

Generation Z is more diverse and highly educated than previous generations. They are fluid as to sexual and demographic orientation. They often do not think of themselves as gay or straight, male or female, religious or agnostic. They are concerned about self-actualization and their own personal definition of fulfillment and happiness.

MILLENNIALS AND GENERATION Z ARE THE FUTURE

We all need to be able to manage, support, and motivate millennials and Generation Z. Obviously, they are the future. Both are comfortable with tech interaction and solutions, but they may need an introduction to traditional business protocols, which are changing as we speak. They will accelerate technology-driven wealth in the new roaring twenties. Do not underestimate the impact of these young people.

TAKEAWAYS

1. Understanding how millennials think will be a key to success in the new roaring twenties. Millennials are going to be the majority of your customers, your suppliers, and your employees (and perhaps your employers). Don't cut in line, or at least not when anyone is watching!

2. Millennials are ready to walk off their job rather than violate their sense of fairness and sincere caring for other people.

3. If you are a millennial, consider a lucrative-upon-graduation major like computer science, engineering, accounting, or applied science. A major in liberal arts can be economically challenging unless you have a concrete and realistic plan for financial support upon graduation.

4. Millennials and Generation Z will rule during the new roaring twenties!

Chapter Ten

THE SHARING REVOLUTION

On résiste à l'invasion des armées; on ne
résiste pas à l'invasion des idées.
(One resists the invasion of armies, one does
not resist the invasion of ideas.)
—Victor Hugo (1802–1885)

oday, entrepreneurs use information technology to create new, better, and sometimes unregulated methods of distribution. This typically results in consumers reducing the cost and/or getting up to twice the value on anything from a taxi ride to overnight lodging.

The sharing economy is about more than just improving economics. It is changing everything–how we work, how we drive, what we eat, where we sleep—everything! This is why I call it "the sharing revolution"—arguably the most significant change to our lives since the nineteenth century, when the affordable automobile led to the creation of roads, hotels, restaurants, and suburbs.

The act of sharing something with another person is one of the most divine experiences in our lives. In most cases, the part left over for us of whatever we have shared often becomes more valuable to us than the whole original—whether it be sharing a meal, sharing a house, sharing love, or sharing knowledge. Ultimately, sharing is the foundation of human existence. That's why the sharing revolution is one of the pillars of the new roaring twenties.

In this chapter, we will examine the sharing economy from the standpoint of creating economic value and see how sharing can be a veritable revolution in the way we live. Sharing can create value in many ways. One way is when two or more separate entities share a tool that neither needs to use at the same time. Another way is when you're enjoying an experience, like a movie or a prayer service, that you enjoy even more once you share the experience with someone else.

Until the recent advance of social media, it was only feasible to share your bounty with your immediate family, your tribe, your colleagues, or some predefined group or friend. Social media allows us to share almost anything with anyone, with potentially everyone reaping the rewards that come from sharing. However, social media can also be stressful and addictive and disrupt our need for privacy and contemplation. See chapter six, "The Robots are Coming."

Ultimately, social media connects everyone on the planet in real time, resulting in a potential exponential expansion of world wealth. I originally began writing this chapter as "The Sharing Economy," and then I renamed it, for reasons you'll see in a moment, to "The Sharing Revolution"—which is how I've referred to the sharing economy since the term was first coined in 2008 during the Great Recession.

AHEAD TO THE PAST – THE SHARING REVOLUTION

The ride-hailing industry of tomorrow may be a throwback to the ride-sharing boards at colleges of forty years ago. Ah, the good old days.

In 1971, I enrolled in Lehigh University in Bethlehem, Pennsylvania—ninety miles from New York City, fifty miles from Philadelphia, and 120 miles from my parents' home in Long Island. I needed to get to NYC about twice each month to help my father with our family business, but there was no direct public transit available from Bethlehem. Thus, one of the most important places I frequently visited on campus as a freshman was the ride-sharing board in the basement of the University Center (UC).

A typical ad on the board said:

Riders Wanted: Bethlehem–NYC. Depart Friday, September 18, at 2 PM from UC. Return Sunday, 5 PM. Share gas and tolls, est. at $5–$11 each for two to four passengers. Call 215-758-8549 (Paul) or campus PO box 509.

Freshmen weren't allowed to have a car on campus. So, if I needed to be in NYC on an upcoming weekend, throughout the week I would check ads from drivers wanting riders to share their expenses. Then, in my sophomore year, I got my own car and put up my own ads wanting riders to share *my* expenses. It was tremendous fun. I met new people, whom I almost always had a lot in common with because we were the same age, went to the same college, and probably grew up in the same place (New York). This foreshadowed where the ride-hailing industry is about to go today: a driver-is-your-friend future as we move from Uber cars driven by strangers to Uber cars driven by people within our social networks.

In the sharing economy of the 2010s, you could get many of the things you wanted at half the price because you shared the cost and use with a stranger. In the sharing revolution of the 2020s, you will get the same price benefit plus the product may be up to twice as valuable because you've met a new friend or potential business associate.

My parents often reminded me that "sharing is caring," but I never dreamed that one day I could be such an enthusiastic booster of the sharing revolution. Thanks to this pillar of our economy, products and services aren't just cheaper, they are up to 200 percent better. Take Uber, for example. I use Uber and its competitors like Lyft and Didi (China) all the time. After decades of waiting outside airports for dirty taxis that charged exorbitant prices, today when I fly, I simply pick up my smartphone when my plane lands. My Uber driver or signage tells me exactly where they are waiting for me as I exit the airport.

The sharing revolution is all about transparency: real time, honest, and open communication, including performance ratings between providers and customers. Never in the days before the sharing revolution would I have purchased a used technology product from a stranger, rented a stranger's vacation home I had never seen for my whole family in a foreign country, or accepted a ride from a stranger who promised to get me to the airport in time for my flight. Now I do all these things and more, weekly, and especially enjoy the cordial relationships developed with my newfound seller, landlord, or driver.

When Uber and similar services started, to get around local taxi regulations, they called themselves "ride-sharing" services that allowed two consumers to connect online to share rides and pool expenses. The truth was there was no common desired ride for two consumers to share—there was only one consumer needing a ride and one driver willing to give you a ride for a fee.

Eventually, they became known more accurately as "ride-hailing" services, in which a rider hires a personal driver to take them and usually only them, to an exact destination. More recently, Uber and its competitors have added UberX Share, a carpool service where, for a reduction in price, the Uber driver adds one or more additional passengers, strangers, to the trip—making the original ride-sharing name more technically accurate but in a different sense.

Ride-hailing companies are currently developing ride-sharing second-generation products to cater to customers' specific needs, desires, and criteria while matching them up with other passengers to make the ride more enjoyable for all. This is a level of service similar to the service on luxury Windstar sailboat cruises that my wife and I have enjoyed.

RIDE-SHARING FUTURE FOLLOWS THE CRUISE INDUSTRY

Before sailing on our first Windstar Cruise in the Mediterranean, we filled out a questionnaire about our hobbies, children, food and wine preferences, work interests, and tastes in the arts. Then, when we when we arrived at the dining room for dinner, our maître d', Pierre, presented us with a choice of tablemates who'd been selected based on our shared interests and tastes.

Mr. and Mrs. Pilzer, would you like to dine alone tonight, or would you like to meet someone new? If so, I have three different tables I could seat you at: a six-top table with two couples from New York who are gastronomes, a two-top table with one couple where the wife used to work at Citibank, or a two-top table with a Vietnamese family who speaks French and Vietnamese and asked about you.

Over the course of our seven-day cruise, we ended up sharing a meal with all three. We made several good friends from those dinner matchups. In the decades to come, more and more people will have similar experiences thanks to Pierre-type services provided in the sharing revolution.

Let's suppose you have to take a longish Uber or Lyft ride to the airport or to a neighboring city. In the near future, you may be able to share the cost and the ride with someone who matches criteria that you choose, such as someone who:

- has children who attend the same school as your child,
- is a member of your local church,
- is working for the same employer,
- is being interviewed for a job at your company,
- has the same golf handicap as you,
- is a trustee of your child's desired college,
- could be a customer for your company,
- vacations in a place you'd like to learn about, or
- has similar tastes in books or music.

The keys to making this happen are the AI private-sharing networks currently being developed by Uber, Google, Apple, and Tesla—each determined to be a leader in transportation software for future self-driving and ride-sharing vehicles.

Here's how a private Uber sharing network might work. Currently, when you sign on to Uber and request a ride, you see available vehicles in the entire Uber network of all types in your immediate area, mostly working entrepreneurs, some of whom used to drive taxicabs. However, with a ride-hailing private sharing network:

1. You could choose to ride in an Uber vehicle where the driver meets one or more of your selection criteria.

2. You could choose to ride in an Uber vehicle where a passenger, say heading to the airport or a nearby city, meets one or more of your selection criteria.

3. You could opt to ride in an Uber vehicle where the driver donates an advertised percentage of the fare to a common charity, school, or church—you are donating your money and the driver is donating time in kind.

4. The more criteria you select, the more likely you get a driver cut from the original mold for ride-sharing—a peer with whom you might have so much in common that you become fast friends.

The phenomenon of ride-sharing or ride-hailing has become ubiquitous, whether it be via Uber or any of the other available services. This has made transportation via automobile more efficient, convenient, and cost-effective. The application of AI may make a shared trip a social experience with a compatible driver or passenger. Eventually, self-driving vehicles may create yet a different experience.

SHARING SPACE BECOMES A THING

Early in the sharing revolution, in 2012, I asked my employees in our ski town if anyone had tried Airbnb, a virtual hotel company that back then was known mostly for helping people rent out unused rooms in their homes. One young woman, age twenty-five, told me that she rents out the couch in her studio apartment for $90/night, sometimes clearing enough after a few nights to pay her entire $550/month rent. I asked her if she was concerned about her safety by renting to strangers. She explained that she mostly rented only to recent graduates of Oberlin College. She was a recent graduate herself and would log in to the college website to verify the bona fides of a prospective guest. Like many graduates of the nation's oldest conservatory, she was a musician and enjoyed jamming or attending concerts with her paying guests. The financial details weren't awkward for her because Airbnb, like Uber, handles the money exchange for each transaction—holding funds until the host and the guest verify that everyone is satisfied.

Over the last ten years, my family has used Airbnb to rent dozens of houses from Sarasota, Florida, to Jerusalem, Israel, to Coronado, California–for much less than the price of a hotel. If you've ever taken four children plus their friends on a vacation, you know how much better a fully equipped house is than a block of hotel rooms. The sharing hosts were of additional value to us; they helped us plan our vacation activities–sharing with us their favorite restaurants and surfing locations.

I will always remember a fascinating religious host in Jerusalem whose home we rented for a week in 2013 and again two years later. When we were negotiating the terms of our initial stay, our host mentioned that the reason they had built this home twenty-two years earlier was to always have a place to stay near the Mount of Olives. This is the place where religious Jews are buried and from where it is believed the Messiah will rise up when He returns to earth. Our host was concerned that every hotel room in the city will be occupied when the Messiah comes. Therefore, they insisted on a clause in the lease stating that we would vacate the premises on twelve hours' notice with a full (not prorated) refund if the Messiah arrives during our stay. Normally, this clause could have been a deal breaker for me, but I agreed to it after I contacted my Jerusalem religious relatives and received assurances that: (1) this is a commonly accepted clause in Jerusalem rentals from religious hosts; and (2) we could stay in my Israeli relative's homes if we were evicted by the arrival of the Messiah. I also figured that they had already owned this home for twenty-two years without the Messiah coming yet, so I was willing to take the chance.

This same host contacted us a few days before our trip to say that they were concerned we were not "frum" (observant) enough to be able to properly respect the rules of their kosher kitchen—but, not to worry, they would be supplying us, gratis, a full-time kosher cook to prepare our meals and keep the kitchen clean. The "cook" turned out to be a delightful young woman who befriended our family and has since visited us for skiing in Utah—exchanging Hebrew lessons for our children for lodging and skiing with our family.

THE UPS AND DOWNS OF BEING AIRBNB

Airbnb began in 2007 when founders Joe Gebbia and Brian Chesky couldn't afford their San Francisco rent and realized that visitors to an upcoming convention might have a problem finding an affordable place to stay. They created a bed-and-breakfast on their living room floor with air mattresses and spent the next few years refining their app and concept, and along with it the rules for much of the sharing economy itself.

The beginning of 2020 was no picnic for Airbnb. In March 2020, most planes stopped flying, and social distancing and other pandemic restrictions decimated Airbnb's revenue by 95 percent. Tens of thousands of Airbnb hosts worldwide went from being successful sharing economy landlords to being potentially bankrupt.

In March 2020, Airbnb was running out of cash, and it had to arrange an emergency loan of $1 billion just to keep the company alive, in a deal that valued the company at $26 billion—a 32 percent, $12 billion drop in value overnight! On May 5, 2020, Airbnb cut 1,900 employees, 25 percent of its workforce, and was predicting that 2020 sales would be less than half of its sales in 2019.

The decline was short-lived—mostly because Airbnb, like many of the important players in the sharing economy, provides a very real and valuable service to its two types of customers: hosts that rent out their homes and guests who stay in them.

By late 2020, the US demand for vacations soared after many months of coronavirus-related restrictions. Airbnb went from being worth $26 billion in March 2020 to $47 billion at their IPO date of December 9, 2020. Then, incredibly, in just two more months, on February 11, 2021, their value almost tripled to $134 billion or $219/share. In the aftermath of the Russian attack on Ukraine and stock market gyrations, the value went to $74.5 billion or $117/share as I write today. These types of wild swings in value are typically unheard of for companies worth $1 billion, let alone $100 billion or more. Welcome to the new roaring twenties!

Airbnb Discovers the Business-Opportunity Business (BOB)

As we'll discuss later on in chapter sixteen, "Business-Opportunity Businesses," there is something else going on inside Airbnb, something I first noticed when I rented a nine-bedroom Airbnb home in Sarasota, Florida, in November 2019. My daughter was attending college in Sarasota, and we had decided at the last moment to take our entire family there to celebrate Thanksgiving by the beach. We didn't need nine bedrooms, but while we were searching, the host lowered the price of this nine-bedroom to that of a competitive seven-bedroom house nearby. When we arrived at our Airbnb rental, I couldn't find the key and texted our host. The host helped me locate the key and then texted comments about the seven-bedroom home nearby, the home that we had also considered renting before we chose his home. His comments made me concerned that he somehow had access to my texts earlier that week with his competition. I asked him to call me on the phone. On our phone call I learned that he owned, or at least managed, nine luxury beach homes of different sizes in the immediate area. Three days earlier, when I was searching for a rental on Airbnb, I thought I was texting and emailing with a different host for each property—but in effect the person I was corresponding with for at least three properties was one and the same. Upon learning that my daughter was a college student nearby, and thus I might be a repeat client, he told me he would send me a list of his nearby properties, and that I should expect a 10 percent discount on future rentals as a repeat customer.

Up until that moment, I had thought that each Airbnb rental was the "home" of the host—or that's what Airbnb and their hosts wanted their rental customers, and local regulatory authorities, to believe. Boy, was I wrong. According to AirDNA, a website that tracks information about Airbnb properties, only one-third of hosts have a single property listing, one-third have between two and twenty-four listings, and a third have more than twenty-four listings.

UBER AS A BOB

A similar phenomenon exists at Uber, where the parent company, Uber, or an entrepreneur with multiple Uber vehicles, supplies certain drivers with vehicles if they don't have a suitable car for Uber ride-hailing. Uber may look like you are "sharing" a ride with a driver-owner, but the future of Uber, particularly as Uber shifts to autonomous (driverless) vehicles, may well be with more owners with multiple vehicles.

Uber developed their proprietary GPS-based, transparent-on-both-sides software as a better way to serve their high-end limo customers who were often worried they'd miss their flight. Then Uber realized the bigger opportunity was to license their software app to their competition and expand the list of potential competitors all the way down to an individual driver with an ordinary vehicle. Today Uber calls their traditional regulated town-car business with licensed, uniformed chauffeurs "Uber Black," and their non-regulated business "UberX." Both UberX and Uber Black use drivers whose backgrounds have been extensively checked, and they automatically suspend drivers whose consumer ratings average less than 4.5 on a 5.0-point scale.

NEXT IN THE SHARING REVOLUTION

This chapter was originally going to be about the future, until the future became the present during the 2020–2021 pandemic lockdown. Changes that I expected would take five to ten years to happen in the new roaring twenties, like ubiquitous video meetings for everyone, took place in 2020—and there's no turning back.

Your entrepreneurial mind is probably racing with ideas on how to use social media and information technology to improve everything, just as Uber and Airbnb have improved transportation and lodging.

Let's take a look at a few examples.

Medicine at Home

Suppose your child wakes up not feeling well, and you don't know whether to keep them home from school. You could get an affordable, virtual online or in-person house call from your own physician or nurse practitioner. If you are a medical professional yourself, you may wish to make $100–$200 an hour visiting someone in your own neighborhood on your own time—you're already licensed in your state so you could start a mobile medical service or something similar. If you're a techie, perhaps you could start a business offering consumers a $99 medical hardware package including a pulse oximeter, blood pressure monitor, and thermometer all connected to your smartphone with a simple application. Your future nanny cam for a child may be monitoring your child's vital statistics as if they were in an ICU—sharing the information in real time with you and your hospital or doctor (who may be a robot).

Food Entrepreneur

The next big thing in the sharing revolution has already started: using an Uber-like software platform that turns any home or space with cooking equipment, or existing restaurant, into a take-out kitchen. If you've dined out at all during 2021, you are already comfortable using an electronic menu on your smartphone for ordering and payment. A foodie entrepreneur would create their daily menu including pictures, quantity, and availability. Diners and chefs would use smartphones and home computers to make selections online and watch the provider in real time drive to the diner's home for delivery, or watch the diner (or Uber Eats driver) drive to the foodie entrepreneur's location.

Plumber

Suppose you need a plumber in fifteen minutes or less to fix a leak? You can probably get an approved plumber to meet you in ten minutes while you watch him or her drive over to your house on an Uber-like app on your smartphone. This recently happened to me when I used an app to find a plumber at 9 PM on a Sunday evening, and we watched him drive to our house on my smartphone by 9:30 PM—asking all the right questions from his truck's speakerphone so he was instantly productive upon arrival.

Math Tutor

Suppose your child, and you, can't understand his math homework, and it's the night before a final exam? How would you like to get an "approved" local math tutor, who might be a student in your child's class, to show up at your door in ten minutes or less? You've been able for years to find a tutor online, but now you can take advantage of a model partially online and partially in person, based on what's best for your child.

Affordable Restaurant Table

Suppose you want a restaurant willing to sell you a vacant table for 50 percent off—but only if you guarantee that you will arrive in fifteen minutes and that you will spend at least fifteen dollars a person. How would you like to see all the seats available nearby at a discount and pick your table? If you're a restaurant owner, wouldn't it be nice to only give this discount to approved regular customers, one at a time, until you fill up the tables you can't sell at full price?

Banking

Unregulated banking services like Venmo have arrived and are already the banking platform of choice for millennials and Generation Z. But the next wave of banking will be single-purpose shared platforms for specific events, like financing a multiperson group ski trip with free tracking of each participant's payments.

SUCCESS IN SHARING REQUIRES A GREAT IDEA AND GREAT EXECUTION

Note that a keyword in many sharing success stories is "approved"—approved and rated by both the service provider and by the customer. Uber, Airbnb, and hundreds more sharing-economy success stories are not just companies with a good idea, they are companies with great execution of their ideas, transparency, and fabulous customer service. People like Jeff Bezos (Amazon) and Brian Chesky (Airbnb) either attended the best computer and engineering schools in the nation or quickly hired as their partners other people who had top engineering backgrounds.

Great execution of a sharing business often requires a different skill set than conceptualization. This is where management ability, critical path analysis, and people skills come into play.

As an entrepreneur, you will want to understand the sharing revolution and its applications. Are there refinements in concept or execution that can make a good idea better? What are your skills and interests? How can they fit?

TAKEAWAYS

1. In the sharing economy, consumers save up to twice the traditional cost of a product or service by sharing the cost with others—a 2x lift. In the sharing revolution, consumers not only save half the cost, they get a product or service that is up to twice as good by meeting other like-minded individuals—a 4x total lift.

2. Similar technology for private networks will allow you to one day choose restaurant tablemates based on your own criteria. While today you primarily select a restaurant for the great cuisine and atmosphere, tomorrow you may choose a restaurant for the potential great dinner conversation.

3. Ahead to the past! Most of the products and services in the sharing revolution have been around for years but in a far inferior form. The college ride board has been replaced by Uber et al., and the "roommates wanted" board has been replaced and greatly improved by Airbnb and some of its derivatives.

4. The sharing revolution presents extraordinary opportunities for creative entrepreneurs who think outside the box or who may not even believe that a box exists.

Chapter Eleven

CONSUMER SURPLUS

"Consumer surplus" is the price a consumer is willing to pay for a good or service when the price that they actually do pay is less.

In this chapter, we will examine an old concept, but a relatively new term, "consumer surplus," which has taken our economy by storm the past few years and formed part of the foundation for the new roaring twenties. Technically, consumer surplus is the price that a consumer pays for a product or service less than the price that they were willing to pay. In the past, this was a purely academic discussion. How could you measure what a consumer *would* have paid and what would you do with this measurement if you could? Today, consumer surplus is one of the most valuable tools a business has, and it's largely responsible for the success of many iconic companies, including Neiman Marcus, Amazon, and Uber.

WHY MANY BUSINESSES DELIVER THE BARE MINIMUM

Successful businesses in the last century delivered the minimum product or service a consumer would be willing to accept for the largest possible price—in business school we called this "short-term profit maximization." Where's the fun in that?

Think about your last ride in a conventional taxi—were you happy with the driver, the vehicle, or the price? Probably not. Think about your last trip to a dated fast-food chain—were you satisfied with the personnel, the cleanliness, the taste, or the price? Why did you go there? Probably because you were very hungry, had to get somewhere in a hurry, or had no other choice.

No wonder so many young people, especially millennials, don't like business. Most of us, especially those who excel in sales, enjoy making other people happy, not squeezing them against the wall until they cry "uncle"—or in this case, "sale."

In the past, in a world where physical resources were scarcer than they are today, most goods and services used to cost retailers 50 to 80 percent of their retail price. The only way a store could afford to stay in business was by cutting every corner and selling at the maximum price its consumer would pay, regardless of the retailer's actual cost.

STANLEY MARCUS DISCOVERS CONSUMER SURPLUS

This changed at the beginning of the twentieth century when my late friend, the entrepreneur and Renaissance man Stanley Marcus (1905–2002), figured out "long-term profit maximization" by giving consumers more than they expected for a given price—what the economist Alfred Marshall (1842–1924) called "consumer surplus."[1]

In 1925, Stanley Marcus graduated from Harvard at age twenty and returned to his hometown of Dallas to work for his family's single-location retail store, Neiman-Marcus. Back then, customers typically shopped only once each fall to purchase a winter coat that they expected would last two years.

---

1   The term "consumer surplus" was originated by Italian-born French economist Jules Dupuit (1804–1866) but was popularized by Alfred Marshall in his classic work *Principles of Economics* (1890).

Noting that most of their customers were affluent, Stanley theorized that if Neiman-Marcus made shopping an exciting, fun experience with an enjoyable outcome—consumer surplus—every time, they could sell the same single-coat customers more goods throughout the year. The strategy worked. It took most US retailers decades to figure out Stanley's consumer surplus formula for success.

Let's say you need to purchase a new dress for a friend's wedding, and you've budgeted yourself $200. You go to the store and find exactly the dress you want for $179.99, the highest amount you're willing to pay for it. You go to the register to check out. Thinking you are saving yourself $20.01, you find that the item has been marked down in the store's computer to $119.99—but the markdown wasn't marked on the sales floor or on the price tag!

Not only do you happily purchase the item for 40 percent ($80.01) less than your original $200 budget, you also probably buy $80 worth of accessories, and you plan on returning next month for lunch with your girlfriends for more shopping!

Stanley Marcus applied the concept of consumer surplus back in the 1930s when wholesale prices on manufactured goods, like dresses, were falling due to automation, the Great Depression, and lower labor costs. This made it possible for Stanley's stores to deliver consumer surplus.

In the new roaring twenties, due to advances in technology, wholesale prices will fall so fast that many products and services will have effectively a zero marginal product cost (ZMPC) for their retailer. This means that the selling price of each additional product, computer program, movie ticket, dinner, dress, etc., will or will almost equal its profit. This will allow retailers to lower prices even more, especially when the customer is purchasing two-for-the-price-of-one of a similar item. The price of the first item covers all the seller's wholesale, sales, and marketing costs, and thus the second item in many of these cases is almost pure profit. No wonder so many items today offer a "second for 50 percent off" or "two for one."

NET PROMOTER SCORE (NPS)

In today's highly competitive online world of social media, where virtually every person's shopping experience can be shared in real time with their demographic peers, no business can afford to have a customer leave merely "satisfied." Every customer must be "extremely satisfied" and then serve as an enthusiastic sales agent for the business.

This is measured with a scale called a Net Promoter Score (NPS), developed in 2003 by Fred Reichheld, which is today used by two-thirds of America's Fortune 1000 companies. You've probably noticed follow-up prompts or surveys used to determine this score on many of your recent online purchases and even sometimes on in-store purchases.[2]

After purchasing a product or service, you are asked one simple question: "On a scale of zero to ten, how likely is it that you would recommend [company name] to your friends, family, or business associates?"

Customers responding 0 to 6 are called "detractors," 7 to 8 are called "passives," and 9 to 10 are called "promoters." A company's NPS is its percentage of promoters less than its percentage of detractors. Companies, employers, retailers, manufacturers, and almost everyone today uses NPS to compare themselves to their competitors and to compare themselves to themselves over periods of time.

The concept of NPS is ubiquitous in large companies, but it's so simple and accurate that it can be applied to all sizes of providers of a product or service. Let's say you own a restaurant or a retailer. First, set up an NPS benchmark that you think is reasonable. Remember, it's not important where you start with NPS; it's important where you are going. Then continue to watch NPS using your benchmark to tell you how you are doing over time, and how to make corrections before you get into trouble—such as if and when your customers stop promoting your business. Depending on how you set up your appropriate data collection process—with a simple questionnaire

---

2   "Would You Recommend Us?" *Business Week*, January 29, 2006; Patrick Wierckx, "The Retention Rate Illusion—Understanding the Relationship Between Retention Rates and the Strength of Subscription-Based Businesses," *Journal of Applied Business and Economics*, October 11, 2020; "The Simple Metric That's Taking Over Big Business," *Business Week*, February 2021.

or a free item for responding—NPS can be priceless information delivered to you on a monthly, weekly, daily, or even hourly basis. This could alert you in real time to a new problem, like bad food or a difficult employee, before your new problem becomes a catastrophe.

In the Bible, Matthew 5:41 tells us to overdeliver—to go the extra mile when doing something for our fellow man. This is no longer just something to do because it is good policy. It is something to do because it will create consumer surplus, leading to lifetime customers and long-term higher profits.

WHY BUSINESS USED TO IGNORE CONSUMER SURPLUS

Consumer surplus has not been a heavily researched field, mainly because it has been so difficult to measure, but this is rapidly changing. The traditional supply-demand curve you studied in high school shows only the equilibrium point (the price) where the supply of a specific item equals the demand. It does not capture how much more a consumer would have paid if the item had been offered at a higher price. Moreover, the traditional supply-and-demand curve equilibrium point inherently assumes that there is a limited supply—something that will almost never happen in the new roaring twenties due to a limitless supply of eventually everything thanks to advancing technology.

Consider what would happen to your company's bottom line if you knew the highest price a consumer would be willing to pay before you set that price—individually for each customer.

Think of a simple transaction like purchasing a shirt online. You see the shirt in an online store for $29.99 and either you purchase it or you do not. If you buy it, and you feel later on that the shirt is worth more than the $29.99 you paid, you experience consumer surplus and you generate a relatively high NPS, making you a long-term customer and a promoter of the store. My father called this "the price at which you leave something on the table for your customer."

My father was especially happy when he saw something for sale at a higher price than he had already paid for it. He was especially distraught when he saw one of his own products for sale at Macy's at a higher price than it was available across the street at Gimbels.

Returning to your shirt, no one asks you, or any purchaser, how much more you would have paid if the shirt was offered at a higher price. Nor could they, because they'd have to ask you many questions about many different price points, and each customer would have a different response about how much more than the selling price the shirt was worth to them. Most importantly, what about your noncustomers who thought $29.99 was too high in the first place to even make the purchase— how would you find these answers for those who didn't buy the product?

UBER TAKES CONSUMER SURPLUS TO A WHOLE NEW LEVEL

Businesses' level of interest, or really lack of interest, in consumer surplus, recently changed when technology allowed some producers and retailers a way to automatically track the behavior of their customers, along with the behavior of their noncustomers. It really took off with Uber around 2016.

Uber has a unique business model of surge pricing based on demand for the exact same service at a particular time. Uber even knows the price at which a transaction is not consummated because it was too high. Here's how Uber and surge pricing work to ensure that Uber can virtually guarantee almost every potential rider a ride when they absolutely need it, especially in bad weather.

A consumer seeking a ride creates an "Uber session" (a company defined term) by logging onto Uber with her smartphone and entering her location and desired destinations. Uber instantly calculates internally the "no surge" or "one-time" price for the requested ride and is about to tell the customer the price, and how many minutes away are her potential drivers and eventual destination. Instantaneously, before displaying this one-time price, Uber looks at the volume of other potential customers seeking rides from the same area and uses an algorithm to predict at what higher price she, and many other potential customers, will cancel their request because the price is too high. In this manner, Uber is able, in real time, to increase revenue and ensure that it almost always has enough drivers available to meet the demand for customers who must have a ride from that area within a reasonable number of minutes, at any price—either because they are late for work or because a thunderstorm just began.

In 2016, a fascinating study of Uber was coauthored by the economist Robert Hahn at the University of Oxford, who coincidentally was my high school classmate. Robert and his team looked at fifty-four million Uber sessions containing rides and requested-but-unconsummated rides, over a five-month period in Uber's four largest US markets (San Francisco, New York City, Chicago, and Los Angeles). The study noted that about 21 percent of UberX sessions experienced surge pricing between 1.2 times and 1.5 times, 4.1 percent experienced surge pricing exceeding three times, and 0.65 percent experienced surge pricing greater than four times. Extrapolating this data to Uber's 2021 $26 billion sales worldwide, Uber generated roughly 10 percent ($2.6 billion) additional revenue for itself and its drivers through surge pricing. This $2.6 billion extra revenue benefits Uber and Uber drivers. Uber drivers receive approximately 75 percent of the increased fare and Uber receives 25 percent. Surge pricing helps Uber ensure that potential customers who really need a ride, and are ready to pay for it, get one—although at a higher price.[3]

Importantly, since most Uber rides are to and/or from the same location, typically work or home, Uber is able to accurately measure consumer surplus for most of its rides. Because of surge pricing, Uber knows almost exactly how much and at what time of day a potential rider was (and probably still is) willing to pay for a specific ride—any amount paid below this price is consumer surplus.

By knowing how high a price a customer would pay due to surge pricing and did pay under regular pricing, the authors of the study concluded that Uber generates approximately $1.60 in consumer surplus for every dollar in revenue—that's $2.60 in value for every dollar spent. In other words, consumers paid Uber in 2016 approximately $16 billion for rides, and for those same rides, consumers would have paid approximately $41.5 billion if Uber

3   Robert Hahn, Peter Cohen, Jonathan Hall, Steven Levitt, and Robert Metcalfe, "Using Big Data to Estimate Consumer Surplus: The Case of Uber," National Bureau of Economic Research, September 2016.

had unilaterally raised its prices 260 percent. In 2016, Uber riders received $25.5 billion in consumer surplus.

Currently, Uber shares its revenue 75 percent to its drivers and 25 percent to Uber. This is before the real promise of the new roaring twenties: autonomous driving. Uber vehicles without drivers could potentially generate an up to 300 percent increase in corporate revenues from the same passengers, every $100 in total passenger revenue goes $25 to Uber; with autonomous vehicles, every $100 in total passenger revenue goes $100 to Uber (although Uber will need to create a new opportunity for gig-economy entrepreneurs to own and maintain Uber driverless autonomous vehicles). Of course, Uber has several formidable competitors in each of its markets. I suspect competition will drive down the price for Uber and other ride-hailing services more than 50 percent once autonomous vehicles replace drivers with robot vehicles. Now that's consumer surplus!

AMAZON SUCCEEDS BY MANAGING CONSUMER SURPLUS

Amazon is the richest retailer in the world today, with a market capitalization of approximately one trillion dollars. No other retailer comes close—even Walmart, the largest retailer in the world, has a market cap of about one-third of Amazon! There are so many amazing things about Amazon, but the most amazing is how quickly it rose to the top and made its founder, Jeff Bezos, one of the richest men in the world. As we shall see, much of Amazon is comprised of a network of small businesses.

Jeff Bezos was born in Albuquerque in 1964 and graduated Princeton University in 1986 with a degree in electrical engineering and computer science. He had several jobs on Wall Street before he focused on online retailing as potentially the fastest growing sector in the economy. He moved to Bellevue, Washington, in 1994 and founded Amazon in the garage of his parents' home. He methodically created a list of twenty products that could be marketed online based on consumer reviews, then he narrowed that list to five products: compact discs, computer hardware, computer software, videos, and books.

The company began selling books based on online customers' reviews in July 1995, and within two months, its sales were $20,000 a week! In 1996, sales grew about 3,000 percent from $511,000 to $15.75 million, and the company did an IPO on May 15, 1997, at $18 per share—an investor buying shares back then would have an investment today worth over $100,000 for every $1,000 invested.

Three days before its IPO, Amazon was sued by Barnes & Noble for claiming that Amazon was the "world's largest bookstore"—Barnes & Noble claimed they shouldn't be allowed to use the term "bookstore" since they had no physical store. Separately, Walmart sued Amazon on October 16, 1998, for stealing trade secrets by hiring former Walmart executives. Both suits were settled out of court.

In 1997, Amazon started the Amazon Affiliate program (now called the Amazon Associates Program), which allowed owners of any website to earn commissions by referring their visitors to specific products and pages on Amazon.com. As a book author since the 1980s, I was pleased by the opportunity to communicate online with my readers and directly refer them to Amazon "buy" pages from wherever I desired. I became an Amazon Associate in 1999.

In 1998, the company began selling more than just books: electronics, software, video games, apparel, furniture, food, toys, and jewelry. In 1999, *Time* magazine named Bezos its "Person of the Year" for Amazon's contribution to online marketing. We'll examine the Amazon Associates Program more in chapter sixteen, "Business-Opportunity Businesses (BOBs)." In all of its sales and business practices, Amazon focused on always offering the customer consumer surplus in the tradition of Stanley Marcus.

I saw firsthand Amazon embracing this time-tested formula for success one day when I purchased my first nonbook product on Amazon in September 2002.

I shave using a five-blade Gillette Fusion5 razor—a starter-pack bundle typically includes a free electronic razor handle worth ten dollars, plus five to twelve individual blade cartridges priced at about three dollars per cartridge. Three days before this day in September, I dropped and broke my razor handle, so I went on Amazon.com and purchased, for $9.99, what I thought was a three-cartridge bundle with a free razor handle. Three days later my purchase arrived: three five-blade cartridges but no razor handle. So I phoned Amazon and a customer representative answered right away.

I explained that I had purchased the bundle but not received the razor handle. She showed me on the Amazon website that it was clearly marked "cartridges only—handle not included" even though there was a picture of the handle. I apologized for my mistake, and asked her if she could help me reorder a bundle with the handle.

Instead, she said: "No, this is our mistake. We don't care what it says, we care about what you expected after reading about it or what you thought it says. To correct our mistake, we will ship you today the 'correct' item, a razor-handle bundle with the three cartridges, and you can keep the three cartridges you've already received as an apology for our mistake in having a website that misled you."

Amazon's attitude and amazing return/refund policy back then was just the beginning of their policy when it comes to consumer surplus. Today, when I need almost anything for our household on a recurring basis, Amazon is my first stop to shop for multiple reasons—starting with the list they keep of all my past purchases.

Amazon has a Net Promoter Score of 73. In general, 50 and above is excellent, and 70 and above is world class. No wonder they have had some success.

MAKING CONSUMER SURPLUS A PERSONAL PRIORITY

Whether you are an employee or own your business, you should make consumer surplus a priority. This means providing an excellent value to your employer or customer, i.e., much more than expected. This is the way to build a successful relationship or business.

Just doing enough to get by is disrespectful to others and also to yourself. Take pride in what you are doing. If it is worth doing, it is worth doing as well as you can, utilizing all available resources and efforts. And providing consumer surplus in the new roaring twenties.

TAKEAWAYS

1. Consumer surplus is the highest amount a consumer is willing to pay for a product or service less the amount they actually do pay.

2. Consumer surplus used to be almost impossible for sellers to deliver but today is a realistic goal because so many products have a zero or virtually zero marginal product cost. Examples include an extra ticket to a movie theater, an extra seat in a shared Uber car, or an empty bedroom in an Airbnb host's apartment.

3. Customers receiving consumer surplus become promoters of the product, the retailer, and the provider—so much so that the empirical scale used to measure consumer surplus is called NPS for Net Promoter Score.

4. Uber became a valued participant in the sharing economy by giving consumers $1.60 in consumer surplus for every dollar in revenue. Uber is just getting started in the new roaring twenties, when it will hope to switch to autonomous, driverless, no- to low-maintenance electric vehicles.

5. Amazon's success is largely based on consistently providing consumer surplus and then measuring it with NPS.

Chapter Twelve

GROSS NATIONAL HAPPINESS

We hold these truths to be self-evident, that all men are created equal,
that they are endowed by their Creator with certain unalienable Rights,
that among these are Life, Liberty and the pursuit of Happiness.
—The United States Declaration of Independence, July 4, 1776

One of our nation's greatest founding documents first declares the signers' independence from Great Britain and then declares the *raison d'être (*the reason to exist) for the United States: to allow people to pursue happiness.

The Declaration of Independence says that people should be able to pursue whatever dreams they want, provided they don't hurt someone else or prevent others from pursuing their own dreams. The word "happiness" is capitalized, but its definition is left ambiguous and for every citizen to define for themselves, based on what they wish to pursue.

In the early twentieth century, however, the national focus for the US and most other nations shifted from the pursuit of happiness to the pursuit of economics. In 1934, economist Simon Kuznets developed a uniform methodology for measuring economic output and, almost overnight, Kuznets's index for gross national product (later renamed gross domestic product or GDP) became the dominant index used worldwide to measure national success.

In this chapter, we introduce a new concept for the 2020s and beyond—gross national happiness (GNH), a term that shakes our values to their core. For almost one hundred years, we have judged ourselves, our careers, nations and many of our fellow human beings by their amount of material wealth produced annually. We even awarded a Nobel Prize to Kuznets, who defined the scale we use to measure material wealth. Successful entrepreneurs having often achieved the material wealth they sought, many of them find that the ultimate goal, happiness, has proven elusive. Moreover, as explained herein, in producing great wealth measured by GDP, we made a tragic calculation mistake. We failed to include the true costs of the raw materials we appropriated from others without fair compensation, such as charging ourselves for the amount of pollution or climate change we caused.

EARNINGS VERSUS LEARNINGS

In the post-World War II era, in response to consumer demand from returning veterans and the GI bill, colleges shifted resources from teaching liberal arts to teaching business. The emphasis on earnings versus learnings took off. In 1974, just before I left New York for school in Philadelphia, my parents hosted a gathering for our extended family. My father told our assembled relatives: "Paul's going to Wharton Business School to learn how to make a living." My embarrassed mother responded to him saying, "Paul's going to the University of Pennsylvania to learn how to live."

By the 1980s, Americans were achieving financial prosperity and acquiring more possessions than previous generations had ever thought possible. US GDP per capita doubled from about $34,000 in 1999 to $68,000 in 2021. Meanwhile, a smaller percentage of Americans each year were sharing in those riches.

Although US average individual wealth per capita skyrocketed, overall US and world happiness has suffered. Almost 50 percent of first marriages now end in divorce; anxiety disorders affect about fifty million adults; depression affects about seventy million; and obesity, mostly caused by overeating and unhappiness, now affects 233 million or about two-thirds of the US population. In the pursuit of financial gain, happiness has taken a hit.

Until recently, no one yet had developed a universal index, like Kuznets's GDP index, to measure happiness on an individual and on a national scale—an index for GNH.

Without such a universal index, nations continue to make ill-advised decisions like China's 1979–2015 implementation of one-child policy (OCP). We'll examine in the next chapter how Deng Xiaoping's 1979 decision on OCP may go down as perhaps the best decision ever made in the history of the world in terms of increasing GDP and one of the worst decisions ever made in terms of increasing GNH.

THE ORIGIN OF GNH

Here's how GNH, now the world index for happiness, came about.

In 2008, the Kingdom of Bhutan decided that private- and public-sector decisions should be made based on the happiness they can generate versus the profits they will make. Moreover, any scale, like GDP, used to measure economic output should have deductions for nonrenewable resources depleted and for pollution created. Bhutan's 2008 constitution outlined the nine domains of happiness and four pillars of GNH. In July 2011, the United Nations adopted much of Bhutan's work on GNH.[1]

Since 2012, the UN has released the World Happiness Report (WHR) every year on the state of global happiness, ranking 156 countries by how happy their citizens perceive themselves to be. These annual WHR reports are insightful for the way they rank each nation compared to other nations, and for how they rank each nation against itself in prior years—giving each nation a happiness scale by which to monitor its own improvement. The WHR is issued on the twentieth of March, the United Nations International Day of Happiness.[2]

---

1   The Constitution of the Kingdom of Bhutan, Royal Government of Bhutan.

2   Bhutan, *Defining a New Economic Paradigm: The Report of the High Level Meeting on Wellbeing and Happiness* (United Nations 2012); "A Resolution Adopted by the General Assembly, International Day of Happiness," June 28, 2012.

Separate from just the data, each annual report also includes related articles and research by the world's top economists, scientists, and leaders. For example, WHR 2018 featured an article by economist Jeffrey Sachs on the "Easterlin paradox"—which was developed by University of Pennsylvania economist Richard Easterlin. This 2018 article analyzed how US per capita real income had more than doubled in the forty-six years since 1972, while happiness had remained roughly unchanged. Back in 1974, the Easterlin paradox postulated that happiness increases directly with income up to a certain point, but that above this point, happiness no longer increases with income.[3]

THE ANNUAL WORLD HAPPINESS REPORT

Each year since 2012, I look forward to the annual WHR report. Readers who want more detailed information, and the latest reports, should go to: www.worldhappiness.report.

Here are the top twenty countries ranked by happiness from WHR 22, the tenth anniversary of the annual report. These rankings are averaged over 2019–2021 to account for nations that did not do an annual survey.

World Happiness Report 2022	
RANK/COUNTRY	SCORE
1. Finland	7.842
2. Denmark	7.620
3. Iceland	7.557
4. Switzerland	7.512

3   Richard Easterlin, "Does Economic Growth Improve the Human Lot? Some Empirical Evidence" (1974), contained in *Nations and Households in Economic Growth: Essays in Honor of Moses Abramovitz* (Academic Press, 1974); Jeffrey Sachs, D.W.B. Stevenson, and Justin Wolfers, "Subjective Well-Being, Income, Economic Development and Growth contained in . . . and the Pursuit of Happiness: Well-Being and the Role of Government," Institute of Economic Affairs, 2018.

5.	Netherlands	7.415
6.	Luxembourg	7.404
7.	Sweden	7.384
8.	Norway	7.364
9.	Israel	7.365
10.	New Zealand	7.200
11.	Austria	7.163
12.	Australia	7.162
13.	Ireland	7.041
14.	Germany	7.034
15.	Canada	7.025
16.	United States	6.977
17.	United Kingdom	6.943
18.	Czech Republic	6.920
19.	Belguim	6.805
20.	France	6.687
72.	China	5.585
80.	Russia	5.459
146.	Afghanistan	2.404

There are a few things to note about these rankings:

- The numbers represent each nation's total score on fifteen scales used to measure happiness, including GDP per capita, freedom from corruption, and economic safety net.
- Finland finished at the top for the third consecutive year, beating out Denmark, although all of the top six are close enough to be statistically the same.
- Citizens of developed nations each year are valuing the quality (stability) of their income—their personal economic safety net—more than the quantity of their income, their per capita GDP.
- This statement has enormous implications in the 2020s for financial service providers and for employers—people prefer stability over quantity when it comes to economic rewards.

- While it would be expected that GNH would decrease with the pandemic, several scores actually rose due to an increase of social support.
- When I began my research on GNH in 2012, one of my colleagues said, "Drop a pin at Copenhagen and draw concentric circles over the globe, the further you go any direction from Denmark the lower the GNH." I believe this is because the Scandinavian countries and their immediate neighbors have always led the way in providing their citizens with an economic safety net.
- The US has fallen one level since 2018 and five levels since 2017. Despite having a significantly larger GDP per capita, the US has one of the lowest economic, social, and crime safety nets. This accounts for the US lower GNH rankings.
- Physical safety and freedom from corruption are more highly valued each year in all nations.

ENVIRONMENTAL, SOCIAL, AND GOVERNANCE

Investors are increasingly applying environmental, social, and governance (ESG) nonfinancial metrics to their investment analysis. They believe that this can help understand companies and evaluate risks. Organizations such as the Sustainability Accounting Standards Board, the Global Reporting Initiative, and the Task Force on Climate-Related Financial Disclosures are trying to identify standards and the precise impact of such factors. The pandemic increased the awareness of how nonfinancial factors affect companies and entrepreneurs.

"Environmental" looks at conservation and efficiency. "Social" involves consideration of relationships with customers, employees, and the community. "Governance" deals with the actual running of a company including board composition, integrity, and executive compensation.

ESG investing started with various notions of socially responsible investing, but today it looks to avoid value judgments and negative screening. It attempts to look at the value within a company and how it can improve on its ESG attributes to increase its value to shareholders and others.

The famous conservative economist Milton Friedman (1912–2006) took the position that the social responsibility of a business is to increase its profits for shareholders. Once armed with profit from a business, shareholders could make their own decisions regarding any social initiatives. This view was criticized after the Great Recession of 2007–2008, which was caused in large part by financial institutions and their employees taking excessive risk to maximize profits and employee bonuses. Nonetheless, the Friedman point of view has been very influential.

I am skeptical regarding current ESG approaches. They have multiple objectives that compete with one another. The measurements are vague and can be manipulated.

ESG advocates the idea that business can be both profitable and admirable. In truth, it is often more profitable for a business to externalize certain costs rather than bear them internally to meet an ESG goal.

I respectfully suggest that ESG should really be "E" and focus on emissions. Under this approach, one would emphasize the impact of emissions technology rather than corporate governance. This would put ESG in a more useful and realistic place.

IMPROVING GNH

The concept of gross national happiness prompts analysis of the nature of growth, as well as the need for growth at all. Throughout this book, we have looked at GDP as a metric of comparison of economies and living standards. What if this is not really the right way to look at the world?

GNH adjusts GDP for the damage done by growth. It also posits that noneconomic factors must be considered to figure out what is real growth.

Scandinavian countries rank high in GNH in part because of their approach to capitalism wrapped in a European socialism security blanket. This is certainly a valid approach, but it probably does not fit everywhere. These countries are not large, sprawling nations like China, Russia, and the US. They do not play an outsized role in the world economy or geopolitical alignment. Perhaps it is easier to create and manage GNH in a more closed-circuit environment.

It is clear that the US could do more to increase its GNH. As discussed in chapter eight, "Universal Basic Income," providing a cash stipend to all Americans is a very good start. Changing entitlements from prescribed and bureaucratic food and housing to a free choice is another positive step. Reforming Medicaid and Medicare so these programs can be understood and readily accessed will be huge. We would all be happier if these systems were less complex and wasteful.

Wishful thinking? I hope not.

TAKEAWAYS

1. Happiness has displaced economics as the item people want most from their lives, a throwback to the "pursuit of Happiness" in the Declaration of Independence.

2. In 1934, economist Simon Kuznets developed the first uniform methodology for measuring economic output, gross national product. In 1979, the King of Bhutan proposed the universal standard for measuring overall well-being, gross national happiness.

3. Since 2012, the UN has released the World Happiness Report (WHR), which ranks the population of 156 nations by happiness—allowing nations to compare the welfare of their citizens to other nations, and to themselves in prior years.

4. After standard of living, the most important criteria for happiness is having a safety net—as evidenced in the 2022 WHR, which

ranked the seven Scandinavian nations at the top of the 156-nation list.

5. Despite having a significantly larger GDP per capita (economics), the US has one of the lowest economic, social, and crime safety nets, which accounts for the lower US GNH rankings.

Chapter Thirteen

THE CHINA CHALLENGE

In the history of the world, there is no greater economic miracle than what China accomplished between 1980 and 2000: lifting one billion people out of poverty—more than the entire population of Africa! In terms of improving the worldwide human condition, the combined efforts of all the other nations, charities, and religious organizations, since the beginning of time, don't come close.

I n this chapter, we will examine how, in the new roaring twenties, the economy of China presents the greatest challenge to the economies of the United States and most other developed nations.

We will also examine how China presents the world with the greatest economic and social opportunities. There may well be nothing more important to the future than the Chinese-American relationship.

If you are an entrepreneur or business executive, China presents the greatest business challenge you have ever faced. China has the ability to deliver your existing products to your existing customers at lower prices than you can ever hope to achieve. All they have been missing so far are the distribution channels, which they are now rapidly building and/or acquiring.

In the new roaring twenties, China will emerge as the world's largest homogeneous nation of consumers: ripe with disposable income, ready to purchase your products and services. This is despite the fact that India will surpass China in population. While India remains very important to the world economy, it has not experienced China's amazing success in raising its population out of poverty.

We will begin with the history of modern China—how the poorest nation became the richest in just the last few decades. We'll examine how our two nations together, China and the US, can bring a new, stable order to world markets.

THE CHINA CHALLENGE AND THE CHINA OPPORTUNITY

The most significant event for the world economy in the next decade will be the emergence of China as the largest consuming nation on earth, even as it maintains its current position as the largest producing nation on earth. How shall the US and other nations deal with this threat and opportunity?

China, more specifically the China-American partnership, will dominate what happens economically in the US on Main Street as well as on Wall Street. The dynamics of this relationship will affect every nation on earth.

I've been working in China since 2009. I first visited the nation as a student in 1969, and each time I returned to the US from China, I saw new things that we could improve in America. Despite my admiration and affection for the Chinese people, I've learned firsthand that China can be the unhappiest of all major nations on earth. Of the 156 nations ranked in the World Happiness Report for 2022, the US ranks sixteenth and China ranks seventy-second. We'll talk about why this is so in a moment.

Interestingly, the enormous wealth China has created is continually cycling back into the US economy. Over five million Chinese people live in the US, and 360,000 Chinese students attend college in the US. Whatever your business is in the West, the key to your future success may depend in substantial part on how you purchase your goods from, or sell your goods to, China.

A little history is in order. The founder of the People's Republic of China (PRC), Mao Zedong, died in 1976. Then, Deng Xiaoping (1904–1997), the founder of modern China, and one of the persons most responsible for China's recent economic miracle, effectively became the leader of that country for twenty-three years until his death. He was a political genius who put China on a capitalist road. He was a pragmatist unencumbered by history or ideology. Accordingly, after Mao's disastrous Cultural Revolution, which brutalized the Chinese people, including its cultural elites, Deng built in checks and balances to prevent any single leader from asserting dominance over the others.[1]

From 1978 to 1997, China's GDP rose from approximately $260 billion to $962 billion, a 3.7x increase over nineteen years. US GDP during this same period, 1978 to 1997, rose from approximately $2.4 trillion to $8.6 trillion, a similar 3.5x increase.[2]

While this initial period of Chinese growth paralleling the US was laudable, it didn't affect the average Chinese person much because the US economy was ten times the size of the Chinese economy back then, with only one-fourth the population. That meant the average American in the 1980s was theoretically forty times better off economically than their Chinese counterpart—ten times the annual wealth distributed over one-quarter as few people.

Deng's reforms had a large impact on China, and because China has today almost one-fifth of the world's population, also on humanity. Deng was named *Time* magazine's "Person of the Year" in 1978 and again in 1985.

In 1997–2020, China's GDP rose from $962 billion to $18 trillion, an incredible 18x increase. In contrast, in 1997–2020, US GDP rose from $8.6 trillion to $22 trillion, a 2.5x increase.[3]

---

1   Joseph Torigan, "The Shadow of Deng Xiaoping on Chinese Elite Politics," *Texas National Security Review*, January 30, 2012; Patrick Tyler, "Den Xiaoping: A Political Wizard Who Put China on the Capitalist Road," New York Times, February 20, 1997.
2   World Bank and Organization for Economic Co-operative and Development data; "China GDP: How It Has Changed Since 1980," *The Guardian*, November 2012.
3   World Bank and Organization for Economic Co-operation and Development data; Macrotrends.net; CEICdata.com.

You are reading these numbers correctly. GDP in China over this twenty-two-year period increased eighteen times, whereas GDP in the same time period in the US increased only two and a half times.

In 2014, China's GDP became the largest in the world, adjusted for purchasing-power parity (cost of living). Today, China ($18 trillion real GDP) and the US ($22 trillion GDP) combined account for almost 50 percent of world GDP with only 22 percent of world population (1.5 billion and 330 million respectively).

The real strength of the Chinese economy lies in its current economic growth rate, its efficient central management, and its commitment to building infrastructure. This combination will very likely produce ever-rising GDP for decades.

A 2016 report by the McKinsey Global Institute stated that China spends more on infrastructure than North America and Western Europe combined.[4]

Here's how some of that infrastructure spending breaks down:

Office buildings – In 2015–2018, China built 310 new skyscrapers compared to thirty-three during the same period in the US.

Space program – In 2018, China successfully launched thirty-five satellites compared to thirty by the US.

Online sales – In 2019, China had the largest online marketplace in the world, exceeding $1 trillion and accounting for 42 percent of its national sales.

Cell phones – In 2018, China had more than one billion 4G cell phone users, 40 percent of the world's cell phones with only 18 percent of the world's population. Huawei surpassed Apple as the world's

---

4   Jonathan Woetzel, Nicklas Garemo, Jan Mischke, Priyanka Kamra, and Robert Palter, "Bridging the Infrastructure Gaps: Has the World Made Progress?" McKinsey Global Institute (2016). McKinsey and Company is a global management consulting firm that advises major corporations and governments.

largest phone maker in 2018, although US sanctions have since interrupted its growth.

Renewable energy – China is expected to account for 40 percent of global renewable energy by 2022. China is already number one in the world in solar power capacity, hydropower, and wind power. See chapter four, "An Energy Revolution."

Efficient railways – China has the busiest railroads in the world with only 6 percent of the world's tracks. In 2017, China had 1.3 trillion passenger kilometers versus 10.6 billion for the US.

Health insurance – China has had basic health insurance provided by the government for 95 percent of its citizens since 2011. In contrast, the US had basic health insurance for 85 percent of its citizens in 2011, although this number has risen to about 91 percent today. In the US, this is mostly provided by private companies.

Poverty population – Over just a thirty-year period, 1981–2011, China reduced extreme poverty from 1.2 billion people to 26 million people. That's over a billion people lifted out of poverty, more than the entire population of Africa. This single achievement has improved life more on earth for more people than the philanthropic efforts of virtually all other nations of the world combined over the past one hundred years.

Middle-class population – China today has the largest middle class in the world, estimated at 400 million in 2019, and expected to grow to 600 million people in the new roaring twenties. The US middle class is estimated at 175 million people and declining. This has happened as many US citizens and residents get left behind and sink into near poverty. The rich are getting richer and poor are getting poorer in the US. This is a very unfortunate development for the US economy and democracy.

As the largest consumer consumption block of population in the world, Chinese tastes in goods and services may define world tastes for decades, just as the US tastes defined consumer and commercial tastes since World War II.

Millionaire-billionaire population – In 2018, according to Credit Suisse Research Institute, 626 of the world's 2,754 billionaires were in China and 724 billionaires were in the US—China passed the US on this scale in 2021. There are 3.5 million millionaires in China, and China will be minting new millionaires at three times the rate of the US over the next five years. Thus, China will soon have the most millionaires as well as billionaires.[5]

THE US AND CHINA DOMINATE WORLD ENERGY

World GDP today is about $90 trillion or $12,000 per person. The United States and China (US + China) together account for more than 50 percent of the world's GDP, even though our two countries combined have only approximately 22 percent of the world's population—the average person living in US + China is about 2.3x richer than the average person living outside of these two countries.

This economic discrepancy also applies to energy consumption. The US consumes 17 percent of the world's energy supply with only 4 percent of the world's population, while China consumes 24 percent of the world's energy supply with only 18 percent of the world's population—US + China consumes about 41 percent of the world's energy supply with only 22 percent of the world's population.

China has a long way to go when it comes to improving their production and use of energy—both from fossil fuel sources that poison our atmosphere, locally and globally, and from renewable energy sources: sources that loom as a potential panacea for local air quality and for global climate change. China is the world's largest producer of energy from coal, the world's most polluting

---

5   Anthony Shorrocks, James Davies, and Rodrigo Lluberas, "Global Wealth Report," Credit Suisse Research Institute (2018).

energy source. China is also the largest producer of energy from wind and solar, two of the least polluting sources of renewable energy.

WHAT THE CHINESE LEADERSHIP REALLY THINKS ABOUT THE UNITED STATES

One of the largest overall reforms under Deng was his determination to choose economic efficiency over politics. He rejected political ideology and famously said, "It doesn't matter if a cat is black or white, so long as it catches mice." This philosophy allowed China to generally avoid world politics and appropriate, some would say misappropriate, the world's best technology in every field.

One of Deng's largest reforms after the one-child policy (OCP) was to encourage China's best and brightest to seek out their education overseas, with spectacular results. In 1985, a thirty-three-year-old chemical engineer, Xi Jinping, came to the US to study agriculture and lived with an American farm family in the small town of Muscatine, Iowa. Today, Xi Jinping is the premier of China, and I am told that his time in Iowa is said to have left a lasting positive view of life in the United States. Nonetheless, he feels a strong need to push his country to aggressively compete economically with the US and demonstrate the superiority of its managed economy system. He appears to be very concerned with the role of Chinese technology companies and integrating them into a centrally managed system.

Most expatriate Chinese nationals today desire to attend America's premier colleges, starting with the eight US Ivy League schools, which altogether only admit 13,000 freshman students from all nations. I estimate that 20–25 percent of the freshmen class at the Ivy League schools are of Asian descent.

In 2020, an incredible 360,000 students of Chinese descent attended full-time college in the US although this may decline somewhat in the future. Most of these students, after receiving their US education, still return to China. Yet, after giving a lecture in China, the most common question I get from their parents' generation is: "Where in the US should our family purchase a home for us or our children to live one day?" This question illustrates what many in China's elite really think about the long-term prospects for America.

Premier Xi's immediate predecessor, Premier Wen Jiabao, was a fan of my book *The Wellness Revolution* (Wiley Press, 2007), which was renamed *The Fifth Wave* in China. Wen Jiabao served as China's head of state from 2003 through 2013, and he had a similar admiration for the United States. While he was premier, he sent his only daughter, Wen Ruchun, under the fake name of Lily Chang for security purposes, to attend undergraduate college in Boston. A Chinese presidential security officer told me that one of the premier's favorite activities when he was head of state was to fly to Boston; rent a car at the airport, disguising himself as a Chinese tourist; and with only one bilingual associate as his driver, clandestinely take his daughter and her classmates out to dinner for her favorite American food: Maine lobsters. After graduation, his daughter took a job in New York City working for J.P. Morgan. This, I tell my Sinophobic friends, is what the last two decades of Chinese leadership really think about the United States.

As I write this, China/US relations are in a bad place. However, the typical Chinese businessman doesn't care about geopolitical superiority or Taiwan or Tibet or any of these issues. He wants his children to go to school in the US and perhaps buy a house in the US. Nonetheless, Taiwan is very important as part of the busiest shipping lanes and the largest producer of valuable computer chips.

The tensions between the two nations and the pandemic have prompted US companies to recognize that supply chain management requires multiple sources and back-ups. One cannot depend on a particular country or company to provide necessary materials or expertise. The China challenge requires awareness of competitive challenges and risks, while being open-minded with respect to opportunities.

DENG'S REFORM: THE ONE-CHILD POLICY

The most significant reform that Deng instituted was the adoption of one-child policy (OCP) in 1979. This will go down in world history as one of the best economic decisions ever made in the history of the world in terms of gross domestic product, and perhaps the worst decision ever made in terms of gross national happiness.

Some background. The population of China effectively doubled in the thirty years from the Chinese Revolution of 1949 to Deng's taking control of the nation's highest office in 1978. During this time period, China was locked into a Malthusian never-ending cycle of poverty. Whenever a reform in technology or politics led to an increase in GDP, it was quickly absorbed by an ever-increasing population, locking the per capita GDP at a subsistence level.

Realizing this dire cycle, the Mao communist government, which had traditionally espoused large families that doubled the size of the population, began pushing in the 1970s toward smaller family size with a decade-long "suggested" two-child policy. Nothing really happened until the one-child policy was made into official law by Deng Xiaoping, which took effect January 1, 1980.

The term "one-child policy" is actually a misnomer. For most of the time it existed (1979–2015), about half of the families in China were allowed to have a second child for numerous reasons, including that their firstborn child was a girl, they lived in a rural area, or they had twins. This last criterion led to already-fertile couples using fertility drugs to produce multiple births.

Nevertheless, in densely populated areas and among the most productive, literate citizens, OCP had a major impact—it is estimated today that four hundred million births were prevented by OCP. Or, as some of my Chinese colleagues remind me, four hundred million of their brothers, sisters, uncles, and aunts are missing from their lives.

Before we examine the negative aspects of OCP that are often criticized by the international press, let's look at the positive aspects.

Positive Aspects of Chinese OCP

Economic: OCP allowed the Chinese economy to pause or "take a breath," implement new technologies, build infrastructure, and many other positive economic changes already mentioned.

Popular support: It was widely supported within China, especially among the middle and upper class, who viewed OCP as their civic duty toward a greater China. In effect, every child born from 1979 through 2015 had the economic and child-raising advantages of being a "first born."

Elevated women: OCP changed the role of women in society who were now able to educate themselves and join the workforce, effectively doubling the middle- and upper-class working population with no corresponding increase in this population's usage of services. Educated women in the workforce alone accounted for a significant part of the increase in China's GDP—something that many nations have yet to learn. Chinese women are now visible as leaders in government and in the private sector.

Technology: OCP is leading the fast-paced development of AI robots as caretakers and companions for an aging population, a technology that could eventually benefit billions of people everywhere.

Now for the other side of this controversy, let's look at the negative results.

Negative Aspects of OCP

Family disruptions: OCP created the greatest population distortion ever known on earth, permanently disrupting (some say destroying) family life for the current and next several generations.

The "4-2-1 problem" refers to one child having to care for their two parents and their four grandparents. A typical middle-class, age twenty-five, Chinese couple has twelve seniors to take care of during their most productive working years—four parents around ages fifty to sixty, and eight grandparents around ages seventy-five to ninety. Just think for a moment of the quality of your life today if your brothers, sisters, uncles, and aunts never existed, and you and your spouse were alone responsible to care for twelve senior parents and grandparents.

Male-female imbalance: OCP led to an unequal ratio of males to females, roughly 118:100 today, leading to thirty million more single men than women unable to find a mate, or needing to leave China in order to marry.

Societal fractures: OCP was unequally enforced based on which province you lived in, changing government regulations, sex of your firstborn, and other criteria. This resulted in conflicts within society between those who followed the rules and those who worked around them.

Labor shortages: OCP has resulted in a dramatic labor shortage that will only grow worse as the effect of a "missing four hundred million people over thirty-five years" works its way through the economy for decades, and this effect will have echo effects on succeeding generations.

Civil rights violations: The policy created a dark history for tens of millions of Chinese families as the most basic of human rights, the right to procreate, was taken from them— sometimes via coerced sterilization and abortion.

My First Emotional Encounter with OCP

I first encountered OCP as an economist studying the massive economic growth of China in the 2000s. After I delivered a speech on December 8, 2009, in the Great Hall of the People in Beijing, our group retired to a traditional dinner. My Chinese hosts, especially the women, were fascinated to meet my wife, Lisa, who is three-quarters Vietnamese and one-quarter Chinese. They asked to see pictures of our four Asian American children. One of the translators remarked that our children looked like Vulcans—which was because producer Gene Roddenberry used Asian American actors to play Vulcan children in the 1960s *Star Trek: The Original Series*.

The next morning, one of my hosts, Dr. Yu asked to speak with me.

"Your wife was inappropriate last night," Dr. Yu said through our interpreter. "Don't you think that every Chinese mother at that table wished that they too could have two children, let alone four children, as your wife has? It was rude of you to . . ." He stopped here and paused.

Then he wiped his face. I thought he was about to cry. He composed himself and continued.

"Professor Pilzer," he said. "This is a very difficult time for my people. We all have to make sacrifices for the greater good, starting with limiting our number of children. It was wrong of me just now to criticize your family. I apologize."

He continued. "Instead of being jealous of your four children, we should be proud of you, and you should show us the way to grow our economy so that one day my grandson can have two children. It's too late for my son and his wife." He threw his arms around me and gave me a bear hug.

I can still feel his emotion wrapped around me as I write this story.

This was just the first of hundreds of encounters I had with Chinese nationals over the next decade. The one-child policy was the elephant in the room whenever the conversation turned from public policy matters to private family matters. China may have a long-term growth problem due to the residual effects of the one-child policy and low fertility rates.

On another occasion, a young Chinese billionaire couple, with a home in Los Angeles, told us that they'd always wanted to have a second child—but the husband had forty thousand employees who would walk off the job if their boss defied the OCP that they all had to follow.

Today, China ranks number one in the world in terms of gross domestic product, and an incredible number eighty-six in the world in terms of gross national happiness. No wonder five million Chinese live permanently in the US and 360,000 Chinese college students go to school in the US. They are not just here in the US to learn what they can and take this knowledge back to China. Some of them are here to establish a future base for their family to eventually move permanently to the US.

THE WORLD'S FACTORY AND GREATEST ENTREPRENEURIAL OPPORTUNITY

China has established itself as the world's largest and most efficient manufacturer, producing 28 percent of the world's manufactured goods with less than 18 percent of the world's population. The average Chinese worker is more efficient than his or her international competitor. However, there is much more to Chinese manufacturing than just the price or efficiency of its labor force. China leads the world in manufacturing infrastructure.

Two of my teenage children spend much of their free time in robotics competitions. They are always on the lookout for the newest servomotors (used to control speed and angles), communications devices, interactive machinery, and other components for their latest and greatest robot design. More than any other place, they want to go visit Shenzhen, a thirteen-million-population city in China's silicon valley near Hong Kong that is renowned for its high-technology infrastructure. The electronics market there, Huaqiang North, is the largest electronics market in the world and where tens of thousands of vendors stock virtually every electronic component. My children claim they could draw the schematic in the morning for any type of electronic product and then find all of the components in the next few hours at the Shenzhen COCO Park mall to build it that afternoon. To them, and hundreds of thousands of electronics designers, there is simply no better place to work at than Shenzhen.

You know you're in a different place as you leave the Beijing airport driving to your hotel. The first thing you notice is the twenty-lane-each-direction highway divided into five four-lane sections—the outermost lanes support local traffic and the innermost lane sections only have exits approximately every twenty-five miles. It's sort of like the HOV (high-occupancy vehicle) lane we have in the US but divided by destination instead of the number of passengers.

If you do run a red light, by even a few milliseconds, a high-resolution camera photographs your license plate and instantly sends your phone the traffic citation along with the indisputable photographic evidence—just click once to confess and pay the fine, which increases the longer you delay.

Every person I've recommended to visit China comes back with stories of Chinese efficiency in their profession and ideas on how they can bring this efficiency to the US. My doctor and health-provider friends are amazed by medical and dental centers where the Chinese group the providers on the same floor based on the ailment they seek to treat. Instead of seeing a single doctor, you go from provider to provider where you explain your problem and they each give you an often-unique solution—with both Western medicine and traditional Chinese medicine "alternative" providers on the same floor.

The opportunity to uniquely design and manufacture your Western product in China for US consumption has largely come and gone. However, in the new roaring twenties, there will be an equal opportunity to bring your product or service to China, the world's largest homogenous nation of consumers who speak the same language. They want services such as entertainment, restaurants, specialized Western medicine, entrepreneurial business opportunities, and much more. One can also bring from China better methods of doing everything including dentistry, artificial intelligence, designing and building electric cars, and providing robotic food service.

AHEAD TO THE PAST, THE NEW SILK ROAD, AND PAX AMERICANA/CHINA

One-fifth of the world's population, roughly 1.5 billion people, live in China today. Ethnically, 97 percent of these people belong to one race—the Han people—who identify themselves as the descendants of the Han dynasty.

Today, the Han are the world's largest ethnic group, including not only 1.3 billion Han in China, but also 75 percent of the population of Singapore and 97 percent of the population of Taiwan.

In China, the Han dynasty (206 BCE–220 CE) was the first of China's golden ages, lasting 426 years. In politics, more than one thousand years before the Magna Carta, the Han emperor shared power with his merchants and noblemen and encouraged entrepreneurship. In finance, technology, agriculture, textiles, and especially iron manufacturing—which allowed for plows, horse collars, and wheelbarrows—the Han dynasty led the known world. It even had a sophisticated government and private monetary system. Some of its coins minted in 100 CE were still in use 860 years later in 960 CE.

The greatest initiative of the Han dynasty was the official opening of trade with the West in 130 BCE, and the resultant Silk Road trade routes to Europe and the West developed over the next two centuries. These land routes connected the East and West in economics, culture, politics, and religion. They were critically important to the development of the human race until the efficiency of these land routes was displaced by maritime routes in the eighteenth century.

In September 2013, Premier Xi Jinping announced the upcoming investment by China of more than $1 trillion in infrastructure improvements of the Silk Road and other related land routes connecting China with Africa and Europe. This Chinese "Belt and Road Initiative" (BRI), formerly known as "One Belt One Road" (OBOR) or simply the "New Silk Road," utilizes rail, trucks, buses, and automobiles. The initiative was incorporated into the 2017 constitution of China "to enhance regional connectivity and embrace a brighter future" with a completion date of 2049—construction is substantially underway. It promises potential dramatic improvements to the economies of the cities and nations through which it passes, including

Afghanistan, Kazakhstan, Tajikistan, Turkmenistan, Uzbekistan, India, and Pakistan—since it closely connects them with Europe and (indirectly via water) the US. The New Silk Road initiative also runs parallel to the "21st-Century Maritime Silk Road," a similar project by China to modernize and upgrade the shipping ports between China, Africa, and Europe—including Hanoi, Jakarta, Singapore, Male, Djibouti, Suez, Haifa, Istanbul, Athens, and Trieste (which has an international free port and rail connections to Central Europe).

More recently Premier Xi Jinping has announced to the UN General Assembly a Global Development Initiative (GDI) focusing on sustainable development objectives for 2030. This program has developed in part as a response to the pandemic with goals of reducing poverty and food scarcity, introducing sustainability and affordable clean energy to global development and improving the worldwide human condition by raising living standards.

These massive projects are financed mostly by China lending money to their host countries, which has prompted criticism that this is just an effort by China to improve its economic and military positions worldwide, so-called "debt-trap diplomacy." Conversely, I don't see the US or Europe investing hundreds of billions or more to modernize infrastructure that benefits everyone—even in their own nations. Moreover, this is massive infrastructure, which will be almost impossible to foreclose or take back. I submit that the leverage in this infrastructure relationship often is with the recipient country.[6]

I visited parts of the old Silk Road in Central Asia in the late 1980s when I worked in the former Soviet Union. I cannot think of any current projects in the world that could enhance world peace and prosperity more in the new roaring twenties. True, these will greatly accelerate China's already-incredible economic growth and influence, but this will leave China more money to spend on US products and services and to loan to third-world nations. China has already taken more than a billion of its own people out of poverty in just the last few decades, an unprecedented accomplishment. These Silk Road

---

6   Andrew Chatzky, and James McBride, "China's Massive Belt and Road Initiative," Council on Foreign Relations, January 28, 2020; Frank Umbach, "How China's Belt and Road Initiative Is Faring", *GIS Reports: Economy*, April 8, 2022.

initiatives alone could lead up to another billion African and East Asian people into middle-class lives—mostly people who aren't even Han or Chinese.

I call this new era "Pax Americana/China"—never before have the interests of the world's two greatest powers been so well in alignment for their and the world's mutual benefit. Taking constructive hold of this opportunity will be the greatest challenge, but also the greatest opportunity, of the twenty-first century for both countries. Can the leaders of China and America understand and act on this? The future of the planet may depend on it.

TAKEAWAYS

1. The US and China have similar interests worldwide in promoting world peace through free trade and the exchange of ideas.
2. China is more of an opportunity for US entrepreneurs and professionals than it is a threat.
3. The Chinese economic miracle of the past three decades is a shining example to the world's less-developed nations of what is possible due to economic alchemy—unlimited physical resources and labor due to freely advancing technology.
4. At the highest levels of leadership, the Chinese want to be our trading partners and emulate our lifestyles and technologies. They have no interest in military conquest of the US.

Chapter Fourteen

THE RUSSIAN WILD CARD

World news was dominated in 2022 by the Russian invasion of Ukraine. In order to understand why President Vladimir Putin pursued this strategy, we need to understand the history of Russia and the objectives of President Putin. Russia is the unpredictable (and yet, somehow predictable in its mendacity) wild card in the new roaring twenties.

The Russian Federation is physically the largest country in the world, spanning both Europe and Asia. It has a population of 150 million and a GDP of $1.5 trillion, about $10,000 per person. In contrast, the US has a population of 330 million and a GDP of $22 trillion, about $65,000 per person or 6.5 times the size of Russia.[1]

Russia will be a wild card in the new roaring twenties, disrupting supply chains and changing geopolitical alliances. Most importantly, Russia has the

---

1   Daniel H. Kaiser and Gary Marker, editors, *Reinterpreting Russian History: Readings 860–1860s* (Oxford University, 1994); Geoffrey Hosking, *Russia and the Russians: A History*, Second Edition (Oxford University 2011).

capability and apparent willingness to deploy tactical nuclear weapons for the first time in world history.

Russia and Ukraine have had a long and tortured history, leading to the current hostilities. Ivan IV (the Terrible) was crowned the first tsar (emperor) of Russia in 1547. In the early seventeenth century, famine and occupation by a Polish-Lithuanian commonwealth devastated the nation. The Romanov dynasty took power and gradually reversed the decline during the age of the Cossacks. The country took the Ukraine under its protection and expanded into the vast Siberian frontier.

Russia became a world power in 1721 under Peter the Great. Catherine the Great presided from 1762–1796 over a Russian age of enlightenment and engagement with Europe.

During the Napoleonic Wars, Russia aligned itself with other European powers and against France. In 1812, Napoleon's army ill advisedly attacked Russia, and despite reaching Moscow, was destroyed by dogged and heroic Russian resistance, as well as the bitterly cold winter.

Various socialist movements arose in Russia in the early twentieth century, resulting in the assassination of Alexander II. Major reforms were imposed on Tsar Nicholas II, who was later murdered together with his family in 1917. The shaky provisional government was eventually overthrown in the October Revolution by Vladimir Lenin, giving full power to the Bolshevik Petrograd Soviet. This led to years of conflict and terror between the anti-communist White Army and the Soviet Red Army, resulting in at least fifteen million deaths from hostilities and famine.

In 1922, Lenin formed the Soviet Union by joining Russia with Belarus, the Transcaucasian Republics, and the Ukraine. After Lenin's death, Joseph Stalin suppressed any opposition and became the country's dictator, imposing a centralized command economy with a draconian transformation from agriculture to an industrial economy. It is estimated that over ten million people died from purges and famine, many of them Soviet Ukranians.[2]

---

2   Martin McCauley, *Stalin and Stalinism*, Third Edition (Pearson, 2003); Sarah Davies and James Harris, editors, *Stalin: A New History* (Cambridge University Press, 2005); Sarah Davies and James Harris, *Stalin's World: Dictating the Soviet Order* (Yale University Press, 2014).

The Soviet Union initially signed a pact with Nazi Germany as World War II began and invaded Poland and the Baltic States. Eventually, Hitler and Nazi Germany made the same mistake as Napoleon and invaded the Soviet Union. Despite initial success, the German army was halted at the Battle of Moscow. Soviet deaths in what the Russians call "the Great Patriotic War" exceeded twenty-seven million, one-half of all World War II fatalities.

The Soviet and Nazi regimes killed over fourteen million people in a zone between Berlin and Moscow, the "bloodlands" of Ukraine, Belarus, and Poland. My father came to the US from Belarus at age eleven, fleeing the deadly oppression. If one feels that our times are scary, simply read some history. It will make you feel better—and worse.[3]

The Soviet Union emerged from World War II as a world power and a member of the United Nations Security Council. It occupied parts of Eastern and Central Europe, including East Germany, and installed satellite constituencies in most of these nations. It became the world's second nation with nuclear weapons capability. An Iron Curtain descended upon Russia and Eastern Europe, and what has been called the Cold War begun. A nuclear weapons standoff of mutually assured destruction staved off Armageddon.

Nikita Khrushchev succeeded Stalin after he died in 1953, but he denounced many of the brutal Stalin-era programs and purges. The 1950s were heady years for the Soviet Union as its centrally managed economic and scientific initiatives surpassed the United States in many areas, including the launch of Sputnik I to take the lead in the space race. Kruschev famously pounded the table with his shoe and declared: "We will bury you!" Many people thought he meant militarily, but he was really referring to economy and science. For a while it looked like he might be right.

The Cold War of this era reached a boiling point in 1962 with the discovery of Soviet nuclear missiles in Cuba, just off the coast of Florida. Hostilities were averted when the US quietly removed its missiles in Turkey, and the Soviet Union abandoned its missiles stationed in Cuba. The Soviet Union, with aging and moribund leadership, began a slow decline in the

---

3   Robert Leckie, *Delivered From Evil* (Harper & Row, 1987); Niall Ferguson, *The War of the World* (Penguin, 2006); Timothy Snyder, *Bloodlands* (Basic, 2010).

1970s and 1980s becoming almost a third-world consumer economy with a first-world military capability.

My mother accompanied me to the Soviet Union in 1967 at age thirteen so I could play in a high school chess tournament. It was an unbelievable experience, learning from the best chess players in the world and meeting new friends.

In 1983, I returned at a time of acrimony resulting from the Soviet shooting down of a Korean airliner, killing all on board. My business in the US was the ownership and management of industrial parks, so I began work in the Soviet Union on similar projects and taught at Moscow State University. I developed close working relationships with a number of Soviet officials including Georgy Arbatov, who served as a senior adviser to five general secretaries of the Communist Party. Mr. Arbatov often stayed at my home when he came to the US and became known for his appearances on US television representing the policies and positions of the Soviet Union.

When I worked in Russia, I was impressed with the technical expertise and intellectual curiosity of my Russian counterparts. Sometimes I would be asked, "How did we do? Are we negotiating in a manner similar to American businessmen?" There was often vodka served, which certainly helped the spirit of Russian-American cooperation.

I learned that Russians and Ukrainians are very similar people. Many top officials in Russia were from Ukraine. However, the relationship between the two countries is complex and filled with blood, sweat, and tears.

The last Soviet leader, the late Mikhail Gorbachev, tried to reform the Soviet system, calling for glasnost (openness) and perestroika (restructuring). This led to separatist movements, eventually resulting in the December 1991 dissolution of the Soviet Union with the emergence of fifteen former Soviet states, including Russia, as independent nations.

Gorbachev was succeeded by Boris Yeltsin. The economic and political collapse of the Soviet Union left Russia in an extended state of chaos and depression. The privatization of most industries unfortunately led to the transfer of massive amounts of wealth to those with inside connections to the government, now known as the Russian oligarchs. Much of the liquidity was moved out of the country. Russia was left with budget deficits and huge debts. The theft on a grand scale, together with a decline in oil prices, led to the financial crisis of 1998. Russia defaulted on its debt and devalued its currency, the ruble. Inflation soared and numerous banks went out of business. Then oil prices increased, and the economy began to recover, surprisingly quickly.

In December 1999, President Yeltsin abruptly resigned and was succeeded by Vladimir Putin, who won the presidential elections in 2000 and 2004. President Putin stabilized the Russian economy but took a much more authoritarian control over the government.

In 2014, Russia annexed Crimea, then part of Ukraine. This led to sanctions against Russia by the US. Russia engaged in multiple cyber-attacks on Ukraine to disrupt infrastructure and elections. Then, in February 2022, Russia attacked Ukraine after recognizing certain Ukrainian separatist movements. The US and the North Atlantic Treaty Organization (NATO) announced extensive sanctions against Russia as a result of the Ukraine incursion.

Why is President Putin attacking Ukraine? What impact will this have on the new roaring twenties?

First, let's look at who Vladimir Putin was and is. He is a native of Leningrad (now St. Petersburg) and a graduate of Leningrad State University, where he studied law. He served in the KGB for sixteen years, rising to the rank of lieutenant colonel. He experienced firsthand the decline and ultimate collapse of the Soviet Union. He left the KGB in 1991 to pursue politics, becoming very close to Anatoly Sobchak, a former professor and eventually the mayor of St. Petersburg, and then Boris Yeltsin, the president of Russia. Yeltsin designated Putin as director of the Federal Security Service, the successor to the KGB. Putin was later appointed as prime minister and eventually elected president.[4]

Vladimir Putin is a student of Russian history. As far as he is concerned, the acquisition of Ukraine and other territories adjacent to Russia is part of a continuum of history wherein his country expands to its rightful borders. He views the collapse of the Soviet Union as a tragedy and completely unnecessary. He considers Ukraine (and the Baltics) as historically part of Russia and

---

4   Mikhail Zygar, *All the Kremlin's Men* (Hachette, 2016); Kathryn E Stoner, *Russia Resurrected* (Oxford University Press, 2021).

eventually destined to return to their rightful place as either within Russia or as satellites.

To Putin, NATO is an existential threat to Russia, not unlike the threat to the United States of missiles in Cuba in the 1960s. NATO, based in Brussels, was founded in 1949 during the Cold War. It is a collective security agreement, and its members agree to defend each other from an external attack. It's the single most powerful world alliance. It has grown from originally twelve countries to currently thirty countries.

Ukraine has been designated an aspiring member of NATO. In 2021, the United States and Ukraine signed the US-Ukraine Charter on Strategic Partnership supporting Ukraine's right to pursue membership in NATO. Putin demanded that NATO never accept Ukraine as a member. From Putin's standpoint, it makes a great deal of sense to attack Ukraine in advance of its admission to NATO membership. If Ukraine were a member of NATO, under the North American Treaty, this would be an attack on all of the NATO nations.

Putin feels completely justified in taking over Ukraine, both historically and strategically. Russian control of Ukraine (and other nearby countries) seems to him to be in the natural order of things.

It makes little sense for Russia to destroy the productive capabilities and infrastructure of Ukraine if Russia intends to control it. Russia will then have a ruined neighbor and will have to rebuild. What's the profit in that? Well, the profit may simply be avoiding a democratic state and the potential of NATO on Russia's border.

Clearly, these actions by Russia have caused international outrage and immense suffering for the Ukrainian people. As a result, this has prompted a much stronger NATO and a more engaged Europe. As I write this, admission of Finland and Sweden to NATO seems likely.[5]

However, what is the impact of the war and Russian sanctions on the international economy? Long term, the answer is less than you might think. Russia is not a critical supplier to the world economy, other than oil and certain minerals like titanium that are also available elsewhere outside of

5   Tunku Varadarajan, "The Two Blunders That Caused the Ukraine War," *Wall Street Journal*, March 5–6, 2022.

Russia. There will be a significant short-term impact on supply chains and food availability, since Russia and Ukraine are important exporters of wheat and related agricultural products. This will contribute to scarcity and inflation for several years. Pursuant to the law of unintended consequences, while the diminished flow of Russian oil and gas to Europe will be inconvenient and temporarily drive up the price, this will also accelerate the changes of the new roaring twenties. Specifically, this is yet another reason to move away from fossil fuels towards electrical and other more efficient energy sources.[6]

Russia will need China as a trading partner, since its other options will be diminished. China will not necessarily need Russia and will tread somewhat carefully in the new roaring twenties because its interests are much more aligned with the US. The deterioration of US/Russia and European/Russia relationships are troubling from a global security standpoint, but ultimately will force a healthy pivot from dependency on Russian commodities.

Russian military performance in the war has been a disaster with reportedly over 80,000 Russian fatalities. This prompts a disturbing reality in the new roaring twenties, the concern that Russia has the capability and willingness to use tactical nuclear weapons.

These would be not big, strategic nuclear weapons, but rather smaller tactical ones, which have shorter range and lower-yield warheads. Russia and America are about equal in strategic nuclear capability, but Russia has an estimated ten times as many tactical nuclear weapons as the US.

In Putin's mind, America is an obsession, being responsible for the ills befalling the Soviet state and Russia. He cannot lose to the West. Without Ukraine, Russia cannot realize his vision of being a truly great power. The potential use of nuclear weapons for the first time since World War II means that Russia (which really means Putin) has become a wild card in the new roaring twenties.

Let us not overlook Russia's ability and willingness to engage in cyber-warfare. The US and Europe are very vulnerable to massive disruptions to critical robotic and other infrastructure. This may have put us in a new cyber cold war whereby multiple disasters are only prevented by a cyber version of mutually assured mass destruction.

---

6   "American Energy Innovation's Big Moment," *The Economist*, March 26, 2022.

As discussed in chapter thirteen, "The China Challenge," the future of the world economy and the new roaring twenties is largely dependent on the relationship between the US and China. Russia is one of the great (and the largest by land mass) countries of the world. I have done business in Russia for over thirty years and greatly admire the Russian people, their technical and intellectual capabilities, and their artists and dancers. However, Putin has increased the geopolitical stakes. This is the wild card.[7]

TAKEAWAYS

1. President Putin views Ukraine as part of historical Russia and the collapse of the Soviet Union as the greatest tragedy of the twentieth century. He believes he must control Ukraine in order to avoid having NATO on his doorstep.
2. The impact of the war and sanctions on Russia is important from a global, political, and security standpoint, but not as significant from a long-term economic standpoint. It may in fact accelerate certain aspects of the new roaring twenties, including better supply chains and the move to alternative energy.
3. The threat of tactical nuclear war will hang over the new roaring twenties, making Russia a scary wild card.

---

7   Peggy Noonan, "Putin Really May Break the Nuclear Taboo," *Wall Street Journal*, April 30–May 1, 2022; Walter Russell Mead, "Another Cuban Missile Crisis?" *Wall Street Journal*, May 3, 2022; Caitlin Talmadge, "What Putin's Nuclear Threats Mean for the U.S.," *Wall Street Journal*, March 5–6, 2022; Niell Ferguson, "Putin Misunderstood History. So, Unfortunately, Does the U.S.," *Bloomberg Opinion*, March 22, 2022.

Strategies for the New Roaring Twenties

PART IV

The six economic and six social pillars provide a framework for the new roaring twenties. They suggest logical strategies for the world economy as well as your personal initiatives. They inform the path that can best reflect your skills, interests, and perspectives.

Should you quit your job before you are laid off? Perhaps, but only when the time is right for you. This can be a bold and important step, requiring you to know yourself and the implications for you of the twelve pillars.

Business-opportunity businesses will present a variety of entrepreneurial possibilities. One may not only be creating business opportunities for others, but also be the beneficiary of a created opportunity.

However, you ain't seen nothin' yet!

The new roaring twenties will be characterized by extraordinary technological developments and an accelerating impact of robots enhanced by AI. There will be an energy revolution of alternative sources and increased efficiency.

And don't forget to find meaning in work and empathy for others.

Chapter Fifteen

SHOULD YOU QUIT BEFORE YOU ARE LAID OFF?

We've discussed the major changes coming in the new roaring twenties, the twelve foundational socioeconomic pillars underlying our brave new world and the opportunities for entrepreneurs and intrapreneurs to start new businesses. Here we explore another reason to become an entrepreneur: You may not have a choice.

In 1931, an idealistic twenty-one-year-old British college student at the London School of Economics won a scholarship to study entrepreneurship in the United States. This young scholar was excited to be coming to the land of the entrepreneur: the home of Cornelius Vanderbilt (shipping), Andrew Carnegie (steel), Henry Ford (automobiles), and David Sarnoff (television), today's equivalent of entrepreneurs like Elon Musk, Jeff Bezos, Jessica Alba, or Oprah Winfrey. These were people who he had read so much about in America, where he thought every person was free to pursue their own dreams.

When he arrived in the United States, he was woefully disappointed. The economy was in the Great Depression, and the British student found that most Americans were hanging on to low-paying jobs rather than taking responsibility for their own welfare, starting their own businesses, or working for themselves. Americans back then didn't want to be entrepreneurs like Henry Ford or David Sarnoff, they wanted to work for entrepreneurs like Ford or Sarnoff. This British economics student wrote a paper, "The Nature of the Firm," that attempted to answer the following question:

Why, in a free enterprise economy, would a worker voluntarily submit to direction by an employer instead of selling his own output or service directly to customers in the market?

This British student was Ronald H. Coase (1910–2013), who won the Sveriges Riksbank Prize in Economic Sciences in Memory of Alfred Nobel in 1991 in part for his explanation of why large companies exist, and why individuals choose to work for them rather than work for themselves. Today, his 1937 landmark paper on this topic is one of the most frequently cited works in economics.[1] If Coase were to write the same paper today, he might well come to exactly the opposite conclusion, that most large companies should not exist—especially in the gig economy.

It is possible that large employers other than those that provide technical solutions or business-opportunity businesses are an endangered species. Much of the unemployment we experience today is actually the permanent dismantling of companies with hundreds or thousands of full-time workers, for reasons precisely described by Coase almost a century ago. This is one of the reasons you should consider starting your own business or becoming part of the gig economy of freelance or contract workers. This is part of what is sometimes called "the Great Resignation."

In "The Nature of the Firm," Coase explained that the large employer exists because of its ability to reduce the transaction costs between individuals working together on the same project. For example, suppose you were a manager back in the 1930s who wanted to dictate a letter and have it typed on your typewriter or today into your computer. You could hire someone merely to type the letter, but the transaction costs of doing so back in the

---

1   R.H. Coase, *The Nature of the Firm, Economics* (Blackwell 1937).

1930s—finding the typist, testing the person's skills, negotiating the price, managing the work, paying the typist—would far exceed the cost of the work itself.

To reduce these transaction costs in the 1930s, and to some extent today, you might trade away hiring only the exact amount of labor when and where you need it. In return, the typist trades away their independence and higher per diem compensation for a guaranteed time and place to work.

Coase also examined why businesses produced goods and services themselves that were available at less cost from outside firms. He concluded that businesses are often better off if they produce themselves what they need because of the delays and transaction costs of dealing with outside suppliers. Coase's work became the mathematical justification for enormous factories such as the Ford River Rouge plant (1918–2004) in Dearborn, Michigan, which employed more than one hundred thousand workers over more than sixteen million square feet of factory floor. This plant had its own rail lines and was famous for "in comes coal (to make steel) and out comes cars."

Of course, this was in the 1930s before social media, ubiquitous free (and sometimes annoying) communication, and the gig economy. Back then, large employers existed as an efficient form of business organization because they reduced the transaction costs of doing business between individuals and firms.

However, as the employers continued to expand in size, different costs increased, including the costs of managing workers, the costs of making erroneous decisions, and the costs associated with hiring personnel whose compensation was not directly based on their performance.

Coase wrote in the 1930s that the optimum size for a firm is a size at which these inefficiency costs (the costs inherent to being a large employer) equal the transaction costs (the costs that the individuals would have to incur among themselves if they were free and independent agents).

According to Coase, an employer will continue to hire employees as long as the reduced transaction costs of having more people working for the single entity exceed the increased inefficiency costs of having a larger organization.

Today, however, for exactly this reason, most large employers have far fewer employees and many heavily staffed businesses should not exist at all. This is because over the past ninety years, the transaction costs of doing business between different entities have fallen, while the inefficiency costs of being a large employer have risen. This was even before the pandemic changed everything by allowing millions more employees to work efficiently from home in the gig economy.

The transaction costs of working with outside suppliers and workers—communicating, delivering, accounting—are now so low relative to the value of the services or the materials being acquired that they are often no longer part of the decision-making process. These transaction costs—directly connected robots, emails, texts, same-day delivery services, real-time invoicing, AI-powered cameras, and electronic payments—will continue to decline.

Meanwhile, inefficiency costs have become a major component of doing business for large employers. Since the inflationary 1960s and 1970s, employees have grown accustomed to receiving annual raises independent of their annual performance. It is now common in many firms for two employees performing the exact same job—one newly hired and one with seven to ten years' experience—to have a 100 percent or greater difference in their salaries. This results from the fact that those employees receiving 10 percent raises each year see their salaries double every seven years.

Moreover, large employers have become obligated to provide their employees with healthcare and retirement benefits. These costs increase each year independent of the productivity of the employees.

Another reason that inefficiency costs have risen dramatically is the relative ineffectiveness of the large employer compared to the individual gig-economy entrepreneur or lean small business in implementing technological change.

Traditionally, the very term "large employer" connoted being on the cutting edge of technology. Computers were once huge mainframes that were only used by large employers, and only large employers could afford to develop this technologically advanced equipment.

Today however, most of the wealthiest and largest firms in America—Apple, Alphabet (Google), Microsoft, Amazon, Meta (Facebook)—are themselves giant providers of technology to third parties. These companies don't provide you with any of the necessities you need that can feed you when you're hungry, clothe you when you're naked, house you when you're cold, or transport you when you travel.

Instead, these technology providers make the companies that do provide these necessities so much more efficient that they, the technology providers, are worth more than their customers who actually do provide these necessities of life.

The cutting-edge technology in most industries no longer belongs exclusively to large employers who develop it for themselves. Instead, large companies purchase the technologies they need from the giant technology providers and gig-economy professionals. The process of bidding out each job on a continuous basis ensures that the company gets the best price and the newest technology. Too often, it seems, companies with big staffs are the last to master new technologies because their employees are paid more based on their duration than on their innovation. It can be argued that certain projects require the vast resources of a large company. However, these projects often need to overcome the inertia of size and bureaucracy.

If you are currently employed full-time, it may be appropriate for you to get a handle on the viability of your current employer. Look back on your raises over the years. If the company made at least enough in additional earnings to cover your raises (and those of your colleagues) over the same time period, your job might be secure. If not, it may be time for you to quit and join the gig economy before you are fired or laid off. Do so thoughtfully in order to take care of your family's economic well-being.

As I write this, we are in the middle of the Great Resignation as predicted by Keynes 90 years ago. There are more jobs than qualified and motivated workers. It has become difficult for businesses to find the employees and gig workers they need. If you are trained and competent you are in great demand.

In addition, ask yourself some questions. Does my job fulfill my most basic subsistence and security needs? Is the workload manageable and suitable? Am I being asked to run a marathon at a sprinter's pace? Do I have a trusted community at work? Am I dealing with apathy, lack of empathy, hostility, discrimination, or bullying? How does my job fit into the rest of my life? Does my job provide me with purpose beyond a paycheck?[2]

---

2   Jolena Kecmanovic, "Thinking about quitting your job?" *Washington Post*, January 20, 2022.

SHOULD YOU GET YOUR HEALTH BENEFITS FROM YOUR EMPLOYER?

Traditionally, from World War II until the beginning of this century, working for a large company was almost synonymous with getting free health-care benefits. This is no longer the case. Over the past twenty-five years, I've written four books and started two companies that have helped millions of individuals purchase their own health benefits—health benefits that are better, cheaper, and more secure than health benefits they could get from a large employer. As unusual as it may seem, I started on this path while working part-time as a guest lecturer at Moscow State University in 1985.

My Soviet hosts asked me to give a series of lectures explaining sovereign debt. Premier Gorbachev had just visited South America, and several Latin nations were in default on their debts to the West—defaults the Soviets wanted to exploit for political advantage. After one of these lectures, a Soviet economist stood up and asked: "How can you, the son of a God-fearing, Russian-born father, work for such an evil nation as the United States?"

I responded aggressively, pointing out Soviet military actions in Afghanistan and Nicaragua, and we went back and forth on the alleged bad deeds of the US versus the USSR. Finally, he said, "I hear that in the United States if you lose your job, even if it's not your fault because your employer goes out of business, they take away your health insurance and the health insurance of your children and your wife—even if she is pregnant!" I assured him that wasn't the case and took another question on a different subject. However, his question bothered me on the flight all the way home and caused me to study this issue more clearly.

When I got back to Washington, I learned that he was 100 percent correct. Most Americans back then, and still today more than thirty-five years later, get their health insurance from their employer and lose their health insurance when they lose their job, even if they lose their job because of illness. This realization began my quest in the US to separate a person's health insurance from their employer, just like their auto, home, and life insurance, which have nothing to do with their employer.

The following year, in 1986, I supported COBRA, a law enacted by Congress that allows a person to stay on their employer's health plan after employment, although only for eighteen to thirty-six months and at substantial cost. This issue of employer group-health insurance being "temporary" really came home for me personally thirteen years later in 1999. My wife was pregnant and our family lost our employer-provided health insurance due to my leaving a Wall Street firm where I served as a director. Failed employer-provided health insurance was and still remains the number one cause of US personal bankruptcy, affecting more than one million US families (four million Americans) each year.

These experience led me to found two health benefits companies and research and write four books— dedicated to showing employees how to purchase their own individual health insurance policies paid for, tax-free, by their employer. The first company, Extend Health, was sold in 2012 to the largest provider of group employer–based policies.[3] The second company, PeopleKeep, Inc., focuses mostly on employers with less than fifty employees.[4]

A similar story to getting health benefits for individuals is still being written for retirement benefits. Progress has been made to make individual IRA accounts for individuals financially competitive and flexible when compared with large corporate pension plans and 401(k)s. Much more needs to be done.

TAKEAWAYS

1. Most of the new unemployment we see occurring today is not temporary. It is caused by the permanent dismantling of large employer organizations into smaller, specialized, and more efficient providers of goods and services—especially in the gig economy.

2. The very same economic algorithms that once guided employers into becoming large, vertically integrated organizations now predict and explain the demise of the large employer. The pandemic

---

3 "Tower Watson Acquires South Jordan-Based Extend Health for $435 Million," *Desert News*, May 12, 2012.

4 PeopleKeep provides easy-to-use health benefits administration and software. See People Keep.com.

economy, particularly the ability to work from home, has had the effect of pouring gasoline on this trend.

3. The term "large employer" used to be synonymous with proprietary cutting-edge technology, but today the exact opposite is often true. The wealthiest and largest firms in America—Apple, Alphabet (Google), Microsoft, Amazon, Meta (Facebook)—are themselves simply providers of the best technology to large legacy companies as well as small businesses.

4. Health benefits are now available to individual entrepreneurs in the gig economy with almost the same advantages as if they worked for a large company.

5. For many employees worldwide, the answer to the question "Should you quit before you're laid off or fired" is not yes or no but "when the time is right."

Chapter Sixteen

BUSINESS-OPPORTUNITY BUSINESSES (BOBS)

One of the greatest opportunities for entrepreneurs and large businesses in the new roaring twenties is creating employment paths for success for other entrepreneurs and small businesses.

In this chapter, we will explore how, because of the twelve pillars, the landscape is blurring between large and small businesses and between employees and contract labor. This blurring will be a major driver of prosperity in the new roaring twenties. The core product of the largest companies in the world today is providing a turnkey small business for an entrepreneur.

Let's review an axiom introduced in chapter five, "Structural Unemployment":

Unemployment due to technological change is the first sign of true economic growth.

When a machine or better method displaces a worker, we, society, still receive the work output of the displaced worker, now performed by the machine or better method. True growth occurs when the displaced worker gets a new job, and we, society, receive the economic benefit (GDP) from both their former and new job.

Thus, the greatest need, and opportunity, for society in the new roaring twenties is getting the displaced worker back to work either as an entrepreneur or as the employee of a new entrepreneur.

Many successful multibillion-dollar businesses today began in the sharing economy as better ways for people to share assets or information but quickly evolved into business-opportunity businesses (BOBs) that offered unemployed people new ways to earn money.

AMWAY LEADS, AIRBNB AND UBER FOLLOW

In 1959, Rich DeVos and Jay Van Andel started Amway, the world's first major direct-sales, multilevel marketing company, offering a business opportunity to anyone who would follow their formula for distributing health, beauty, and home-care products. Over the next sixty years, thousands of these Amway entrepreneurs became millionaires. As a former vendor to Amway, I have personally met hundreds of them. As told in a cover story in *Success* magazine in June 1997, Amway became a large distributor for an educational publishing and consulting company I founded called "Zane Publishing." Today, Amway has annual sales of $8.8 billion worldwide. The US direct-sales industry enjoys sales of about $114 billion with sixteen million independent entrepreneur representatives.

Thanks to recent advances in social media and technology, the business-opportunity business is just getting started. That was even before the pandemic forever changed the way we work, substituting social media (i.e., Facebook, Instagram, video calls, and Zoom meetings) for retail stores and office buildings. In just the last decade, according to *Forbes* magazine, the sharing-economy business-opportunity business is projected to grow from $14 billion in 2014 to $335 billion in 2025.

As presented earlier in this book, in 2007, Joe Gebbia and Brian Chesky founded Airbnb to rent out extra rooms with air mattresses in their apartment.

Today, Airbnb has seven million units listed for daily rental and is worth approximately $60 billion (June 2022). The explosive growth of Airbnb is coming not from individual homeowners renting out their space, but from a new breed of real estate entrepreneurs buying multiple properties for the sole purpose of renting them out via Airbnb and its competitors like HomeAway, Vrbo, Booking.com, Trivago, and Hotels.com, which collectively are much larger than Airbnb.

Also, as detailed earlier, in 2009, Garrett Camp and Travis Kalanick founded Uber as a smartphone application to add value to their existing "black car" limo and transportation company. Uber quickly morphed into the world's largest ride-hailing (versus ride-sharing) business, in which some entrepreneurs purchase cars solely for the purpose of driving them on demand for strangers as a business opportunity. Some Uber entrepreneurs purchase their own fleets of Uber-powered cars to be assigned to "employees," who are legally independent contractors. Uber Eats already enjoys sales exceeding $2 billion by allowing diners to order prepaid food from local restaurants and have it delivered by Uber drivers. Uber has truly changed the landscape for personal transportation.

THE UBER STORIES

Uber has been tremendous for billions of Uber passengers, changing lives on our planet for its rider-customers. Uber has had a much bigger impact on the lives of its drivers, some of whom might not have found gainful employment before Uber.

In 2014, my wife and I decided to try out Uber by spending three days in Los Angeles without an automobile—despite having to attend twelve different wedding events and business meetings within a twenty-mile radius of the LAX airport.

We used Uber on our cell phones to connect with drivers who took us where we wanted in luxury vehicles that showed up five minutes or less after we texted them. Our total Uber three-day cost was $150—about $11 a ride—far less than the $450 we would have spent paying $60 a day for a rental car, $42 a day for hotel parking, $40 for gas, and $100 or more for parking garages. The main value of using Uber was not the financial savings. Using Uber was so much easier, better, and faster than driving ourselves and hunting for parking or using traditional taxis and limousines.

All this we expected in our new sharing revolution, where technology is decreasing the cost and raising the value of most things we buy. What we didn't expect was to discover a community of Uber entrepreneurs—different types of drivers—who received far more value than the twenty to thirty dollars per hour they told us they were earning driving for Uber.

Each driver had a different story of why he or she became an entrepreneur working with Uber. Here are three of their stories.

Driver Joseph took us in a new Lexus SUV from our hotel to a dim sum restaurant—the Uber trip cost $8.85 including 20 percent gratuity. When we encountered LA traffic, Joseph asked us if he could deviate from the recommendation of the Uber app and take an alternate route. I asked him how he knew LA so well, and he told me he lived all his life nearby in Santa Monica—a neighborhood where I knew the homes started at one million dollars. I asked him why he was driving for Uber if he didn't need the money. He told me he was recently divorced and this was his weekend without his children. Whenever he got lonely he would turn on his Uber app and drive for a while, meeting new people and explaining his favorite places in his town to visitors. He often parked in front of our hotel, the Bel-Air, in hope of picking up a celebrity passenger. He didn't see driving for Uber as a job since he could turn it off at any time if he wanted to do something else.

Driver Constantine took us in his Prius from our hotel to our newest Zaniac Learning Center in Beverly Hills—the trip cost $11.22. Constantine told us this was the first day of his life in Los Angeles. He had arrived the previous night from Arizona, alone, for a mini-vacation—a vacation made much more fun by his taking his "work" (Uber) with him. Not being familiar with LA didn't affect him—or us—since the Uber-supplied GPS and smartphone told him turn by turn where to drive.

Driver Roger took us in his spotlessly clean Chevrolet sedan from our hotel back to the LAX airport—for $22.22, which also included gratuity. The hotel limo would have charged us $139 without tip for the same ride, and a taxi would have cost about $55. I asked driver Roger to share with us his Uber story on the twenty-five-minute drive to the airport. Roger had determined at age fifty that he wanted to be an artist, but he needed to earn $200 cash a day to cover his rent and food. So, he would get up every morning and drive for Uber from 8 AM to approximately noon—just until he cleared $200 in profit after paying for gas and 20 percent commission to Uber (it's now 25 percent)—and then he would spend the afternoon painting in his studio. On some days when he awoke early, he would start at 6 AM. On these early days, he would get very hungry around 8 AM. He liked to eat leisurely, so he would then simply turn off his Uber app and go to an enjoyable breakfast until he was ready to return to driving. He was disciplined about working just enough to clear $200 a day before returning to his art studio.

Since that first LA weekend in 2014, my wife and I have taken hundreds of Uber (and their competitors') rides in more than fifty cities around the globe. It's always been a pleasurable experience, mostly because of the drivers themselves and their personalities. The most common denominator I've noticed among the drivers is that many, if not most, of them would not be working at all if not for the flexibility provided by Uber and its competitors in the sharing revolution.

AMAZON WANTS TO BE YOUR PARTNER

We've already discussed Amazon's successful management of consumer surplus in chapter eleven. Now we'll see how the company creates opportunities for other businesses. Amazon started out in 1995 as an online seller of books based on customers' reviews. In 1998, the company began using this model to sell almost everything, starting with electronics, software, video games, apparel, furniture, food, toys, and jewelry.

The following year, Amazon started the Amazon Affiliate program, called Amazon Associates, which allows entrepreneurs with their own website to earn commissions by referring their visitors to specific products and pages on Amazon.com. Here's how Amazon Associates, which is now the largest affiliate marketing program in the world, works.

Let's say you have a website or a posting on social media that might lead a visitor to want to purchase something on Amazon.com. It could be something you just purchased yourself, often a product you've just reviewed, or a story that might lead someone to want to learn about a group of products, like things to take on a trip to a specific foreign country. After you've signed up for Amazon Associates, you simply put a link on your postings to specific pages or items for sale on Amazon.com. You can also create pages on Amazon describing groups of products. If your visitor clicks on the link and purchases a product on Amazon.com: (1) you get a commission paid to you for referring them to the product, and (2) you get a commission on anything your visitor purchases from Amazon.com for the next twenty-four hours—because you referred your visitor to Amazon's website.

Commissions range from about 10 percent for luxury beauty products down to 1 percent for food and video games, with most items paying about 4 to 6 percent.

Note that this program is completely separate from and in addition to the Amazon traditional retail model where you sell your own products on Amazon, set your own retail price for your products, and receive your retail price less than what Amazon charges you for collecting your money and fulfilling your orders.

BUSINESS-OPPORTUNITY BUSINESSES (BOBS) ARE THE NEXT BIG THING!

While Airbnb, Uber, and thousands of their competitors see themselves as being in the lodging, dining, or transportation industry, I see them as just the beginning of a much larger industry that will soon produce trillions in value for our economy. This industry is the business-opportunity business that will allow anyone with a skill (from knowing how to drive to knowing how to cook customized take-out meals) to start and manage their own entrepreneurial business.

> Take a moment now to think about businesses or industries you've worked for and how you could apply the knowledge you've acquired to building a BOB in your own sector of the sharing economy.

Can you participate by starting your own business under the framework of an existing BOB? Or are you able to envision your own BOB that will create opportunities for others? Or a combination?

TAKEAWAYS

1. The greatest immediate economic opportunity for most societies is to help the unemployed get a job, particularly those people currently receiving unemployment benefits.
2. Unemployment due to technological change, as opposed to war or pandemic, is the first sign of true economic growth. This is because when a machine or better method displaces a worker, we, society, still receive the output of the displaced worker, now performed by the machine or better method.
3. True growth occurs when the displaced worker gets a new job producing new or more goods and services, and society receives the GDP benefit of both their former and their new job.
4. The current system of distributing unemployment benefits was designed during the Great Depression for unemployment caused by downturns in the economic cycle, not structural unemployment caused by technological change. Almost by definition, a job lost to technological change is not coming back—at least not for the displaced worker.

5. The ultimate societal programs for fixing unemployment are programs that offer a business opportunity to a person currently receiving unemployment benefits.
6. The greatest business opportunities for entrepreneurs in the new roaring twenties involve starting businesses that offer a business opportunity to other entrepreneurs.

Chapter Seventeen

YOU AIN'T SEEN NOTHIN' YET

America's best days lie ahead. And you ain't seen nothin' yet.
—President Ronald Reagan, November 5, 1984.

I remember how I felt when I watched President Reagan deliver the above words on television from the Oval Office. It was the night before the presidential election. Almost everyone seemed excited about the prospects for our nation on the two issues that had dominated the campaign: the economy and national security. In 1984, US GDP under Reagan experienced its most dramatic increase (7.2 percent) since the Korean War, and there were possibilities of a future rapprochement with the Soviet Union. The next day, the voters overwhelmingly agreed with President Reagan. He and Vice President Bush captured forty-nine out of fifty states in a landslide, the greatest presidential election margin of victory since the unanimous election of George Washington in 1789.

That night, when President Reagan explained his forecast for his second term, he closed his election-eve speech with the words, "And, you ain't seen nothin' yet!" Sure enough, during Reagan's second term, GDP grew 12 percent, and shortly thereafter we ended the seventy-year-old Cold War with the Soviet Union.

Reagan's optimism back in 1984 is how I feel today about the new roaring twenties. I realize it will be a time of gut-wrenching change and volatility. However, I also believe that there are potentially huge opportunities for you and me. Here are a few of the reasons why, as I completed writing each chapter, I thought, "And you ain't seen nothin' yet!"

TECHNOLOGY AND ECONOMIC ALCHEMY

The theory of economic alchemy explains that we have unlimited wealth due to the acceleration of technology, particularly information technology. While there may be temporary shortages or dislocations due to supply-chain interruptions, inflation, war, or market gyrations, the trend is toward more and better technology resulting in new ways of fulfilling human needs and aspirations.

In fact, we have a huge technology gap—ideas, innovations, and processes that are backed up in terms of their conversion to practical utilization. As we accelerate into the new roaring twenties, the pace of conversion (itself enhanced by information technology) will increase as well. We truly ain't seen nothin' yet when it comes to applied technology.

Our enhanced ability to communicate has been a substantial factor in the large increase in GDP in the last fifteen years. The introduction of the Apple iPhone and its competitors connected half the planet's population in real time.

One hundred years ago, it took weeks or even months for information to travel in a coherent and comprehensive form. Now it takes seconds. We know instantly what is going on in the world, albeit sometimes scrambled by disinformation and outright lies.

Believe it or not, the ability to communicate, process, store, and manipulate information will dramatically expand in the new roaring twenties. On balance, this is positive and will advance economic alchemy—unlimited wealth. But it also poses complex challenges in these volatile times. Again, be positive, but be skeptical.

Cryptocurrency is the tip of the blockchain iceberg. This technology will be part of the new world order of the metaverse and multiple realities. We are really just beginning to understand time and space and the role they play in human narrative.

We live in interesting times. This is a blessing and a curse. *The New Roaring Twenties*!

THE ENERGY REVOLUTION

In chapter four, "An Energy Revolution," we examined how new technologies are developing additional sources of energy: fracking, ocean waves, better drilling techniques, wind, hydroelectric, hydrogen, solar power, and nuclear fission could double our energy supply—a 2x lift—driving down the price of petroleum and thus the cost of many other things made from oil. Over the next decade, energy prices will fall for the first time in history. But you ain't seen nothing yet.

We also examined how an equal amount of potential energy savings, another 2x lift, could come from applying better technology to devices and systems that use energy in order to reduce their consumption. Remember that the price of some sources of energy, like petroleum, are highly elastic—a 25 percent drop in demand could cause a 75 percent or greater drop in price—because few people can afford to get stuck with unsold flowing oil or having to take physical delivery of a contract for oil futures.

These devices and systems include EVs, intelligent heating and cooling systems, home construction, and especially illumination. Illumination alone uses 22 percent of the world's energy. Just switching from incandescent to LED lighting will potentially save the world $2 trillion, 90 percent, on illumination energy costs. That's almost half the total economy of Japan, enough to give an annual stipend of about $1,000 to every family on our eight-billion-person planet.

While writing chapter four, I met with scientists and engineers who helped me understand and appreciate the upcoming developments in solar, wind, waves, nuclear, and other energy technologies. And then there is geothermal, which has the potential to rewrite all of the rules of energy dependence.

The earth, as a result of an astronomical accident, is set up for geothermal energy. Our planet is the right size with a molten red-hot lava core. It is a giant nuclear heater. We find geothermal energy both in the earth's core and from the sun on the earth's crust. Potentially we have unlimited geothermal energy.

During the new roaring twenties, we will begin to develop technology to locate, process, ship, store, and convert geothermal energy into electricity or heat. While the timing of all this is difficult to pin down, it is coming!

More energy savings will come from dispensing with many of the things we do now that use energy, like some business meetings (replaced by Zoom meetings), shopping trips (transitioning to online purchases), dining out (shifting to takeout), and the introduction of self-driving autonomous EVs powered in many cases by Waze AI. The ultimate in energy savings comes from eliminating the task that was using the energy in the first place. All of these changes in energy supply and demand are happening now, and they're happening fast, creating business opportunities worldwide in the new roaring twenties!

THE ROBOTS ARE HERE

I cannot over-emphasize the impact of robots on the economy and the redefinition of work. In the industrial and agricultural sectors, whole plants and farms function with limited human involvement. This trend will accelerate.

In the service and personal sectors we already use robotic applications almost without thinking about it. Cell phones, GPS, automated customer service, and social media have become a part of our daily lives.

Even if you are not an engineering graduate or a tech person, you can understand and appreciate the growing impact of robots. Part of this process is observing the impact of robots on your daily life and not taking anything for granted. One must become self-aware and robot-aware.

We are adding artificial intelligence (AI) to the mix, which will dramatically increase Schumpeter's notion of creative destruction. AI is the ability of a robot to perceive its environment and then alter its behavior to improve its chances of meeting its goals. Often AI becomes routine technology, almost without us recognizing this transition.

Robots will play an important role in the energy revolution. They will enable us to more efficiently extract oil and gas as well as significantly hasten the transition to alternative sources of energy.

While robots improve the speed and precision of almost everything they do, the impact on increased structural unemployment is immense. There is perhaps nothing more important in the new roaring twenties than to help potentially billions of people through the transition to a robot-driven economy.

GEOPOLITICAL ESSENTIALS

The key to peace and prosperity in the new roaring twenties is a productive US-China relationship. The two countries do not need to be the best of friends but only to recognize that, as a matter of national policy, there is much to be learned and gained from each other. Never before has the world depended on two uniquely powerful nations to find a way to prosper together.

This working relationship between China and the US will help defuse and manage the Russian wild card. As China recognizes its future GDP and GNH are better served by working with the US, Russia will become more isolated. While this may cause desperation and acting out by the Russian autocracy, eventually the economic and psychological isolation will take its toll. More nations will clamor to join NATO.

Chinese leadership cares about its people and wants unlimited wealth for them. Current Russian leadership wants only to maintain its personal power and wealth.

The Chinese-US relationship has been plagued by animosity, suspicion, and nationalism. However, it is critical that these two great nations look beyond these differences to the greater good. I firmly believe this is possible during the new roaring twenties.

MEANING IN WORK

The new roaring twenties will be a time of self-examination and reflection in a period of volatility and unprecedented technological advancement. Work is something you do for yourself and for others. Work can give life meaning or reduce it to no meaning. Millennials and Generation Z increasingly want to find meaning in their work, or they would rather not work at all. Even baby boomers are retiring early or seeking new purpose in what they do. They ask whether they truly are of service to others and can contribute to a better future. Technology has created new wealth and opportunities and structural unemployment. While structural unemployment is a natural result of technology-driven wealth, it is devastating to those affected, often the least able to protect themselves.

It appears that Keynes may well have been right in forecasting that only one-third of the population will be working at some point. However, he thought in terms of work that directly contributes to GDP rather than GNH. Work can be important even if it contributes minimally to economic growth.

The partial solutions to the problematic aspect of Keynes's prediction include the explosive growth of the gig economy and the sharing revolution. Both give workers an opportunity to work while being on their own. The US has never really experienced the magnitude of dramatic new work positioning and affirmation that we will see in the new roaring twenties.

I cannot stress too highly the benefits of universal basic income indexed for inflation, in the new roaring twenties. It will soften the effect of structural unemployment and the transition to an economy populated by robots. It will give many people an opportunity and flexibility to start their own business, to become an entrepreneur, to try to find meaning in work. This initiative, together with simplification and common sense in medical and disability benefits, will make all the difference in the world to millions.

I have a great deal of faith in all of the generations: baby boomers, Generation X, millennials, and Generation Z. None of them are indolent or distracted. They simply need to find meaning. Not easy, but possible. I think each demographic will find its footing in the challenges and opportunities of the new roaring twenties. This will be a time of personal growth and reflection, driven by technology.

The media celebrates bitter partisan politics and the cults of personality. Consider, however, that the 2021–2022 Congress has been surprisingly productive with legislation on stimulus, infrastructure, election reform, gun control, taxation, climate change, and healthcare.

We view ourselves in the context of tumult and disruption. If you read history, you will find that it has always been like this. Contrary to popular opinion, our times are not all that unique other than the incredible potential of technology and economic alchemy.

I truly believe you ain't seen nothin' yet. You can prosper during this volatile time of technology-driven wealth and disruption. Invest in yourself. Invest in a business that makes the world a better place and you a better person. *The* new roaring twenties can be your time!

SOME THOUGHTS FOR YOU

I would like to share with you some parting thoughts based on my personal experience about how you might personally thrive in the new roaring twenties.

The new roaring twenties will be unpredictable and volatile. The speed of change will accelerate. Stay centered, focused, and calm. Pretty much everything is out of your control so don't worry about it. Be focused on what is within your power to change.

Try to get on your unique path—that which seems right to you and fits who you are or will be. Don't be bothered if others find your path ridiculous or wrongheaded. It is yours.

Read, really listen to others, be open-minded. Engage those you don't agree with, not to convince them, but to better understand their point of view. Embrace those who are different from you. Appreciate and learn from other cultures and ways. From this you will form a thoughtful and holistic perspective.

Economic success is a worthy goal, but rich people are sometimes not that happy. It's stressful being poor, but it is surprisingly stressful to be rich. Be grateful every day for what you have and the life God has given you.

Try to maintain some personal liquidity (cash) at the expense of investment yield. It is a powerful feeling to be able to write a check to handle an emergency or to take advantage of an opportunity.

Look for opportunities to be of service to others. This is what makes one happy ultimately. Expect nothing in return other than the knowledge you are doing the right thing.

Be a good friend. Reach out to others. Don't wait for them to reach out to you. People become busy with their own lives. However, they will be pleased to hear from you and you will add much to them and yourself.

Be wary of those who think they know. In truth, nobody really knows anything.

Recognize the law of unintended consequences. All sorts of things can happen as a result of an action, much of which you didn't see coming. Expect the unexpected.

Health is so important. All is irrelevant unless you are healthy. The pandemic has been a unique opportunity to recognize this and live it.

There are no simple solutions, but your approach to life can be simple and straightforward. Answer questions directly. Stick with the truth. It's the safest way.

You are living in a time of great challenges and opportunities. Don't be afraid to try different things, to live different lives. Take thoughtful and calculated risks. Expect to succeed, but don't be too discouraged by failure. Generally, a great success is enabled by adversity.

You have skills and determination, persistence, patience. If you can envision something in your mind, you can do it. It probably will work out differently than you planned, but that's all right. Even if you are on the best path for you, it may (will) often be dark and difficult. Stay with it; be resilient. You can get through it. You are on the hero's journey.

You stand on the shoulders of giants. May God be with you.

ACKNOWLEDGMENTS

First and foremost, I would like to thank my literary agent, Jan Miller, and my business manager, Reed Bilbray, who have been by my side since my first book.

I am eternally grateful to my wife, Lisa, the love of my life, and our four incredible children, Miriam, Amethyst, Ashe, and Mark, who inspire me every day. I am also grateful to my brother, Lee Pilzer, and his wife, Meryn, my aunt Gerry Pilzer, and Lisa's brother, Brian Dang. I am grateful to have each of you in my life.

I would like to thank the following people, some of whom are no longer with us, for their unbounded friendship, inspiration, and contribution to this book: Jay Abraham, Rick Alden, Ed Ames, Ayla and Fehmi Ashaboglu, Sheila and Michael Ashkin, Norman Beil, Linda and Neill Brownstein, Ronald Coase, Jerry Coffee, Ruth and Phil Davidson, Peter Derby, Mark Dietzgen, Randy Fields, Laurie and Patrick Gentempo, Roger Goldman, Mimi and Kenny Griswold, Bobby Hahn, Meg and John Hauge, Jan and Don Held, Allan Hunter, Scott Ingraham, Richard Jaffe, Stuart Johnson, Menashe Kadishman, Larry King, Eli Levine, Rabbi David Levinsky, Rick Lindquist, Ken Mabry, Sharon and Bill Macey, Stanley Marcus, Ann Mather, Alan May, Tony Meyer, Eric Morgan, David O'Brien, Bob Petrucello, Uncle Charlie (Charles Jay Pilzer), Lea and Barry Porter, Craig Primo, Ronald Reagan, Russ Reiss, Tony Robbins, Pat Robertson, Randy Sigman, Julian Simon, Michael Smerconish, Howie Spring, Tony Stark, Lisa Evans and Hansell Stedman, Jerome Stern, Ralou and Ronnie Stern, George Stone, Morris Sutton, In-Hei Hahn and Geoff Tabin, Zibby and Jim Tozer,

Brandon Williams, Jason Xu, Dexter Yager family, Caroline Zemmel, Susie Zemmel, and Rabbi Yoshi Zweiback.

I would like to thank my publisher, Matt Holt, and the entire team at BenBella Books. My editor Katie Dickman, cover designer Brigid Pearson, production editor Kim Broderick, marketing manager Mallory Hyde, interior designer Aaron Edmiston, copyeditor Scott Calamar, and proofreaders Jenny Rosen and Isabelle Rubio.

When this book was almost complete, I became seriously ill and was hospitalized over a six-month period. When my publisher suggested that we develop a contingency plan for completing the book, I contacted my intellectual sparring partner, award-winning filmmaker Stephen P. Jarchow, who immediately recognized the need for this book. Steve and I have worked together since 1982, when we both served as contributing editors of the same economics publication. With the support of two of his colleagues, Tasha Compton and Paul Colichman, Steve provided invaluable assistance toward the completion of this project.

And finally, to my students and my readers, who have given me my professional raison d'être.

Paul Zane Pilzer
Park City, Utah

INDEX

A

abundance, 45. *See also* economic alchemy
Act to Encourage Immigration, 124–125
advertising, 118
agricultural sector, robots in, 100
AI (artificial intelligence), 5, 102, 246. *See also* robots
Airbnb, 7, 8, 10, 121, 122, 128, 136, 168–171, 172, 174, 236–237. *See also* gig economy; sharing economy
AirDNA, 171
Akasaki, Isamu, 76
algorithms, 117–118, 120
alien contract labor law, 124
Alphabet, 230
Amano, Hiroshi, 76
Amazon, 10, 38, 114, 118, 126, 136, 174, 230
    consumer surplus and, 8, 177, 184–186, 187
    goodwill and, 59
    Net Promoter Score, 186
    Whole Foods Market, 114
Amazon Associates Program, 185, 240
American Dream, xiv, 159
Americans with Disabilities Act of 1990, 110
Amway, 236
Apple, 25, 38, 118, 126, 160, 230

iPhone, 52–53, 89–90
    during lockdown, 26–27
appliances, 103–104
Arbatov, Georgy, 220
artificial intelligence (AI), 5, 102, 246. *See also* robots
authoritarianism, 221
autocracy, 93
automobiles. *See* cars
autonomous vehicles, 73, 102, 172, 184, 246

B

baby boom generation, xiii, 7, 130, 151, 152, 159, 160, 161, 248
banking, 35, 174
bankruptcy, 233
Barnes & Noble, 185
Belarus, 219
Belt and Road Initiative (BRI), 213–215
benefits, 230. *See also* health insurance
Bezos, Jeff, 174, 184, 185
Bhutan, 191, 196
billion dollars, defined, 28
billionaires, 4, 38, 204
Bitcoin, 54
Black Monday, 19
blockchain, 53–54, 244
blubber, 49
Blue-ray DVDs, 77

BOBs (business-opportunity businesses).
    See business-opportunity businesses
    (BOBs)
bugs. *See* zero-days
business lockdown, 20–21
businesses, small, 2, 20n, 141
business-opportunity businesses (BOBs),
    10, 90, 122, 171, 172, 185, 226, 236, 240–
    241. *See also* Airbnb; gig economy; Uber

C
CAFE (Corporate Average Fuel Economy
    standards), 70
Camp, Garrett, 237
Can Capitalism Survive? (Schumpeter), 93
capital, defined, 101
capitalism, 92, 93, 117
Capitalism, Socialism, and Democracy
    (Schumpeter), 92
caregiving, robots for, 110–111, 208
CARES (Coronavirus Aid, Relief, and
    Economic Security) Act, 20n, 97
CARES PPP SBA, 19–20
Carnegie, Andrew, 126
cars. *See also* Uber
    autonomous vehicles, 73, 102, 172,
        184, 246
    environment and, 72
    EVs, 55, 64, 69, 71–73, 83, 84, 85, 245
    fuel economy, 4, 70–71
    hybrid vehicles, 69–70, 71–73
    internal combustion engines, 55, 70,
        72, 84
    millennials and, 159
    MPGe, 72
    Waze and, 111–112, 246
cash, 251
cell phones, 26, 34, 52–53, 202–203. *See also*
    iPhone
Chamberlain MyQ Smart Garage Door
    Opener., 104
change, speed of, 2, 27
charging stations, 69

Chesky, Brian, 170, 174, 236
China, 38, 215
    billionaires in, 204
    Deng Xiaoping, 201, 205, 206
    digital currencies and, 54
    displaced workers in, 91
    economic miracle, 199, 200, 201, 203,
        215
    economy of, 94
    efficiency in, 212
    energy and, 203, 204–205
    GDP of, 201–202, 204, 206, 211, 247
    Global Development Initiative, 214
    GNH and, 200, 206, 211, 247
    Han people, 213
    health insurance in, 203
    infrastructure and, 202–204, 213–215
    lithium and, 74
    manufacturing in, 211–212
    middle-class population, 203
    millionaires in, 204
    one-child policy, 191, 205, 206–211
    as opportunity vs. threat, 215
    population of, 201, 207, 213
    Russia and, 223
    Shenzhen, 211–212
    trade with West, 213
    transportation in, 203
    US debt held by, 29
    women in, 208
China challenge, 2, 9, 150
Chinese-American relationship, 9, 199,
    200, 205–206, 215, 247
chip robots, 26
citizenship, US, 38
cloud computing, defined, 101
coal, 50–52, 204–205
Coal Question, The (Jevons), 51
Coase, Ronald H., 228–229
COBRA, 232–233
Cold War, 219
colleges, US
    cost of, 157–158

emphasis on business, 190
    students of Chinese descent at, 205
communication, 244. *See also* technology
communism, 91, 120
companies, large. *See* employers, large
construction, 128
consumer behavior, algorithms and,
    117–118
consumer surplus, 2, 8, 34, 114, 177, 181
    ability to deliver, 187
    Amazon and, 184–186, 187
    lack of interest in, 181–182
    Neiman Marcus and, 178–179
    NPS and, 187
    as personal priority, 186
    Uber and, 183–184, 187
consumption
    millennials and, 159, 160, 161
    unlimited, xiii
coronavirus, 2. *See also* COVID-19;
    pandemic
Coronavirus Aid, Relief, and Economic
    Security (CARES) Act, 97
Corporate Average Fuel Economy
    standards (CAFE), 70
COVID-19, 2. *See also* pandemic
    emergence of, 19
    long-term, 2
    vaccine for, 58
creative destruction, 92, 120, 246
Crimea, 221
crowdsourcing, 111, 133–134
cryptocurrencies, 54, 244
cults of personality, 248
customer satisfaction, 180. *See also* Net
    Promoter Score (NPS)
customer service robots, 112–114
customers, existing, 155
cutting in line, 153–156, 162
cyber-attacks, 62, 118–119, 120, 221
cybersecurity, 60–61, 118–119
cyber-warfare, 223

D
Da Vinci surgical robots, 110
Davis, Ken, 133
debt, federal, 27, 28–30, 36–38, 53
debt, sovereign, 232
debt, student loan, 157
debt holders, 29
debt service, 29–30
debt-trap diplomacy, 214
Declaration of Independence, US, 189
Defense Protection Act, 74
deficit, federal, 27, 28
deficit spending, 35
demand
    alchemic, 59
    level of, technology and, 62
    quality, 59
    quantity, 59
    unlimited, xiii, xiv
democracy
    millennials' view of, 159
    threats to, 117
Democratic Party, 31
Deng Xiaoping, 191, 201, 206
Denmark, 193, 194
depression, 25–41
destruction, creative, 92, 120, 246
device, defined, 101
DeVos, Rich, 236
dictators, 93
Didi (China), 165
digital capabilities. *See* technology
digital currency, 54, 244. *See also*
    cryptocurrencies
direct lithium extraction (DLE), 74
disability benefits, 30, 142–143, 145
disabled people, 110, 116
Disney, 160
DLE (direct lithium extraction), 74
Doudna, Jennifer, 58
Drake, Edwin L., 50

E

Easterlin, Richard, 192
e-commerce, 2, 25, 26, 135
economic alchemy, 45, 47, 48–60, 62, 244
Economic Consequences of the Peace, The
    (Keynes), xii
economic crisis, 31. *See also* Great
    Depression; Great Recession
economic forecast, Keynes's, xi–xii
economic pillars, 3–7
economic possibilities, 1
Economic Possibilities for Our Grandchildren
    (Keynes), xi, xii
economics
    scarcity and, 46–47
    traditional, 47, 48
economy, US. *See also* gross domestic
    product (GDP); unemployment
    Great Recession (2007–2009), 16, 19,
        28, 35, 38, 127, 195
    loss of faith in, 19
    major sectors of, 100
    before pandemic, 15–17
    during pandemic, 24–41
    recovery of, 20, 23
    resilience of, 32
    stimulating, 28
education, 92, 115, 205. *See also* colleges,
    US
electric vehicles (EVs), 55, 64, 69, 71–73,
    83, 84, 85, 245
electricity generation, 83–84. *See also*
    energy
employees. *See* workers
employers, large, 228–230, 233–234
    gig economy and, 228–229
    health insurance and, 232–233
    technology and, 230–231, 234
    viability of, 231
employment locations, changes in, 89–90.
    See also unemployment, structural
energy, 2, 4. *See also* coal; fossil fuels; oil
    alternative, 85
    bad actors and, 63, 84–85
    cars and, 71–74
    China and, 203, 204–205
    cost of, 75
    free, 85
    geothermal, 64, 79–84, 245–246
    for illumination, 55, 64, 74, 75–79, 84,
        85, 245
    lithium, 74
    move away from fossil fuels, 63, 81
    in new roaring twenties, 84–85
    reduction in costs, 71
    renewable, 63, 64, 69, 203, 205
    Russian invasion of Ukraine and, 223
    as share of disposable income, 39
    solar, 81
    sources of, 65
    for transportation, 55. *see also* cars; oil
    in US, 204
Energy, US Department of, 79, 82
energy crisis, first, 49–51
energy prices, 63, 245
energy revolution, 43, 49, 245, 246
energy savings, 64, 246. *See also* electric
    vehicles (EVs); LED lighting
entitlements, 7, 141, 196. *See also*
    unemployment benefits
entrepreneurial spirit, 2
entrepreneurs, 6, 134–135, 155, 163. *See also*
    business-opportunity businesses (BOBs);
    gig economy
environmental, social, and governance
    (ESG) metrics, 194–195
Environmental Protection Agency (EPA),
    71–72, 73
ESG (environmental, social, and
    governance) metrics, 194–195
essential services, 25
Ethereum, 54
ethics, 156. *See also* values
EVs (electric vehicles), 55, 64, 69, 71–73,
    83, 84, 85, 245
exoskeletons, 110

Extend Health, 233
Exxon Mobil Corp, 66

F

Facebook, 38, 118, 126, 160, 230
factories, 229
failure, 252
fairness, millennials and, 7, 133, 155–156, 160, 162
Feigenbaum, Mitchell, 48
felons, 144
Fifth Wave, The (Pilzer), 206
financial crises. *See* Great Depression; Great Recession
Finland, 193, 222
FIRST (For Inspiration and Recognition of Science and Technology), 115–116
flexible manufacturing systems (FMS), 89, 107
Flowers, Woodie, 115
Floyd, George, 17
flu pandemic, xiv
FMS (flexible manufacturing system), 107
food, as share of disposable income, 39
food entrepreneurs, sharing revolution and, 173
food stamps, 141
For Inspiration and Recognition of Science and Technology (FIRST), 115–116
Ford River Rouge plant, 229
fossil fuels, 4. *See also* coal; energy; oil
    bad actors and, 63, 84–85
    move away from, 63, 81
401(k)s, 233
Friedman, Milton, 138, 195

G

Galbraith, John Kenneth, 58
gallium nitride (GaN), 77
GDP (gross domestic product). *See* gross domestic product (GDP)
Gebbia, Joe, 170, 236

General Theory of Employment, Interest and Money, The (Keynes), xii
Generation X, 84, 248
Generation Y (millennials). *See* millennials
Generation Z, 7, 84, 149, 151, 156, 161, 248
generations, age definitions for, 152
geothermal development, 84
geothermal gradient, 81
gig businesses, 131
gig consumers, 131
gig economy, 2, 5, 6, 44, 135, 248. *See also* Airbnb; business-opportunity businesses (BOBs); entrepreneurs; Uber
    baby boomers and, 130
    challenges of, 134–135
    characteristics of, 128–130
    construction, 128
    consumers' benefits from, 131–132
    crowdsourcing, 133–134
    displaced workers and, 123, 134
    examples of, 136
    facilitators in, 133–134
    health insurance and, 234
    lack of benefits, 122, 123, 129
    large companies and, 228–229
    millennials and, 130, 131
    parties involved in, 130–131
    restructuring of industries and, 122
    rewards of, 121, 134–135
    size of, 121, 127
gig workers, 6, 122, 123, 129, 130–131
Global Development Initiative (GDI), 214
God Wants You to Be Rich (Pilzer), 88
goodwill, 59
Google, 38, 118, 126, 160, 230
Gorbachev, Mikhail, 220, 232
grain prices, 52n
Great Depression, xi, xii, xiv, 19, 31, 32, 227
Great Recession (2007–2009), 16, 19, 28, 35, 38, 127, 195
Great Resignation, xi, 228, 231

gross domestic product (GDP), xii–xiii, xiii note, 8, 189–190, 248. *See also* economy, US; wealth
  adjusting for damage done by growth, 196
  baby boomers and, 151
  of China, 201–202, 204, 206, 211, 247
  vs. GNH, 48
  increase in, xiii, 52. *see also* growth, economic
  increasing, 196. *see also* universal basic income (UBI)
  information technology and, 52
  one-child policy and, 191
  before pandemic, 15–17
  during pandemic, 32
  predictions for, xv, 1
  under Reagan, 243
  during recession, 24
  of US, 190, 201–202, 204
  Walmart and, 25
  of world, 75
gross national happiness (GNH), 2, 8, 123, 190, 248. *See also* happiness
  of China, 200, 206, 211, 247
  vs. GDP, 48
  millennials and, 151, 160
  one-child policy and, 191
  pandemic and, 194
  US and, 197
gross national product (GNP), xiii note, 8, 189. *See also* gross domestic product (GDP)
growth, economic
  damage done by, 196
  displaced workers and, 236
  retooling for, 43
  structural unemployment and, 44, 87, 98, 236, 241
  technology gap and, 55
Gulf War, 67

H
Hahn, Robert, 80n, 183
Han people, 213
happiness, 190–191. *See also* gross national happiness (GNH)
  in Declaration of Independence, 189
  fundamental requirement for, 34
  income and, 192, 193
  measuring, 193
  millennials and, 160
  safety nets and, 194, 196
  World Happiness Report, 191–194, 196, 200
health, 252
health insurance, 230. *See also* medical care
  in China, 203
  COBRA, 232–233
  connected to employment, 232
  gig economy and, 234
heat pumps, 81–82, 83
heat sinks, 81–82
home offices, 26. *See also* remote work
hotel groups, 122
household net worth, US, 52–53
housing
  GNH and, 196
  low-income households and, 141, 142
  millennials and, 7, 159, 160
  subsidized, 142
housing prices, decline in, 16
Howe, Jeff, 132
Huawei, 202–203

I
Iceland, 80
immigrants, 124–126
immigration laws, xiv
immorality, 30
incarceration, 144
income, xiii, xv, 17, 39, 193
independent contractors, 129. *See also* gig workers
India, 200

Industrial Revolution, 49
industrial sector. *See* manufacturing/ industrial sector
inefficiency costs, 229–230
inflation, 30, 35, 39, 56, 157–158
information technology, 3, 4. *See also* technology
infrastructure, China and, 202–204, 213–215
innovation, xv. *See also* technology
Instagram, 118
interest rates, 30, 35, 36–38, 140
International Monetary Fund (IMF), xiii note
invention, process of, 57
iPads, 34. *See also* technology
iPhone, 52–53, 89–90. *See also* Apple; technology
IRA accounts, 233

J
Japan
　caregiving robots in, 111
　US debt held by, 29
Jevons, William Stanley, 51
Jevons paradox, 51
job loss. *See* unemployment

K
Kalanick, Travis, 237
Kamen, Dean, 115–116
Kennedy, John F., 18, 57
Keynes, John Maynard, xi–xii, xiv–xv, 6, 54, 160, 231, 248
Khrushchev, Nikita, 219
King, Martin Luther, Jr., 138
Kuznets, Simon, 8, 189, 196

L
labor. *See also* workforce
　defined, 101
　during pandemic, 25–26
　scarcity of, 99

labor market, unemployment benefits' conflict with, 138–139
land, value of, 56
lava, molten, 80–81
learning, remote, 26
LED lighting, 55, 64, 74, 75–79, 84, 85, 245
leisure, millennials and, 160
lending at discount rate, 35
Lenin, Vladimir, 218
life goals, reevaluation of, 13
light. *See* LED lighting
Lincoln, Abraham, 124
liquidity, personal, 251
lithium, 74
livestock, 56
living wage, 141
loans, forgivable, 19
lockdown, 20–21, 26
lodging. *See* Airbnb
long-term profit maximization, 178
low-income households, 142
Luddites, 90–91, 96
luxuries, vs. necessities, 58–59
Lyft, 105, 112, 128, 165. *See also* gig economy

M
machine, defined, 101. *See also* robots
macroeconomics, 46
management, 123–124
manufacturing/industrial sector
　Chinese, 211–212
　FMS, 89, 107
　robots in, 100, 106–108, 117
Mao Zedong, 201
Marcus, Stanley, 178
marketing, 47
Marriott, 122
Marshall, Alfred, 178
mass production, 123
math tutor, sharing revolution and, 174
McKinsey Global Institute, 202

Medicaid, 141–142, 143, 196

medical care. *See also* health insurance
   in China, 212
   low-income households and, 141–142
   robots in, 109–111
   sharing revolution and, 173
   telemedicine, 143–144
   waste in, 143–144

Medicare, 143

Meta, 53, 230

metaverse, 53–54

Microsoft, 160, 230

middle class, US, 203

military strength, US, 37

millennials (Generation Y), 2, 7, 149, 156, 248
   challenges faced by, 152
   characteristics of, 159–160
   consumption and, 160, 161
   criticism of, 159
   fairness and, 7, 133, 155–156, 160, 162
   future impact of, 161
   geothermic power and, 84
   gig work and, 130, 131
   GNH and, 151
   housing and, 7
   number of, 151, 156
   social conscience of, 159
   technology and, 152
   transportation and, 159, 160
   trauma experienced by, 158–159
   values of, 7, 156, 160–161, 162

millionaires, in China, 204

minimum wage, 140–141

Minuet, Peter, 56

More, Thomas, 138

mortgage payments, 140

Musk, Elon, 84, 138

N

Nakamura, Shuji, 76, 78

nanobots, 110

nanomedicine, 110

National Origins Act of 1924, xiv

national security, 37, 60

national socialism, 93

nationalism, 93

NATO, 222, 224, 247

"Nature of the Firm, The" (Coase), 228–229

necessities, vs. luxuries, 58–59

Neiman Marcus, 177, 178–179

Net Promoter Score (NPS), 8, 180–181, 186, 187

New Silk Road initiative, 213–215

NFTs (non-fungible tokens), 54

Nichia, 76

9/11, 19, 38, 60, 158

Nixon, Richard M., 18, 138

non-fungible tokens (NFTs), 54

NPS (Net Promoter Score), 8, 180–181, 186, 187

nuclear weapons, 218, 223, 224

O

OCP (one-child policy), 191, 205, 206–211

office space, remote work and, 40

oil, 50. *See also* energy; resources
   consumption rates, 66
   prices, 66–68, 85, 220
   production of, 65–66
   Russian, 66, 223
   type of, 65
   value of, 56

oligarchs, 93

one-child policy (OCP), 191, 205, 206–211

online commerce, 2, 25, 26, 135

Operation Olympic Games, 60

Organization for Economic Co-operation and Development (OECD), xiii note

Oswald, Lee Harvey, 18

Other People's Money (Pilzer), 37

outsourcing, 89–90

overdelivering, 181. *See also* consumer surplus

P

P. See resources

pandemic, 13, 17–21. *See also* COVID-19; stimulus packages

    Airbnb during, 170

    businesses during, 5, 135

    CARES, 97

    CARES PPP SBA, 19–20

    death toll, 21

    economic recovery from, 23, 97

    economy during, 24–41

    GDP during, 32

    GNH and, 194

    interest rates during, 38

    lockdown, 20–21

    millennials and, 159

    oil prices and, 68

    remote work and, 40

    speed of change and, 2

    stock market and, 31

    supply chain disruptions and, 39, 90, 108

    survive-then-thrive phenomenon, 32–35

    US government spending during, 27–31. *see also* stimulus packages

Park City, 35

passwords, 61

Pax Americana/China, 215

peace, 247

pension plans, 233

PeopleKeep, Inc., 233

People's Republic of China (PRC). *See* China

personal information managers (PIMs), 101

pessimism, 51

petroleum, 50, 66. *See also* oil

pillars, 10, 40

pillars, economic, 1, 2, 43. *See also* energy; gig economy; robots; technology; unemployment, structural; universal basic income (UBI)

pillars, social, 1, 7–9. *See also* China challenge; consumer surplus; gross national happiness (GNH); millennials; Russian wild card; sharing revolution

Planet Fitness, 20–21

plumbers, 173

political change, xiv

possessions. *See* consumption

poverty, 17, 140, 141, 203

power. *See* energy

PPP (Payroll Protection Program), 20n

PRC (People's Republic of China). *See* China

price increases, 39. *See also* inflation

prices, wholesale, 179

prisoners, former, 144

productivity, xi, 39

progress, structural unemployment and, 44

Prohibition, xiv

prosperity, 247

prostheses, 110

public-housing projects, 142

purchasing power, 30. *See also* inflation

Putin, Vladimir, 9, 217, 221–222, 223, 224

Q

quitting, 10, 225, 231, 234

R

Reagan, Ronald, 19, 142, 243–244

real estate market, 16, 40. *See also* housing

recession, 40

    avoidance of during pandemic, 25–41

    defined, 24

    Great Recession (2007–2009), 16, 19, 28, 35, 38, 127, 195

Reichheld, Fred, 180

religion, 47

remote work, 26, 40, 230

Rent the Runway, 104

Republican Party, 29, 30

residency, US, 38

resources, 3, 45–46. *See also* energy; oil

resources (*continued*)
　　ability to use, 56. *see also* technology
　　　gap
　　GNH and, 48
　　inventing, 48
　　relative value of, 4
　　scarce, 46
　　technology and, 52
　　unlimited, 48
　　wealth and, 47–48, 56
restaurants, sharing revolution and, 174
retailers, big-box, 25–27. *See also* Apple;
　　Walmart
retraining for displaced workers, 91–92,
　　94–95, 96–97
reverse withholding, 140, 141
RFID-reading robots, 26, 113, 114
rice, as share of disposable income, 39
ride-hailing industry, 165–166, 184. *See also*
　　Uber
ride-sharing boards, 164–165
ride-sharing services, 166. *See also* Uber
riots, 17
risks, 252
R-I-Ts (ready-to-be implemented
　　technological advances), 77
Roaring Twenties (1920–1929), xii, xiv, xv,
　　70
roaring twenties, new (2023–2033), 3
　　economic promise of, 43
　　energy in, 84–85
　　potential of, 13
　　strategies for, 9–10. *see also* business-
　　　opportunity businesses (BOBs);
　　　quitting
Robinson, Mark, 132
robotics, 115–117, 211
robots, 2, 5–6, 99, 108–109, 119, 246
　　autonomous driving by, 73, 102, 172,
　　　184, 246
　　as caretakers, 110–111, 208
　　customer service, 26, 112–114
　　cybersecurity and, 118–119

defined, 99–102
energy revolution and, 84, 246
functions performed by, 103–105
geothermal development and, 84
global supply-chain management and,
　　107–108
humans' competition with, 100
job loss and, 117, 119
in manufacturing/industrial sector,
　　100, 106–108, 117
in medicine, 109–111
online, 114
RFID-reading, 26, 113, 114
semi-autonomous, 102
Waze, 73, 111–112
Rockefeller, John D., 4
Roosevelt, Franklin D., xiv
Russia, 247. *See also* Soviet Union
　　authoritarianism in, 221
　　China and, 223
　　cyber-warfare and, 223
　　financial crisis of 1998, 221
　　government in, 93
　　history of, 218–221
　　international economy and, 222–223,
　　　224
　　NATO and, 222
　　nuclear weapons and, 218, 223, 224
　　oil from, 66
　　oligarchs in, 220
　　sanctions against, 222
　　size of, 217
　　supply chain disruptions and, 217, 223
　　Ukraine and, 9, 39, 66, 85, 170, 217,
　　　218, 220, 221, 222, 224
Russian wild card, 2, 9, 150

S
SaaS (software as a service), 34, 59
Sachs, Jeffrey, 192
safety nets, 1, 137, 152, 194, 196. *See also*
　　benefits; health insurance; universal basic
　　income (UBI)

salaries, 230

Salton Sea, 74

saving, xiv

SBA (Small Business Administration), 20n

scarcity, 45, 46

Schumpeter, Joseph, 92–93, 117, 246

Schwabe, Samuel Heinrich, 52n

security, 60–61

Segway Human Transporter, 116

self-checkout, 26, 113

September 11, 2001, 19, 38, 60, 158

service sector
    millennials in, 156
    robots in, 100, 112–114, 117

service to others, 252

Shabtai, Ehud, 111–112

Shakespeare, William, 11

sharing, 163–164

sharing economy, 7–8, 163, 165, 175.
    See also Airbnb; business-opportunity
    businesses (BOBs); Uber

sharing revolution, 2, 149, 165–166,
    167–168, 173, 174–175, 248. *See also*
    Airbnb; business-opportunity businesses
    (BOBs); Uber

shopping list, permanent, 114

short-term profit maximization, 178

Small Business Administration (SBA), 20n

smartphones, 26, 34, 52–53. *See also* Apple;
    technology

Snow Crash (Stephenson), 53

Sobchak, Anatoly, 221

social change, xiv, 3

social conscience, 159

social media, 120, 164

social responsibility, 195

socialism, 93, 117, 120, 196, 218

software as a service (SaaS), 34, 59

solar panels, 81

solar sunspot cycle, 52n

Soviet Union, 46, 94, 117, 218–220, 232.
    See also Russia

stability, political, 9, 37, 38

Stalin, Joseph, 218

Standard and Poor's 500 (S&P), 31, 32

Stark, Antony, 79n

steel industry, 125–126

STEM (science, technology, engineering,
    and mathematics), 115

Stephenson, Neal, 53

stimulus packages, 5, 27, 28, 30–31, 39, 53,
    138–139

stock market, unpredictability of, 31–32

strategies for new roaring twenties, 225,
    247–248. *See also* business-opportunity
    businesses (BOBs); quitting

student loans, 157

Stuxnet virus, 60–61

success, measuring, 190. *See also* gross
    domestic product (GDP); gross national
    happiness (GNH)

supply chain disruptions, 18, 39, 90, 108,
    217, 223

supply-chain management, global, 107–108

supply-demand curve, 181

surge pricing, 105, 182–183

surgical robots, 110

surveillance economy, 118

survive-then-thrive phenomenon, 32–35

Sweden, 222

T

Taiwan, 206

TaskEasy, 121, 133–134. *See also* gig
    economy

taxation, 91

Taylor, Frederick W., 123–124

T-bills (Treasury bills), 35–36, 37n

technology, xv, 2, 3–4, 10–11, 43, 52, 230
    ability to use resources and, 56
    backlog of unimplemented advances,
      54–55. *see also* technology gap
    cyber-attacks, 62, 118–119, 120, 221
    demand and, 58–59, 62
    FMS, 89, 107
    inflation and, 39

technology (*continued*)
    large employers and, 230–231, 234
    millennials and, 152
    physical resources and, 52
    political stability and, 9
    productivity and, xi
    rapid adoption of, 2
    rate of advancement, 57–58
    risk and, 62
    R-I-Ts, 77
    security risks and, 60–61
    survive-then-thrive phenomenon,
        33–35
    unemployment and. *see*
        unemployment, structural
    wealth and, 4, 45–46, 49–52, 62
technology, quantity, 57
technology, supply, 57
technology, use, 57
technology gap, 54–55, 59–60, 74, 83–84,
    244. *See also* LED lighting
technology providers, 230–231, 234
    threats to democracy from, 117–118
technostate, 118
telemedicine, 144
Tempest, The (Shakespeare), 11
Tesla, 38, 73, 84, 102, 126
thermocouple, 83
TikTok, 118
totalitarianism, 93
transaction costs, 229–230
transparency, 133, 165–166
transportation. *See also* cars; Uber
    Belt and Road Initiative, 213–215
    in China, 203
    energy used for, 55
    millennials and, 159, 160
Treasury, US, 38
Treasury bills (T-bills), 35–36, 37n
trillion dollars, defined, 28
Twenge, Jean, 159
Twitter, 118

U

Uber, 7, 10, 105, 112, 121, 122, 128, 136,
    165–166, 172, 174, 237–239. *See also* gig
    economy; sharing economy
    autonomous vehicles and, 184
    as BOB, 172
    consumer surplus and, 8, 177,
        183–184, 187
    sharing network for, 167–168
    surge pricing, 182–183
Uber Black, 172
Uber Eats, 122, 237
Uber Freight, 122
Uber Health, 122
UberX, 172
UberX Share, 122, 166
UBI (universal basic income). *See* universal
    basic income (UBI)
Ukraine, 9, 39, 66, 85, 170, 217, 218, 220,
    221–222, 224
underemployment, 144
unemployment, xv, 5, 228. *See also* workers,
    displaced; workforce
    Black Americans and, 17
    causes of, 98
    FMS and, 107–108
    health insurance and, 232
    before pandemic, 16–17
    pandemic and, 18
    permanent closure of companies and,
        233
    robots and, 119
    speed of, 88–89
unemployment, structural, 2, 5, 55, 120. *See
    also* workers, displaced; workforce
    creative destruction and, 92
    effects of, 44, 89, 248
    government reaction to, 96–97
    growth and, 44, 87, 98, 235, 236, 241
    political stability and, 9
    proponents of, 137–138
    responses to, 90–92, 94–95
    robots and, 247

stimulus packages, 138
unemployment benefits, 96–97, 144, 241.
   See also entitlements
     conflict with labor market, 138–139
     tied to employment, 139–140
unintended consequences, law of, 252
United Nations (UN) World Happiness
   Report, 191–194, 196, 200
universal basic income (UBI), xiii, 2, 6–7,
   30, 39, 44, 135, 248
     benefits of, 137
     GNH and, 196
     unconditional, 140–141
Utopia (More), 138

V
vaccine for COVID-19, 58
values, of millennials, 7, 156, 160–161, 162
Van Andel, Jay, 236
Venmo, 174
viruses. *See* zero-days

W
W. See wealth
wages, 39, 230
Walmart, 25–26
     Amazon sued by, 185
     customer service robots used by, 26,
       113–114
     e-commerce capabilities of, 25, 26, 114
washing machines, 104
waste, 30
Waze, 73, 111–112, 246
wealth, 3
     defining, 56–57
     measuring, 48
     military and, 37–38
     physical resources and, 47–48
     storing, 35, 37–38
     technology and, 4, 45–46, 49–52, 62
     unlimited, 48, 53, 62. *see also* economic
       alchemy

wealth, US national, xiv, 1. *See also* gross
   domestic product (GDP)
Wellness Revolution, The (Pilzer), 206
Wen Jiabao, 206
Wen Ruchun, 206
whaling industry, 49–50
Whole Foods Market, 114
WHR (World Happiness Report),
   191–194, 196, 200
withholding, reverse, 140, 141
women
     in China, 208
     in workforce, xiii, 208
work, xiv, 13, 247–248
workers, discouraged, 17–18, 144
workers, displaced, 92. *See also*
   unemployment
     in China, 91
     gig economy and, 123, 134
     growth and, 236, 241
     robots and, 100
     training for, 91–92, 94–95, 96–97
workers, gig, 6, 122, 123, 129, 130–131
workers, skilled, 99, 125
workers, underemployed, 144
workers, unskilled, 123, 125–126
workforce. *See also* unemployment
     Keynes's predictions for, xi–xii
     size of, xi, xiii, xv
     women in, xiii, 208
working hours, Keynes's predictions for, xv
work/life balance, 156
World Economic Forum, 119
World Happiness Report (WHR),
   191–194, 196, 200
World War I, xiv
World War II, 57, 219

X
Xi Jinping, 205, 213, 214

Y
Yang, Andrew, 137
Yeltsin, Boris, 220, 221
YouTube, 118

Z
Zaniac, 132
zero marginal product cost (ZMPC), 59,
    179
zero-days, 60–61
Zuckerberg, Mark, 138

ABOUT THE AUTHORS

Paul Zane Pilzer is an American economist, *New York Times* best-selling author, and social entrepreneur. Pilzer earned a BA in Journalism from Lehigh University, an MBA from the Wharton School of the University of Pennsylvania, and taught at New York University for twenty-one years where he was five times voted "best teacher." He was a vice president at Citibank, served in two White House administrations, has written thirteen books, founded six companies, and has been profiled in more than 100 publications including on the front page of the *Wall Street Journal*. He lives in Park City, Utah, with his wife, Lisa, and their four children.

Stephen P. Jarchow received his BBA, MS, and JD from the University of Wisconsin. He has been involved in the production and/or distribution of over 250 motion pictures and television series. Mr. Jarchow's films have won two Academy Awards®. He has been nominated for five Emmy Awards®, winning in 2021 for *Girls Voices Now*. Mr. Jarchow has been a principal in over 100 real estate ventures. He is the author of five books on real estate finance.